We Are in Charge Now

We Are in Charge Now

Corruption and Intrigue in World War II Cheyenne

RICK EWIG

✳

WordsWorth Publishing

Cody, Wyoming

ISBN: 979-8-9939600-3-6

First edition paperback

WordsWorth Publishing
Cody, Wyoming
www.wordsworthpublishing.com

CONTENTS

Acknowledgements

There are many people to thank for their important assistance to this study. I will start with Byron Hirst, who gave me the idea to research this topic. I met him about twenty-five years ago when I worked at the American Heritage Center and he wanted to donate some of his papers to the AHC. I worked with him on the donation and several times he mentioned that he prosecuted Cheyenne's mayor during World War II. He did not tell me the entire story, but enough to pique my interest and I thought when I retired that would make for an interesting research project, which it certainly turned out to be.

For the majority of my research, I spent much of my time at the Wyoming State Archives. I knew the staff from my previous research efforts and the three who went above and beyond in their assistance to me were Suzi Taylor, Robin Everett, and Carl Hallberg. Suzi works with the Archives' many photographs, but she does so much more, and she never tired of answering my questions and directing me towards sources when needed. Robin was so helpful, even finding some sources for me and keeping me headed in the right direction. As for Carl, he and I were colleagues at the department many years ago and he has always been there to suggest sources and find the sources I so desperately needed to document my work. I cannot speak highly enough of the assistance I received at the Wyoming State Archives.

Mike Kassel at the Old West Museum in Cheyenne has been so helpful in my study. The museum holds a Byron Hirst Collection which was vital to my research. Mike discussed the collection and the sources with me providing helpful insights and when I realized there were sound scriber disks and it was important to get those digitized, Mike took care of that and even drove the disks to the business which was able to complete the digitizing project. Also, as you will see, I used extensively Mike's excellent master's thesis to explore Cheyenne's aviation history during the war.

As mentioned, the American Heritage Center also has a Byron Hirst Collection. To utilize that I worked with Ginny Kilander, who is the head of reference at the Center. I worked with her for many years, and I am always impressed by how much she is able to accomplish. In her time at the AHC she has helped so many researchers find what they needed, including me. I also worked with Jessica LaBozetta, a reference archivist at the Center and who works with photographs and audio-visual materials. She was able to scan some large items for me which was important for my research.

One source that must be mentioned is the book *Cheyenne, Wyoming, 1940-1955: WWII National Defense Work Shortage of Living Quarters Justifying the Construction of Federal Housing Projects*, by Robert F. Gish. This is an incredible resource for anyone researching Cheyenne's World War II history. Mr. Gish researched and published this wonderful book.

Leon Reed, the grandson of Lola West, has been a great help. He provided some wonderful photographs of his grandmother and the Black and Tan Club and he also explained to me what it was like for a young African American to grow up in Cheyenne during the 1940s and 1950s. The photographs are from the Alonzo Reed Family.

I also want to thank Jim Johns, Bruce Curl, and Randy Fetzer. These are my coffee group colleagues, and Jim was my first college history instructor for which I am grateful. All three are long-time employees at Laramie County Community College in Cheyenne. Meeting every week for quite a few years now, they often asked about the progress of my research and offered thoughtful comments and suggestions and were an inspiration for me to continue to research the topic and finally to finish writing. I have much to thank them for, especially for their friendship. I also want to thank Lyn Myrick. He was the one who got me into the coffee group. Lyn taught history classes at the University of Wyoming and Laramie County Community College. I wish I had taken some of his classes.

Dave Kathka and Linda Fabian are two of my dearest friends in Wyoming. We have worked together in state government, in the Wyoming State Historical Society and in other capacities. Their knowledge and expertise and their mentoring have helped me extensively in my travels through Wyoming history.

I have written and published several books. This is the first time I have worked with Renée Tafoya at WordsWorth Publishing, and I have so enjoyed working with her. She has edited and published the work and certainly made it a better book.

On a more personal note, I must thank two people who are most important to me. Kristi Wallin, my lifetime partner, has assisted me like she did on my first book, by reading, commenting, and helping me improve the book as well as always being supportive of my efforts to complete the book. Finally, I must thank my daughter, Taylor, for the constant support which has greatly assisted me in this effort.

Introduction

"World War II passed no one by," stated Wyoming historian T.A. Larson in his book *Wyoming's War Years 1941-1945*. That certainly held true for the citizens of Cheyenne as they assisted in the war effort by modifying thousands B-17 bombers, building needed housing, working to produce 100-octane gasoline, or collecting aluminum for the war effort. Everyone was engaged in some way.

Cheyenne experienced an economic boom during the war. The population increased by more than 10,000, including thousands of workers needed for government-funded industries and construction projects. In addition to the growth in the civilian population, Fort Francis E. Warren and the newly built Quartermaster Replacement Training Center (QMRTC), west of the city, trained thousands of soldiers. The two military installations brought millions of dollars into the Capital City.

Cheyenne, like other military communities, saw an increase in vice during the war. Gambling became widespread, as did prostitution and the illegal sale of alcohol. The Capital City had a long history of prostitution, but during World War II, the military leaders and the city administration sometimes were at odds over how successful the efforts were to eradicate the vice.

The QMRTC brought in many "conscriptees" to be trained as quartermasters. Some members of the city administration expressed concern about the center's Fourth Regiment because the unit was made up of African American soldiers, and they realized there were few recreational activities for those troops. The city was segregated at that time. Cheyenne had a small population of Black citizens who mostly lived on the West Side of the city. Those soldiers in the Fourth Regiment often visited the clubs and restaurants in that part of town, which certainly brought more money to the area. That was noticed by some high up in the city administration, who began to make money by threatening West Side business owners that if they did not "pay" for protection, their businesses would be closed.

Those illegal activities by respected members of the community did not go unnoticed and were quickly stopped. All it took to end the corruption and intrigue was a young county attorney and a group of West Side business owners led by an African American woman.

Cheyenne: A Wartime Boomtown

Cheyenne's population in 1940, just before the beginning of World War II, was 22,474 according to that year's federal census. No one could have imagined or estimated what impact the war would have on Wyoming's Capitol City. According to T.A. Larson in his book *Wyoming's War Years*, the city's population increased by ten thousand between 1940 and November 1943.[1] War industries needed thousands of workers, and there was a great increase in the number of soldiers training at Fort Francis E. Warren. Like many other communities across the country, Cheyenne was a wartime boomtown.[2] As one would expect, this abrupt and sudden increase in population led to many issues that those communities had to face, such as housing shortages, perhaps increases in crime, juvenile delinquency, gambling, prostitution in cities near military installations, and perhaps in some cities, something no one expected or could have foreseen.

Even before the war began, Cheyenne began to experience tremendous growth, beginning with activity at the fort. In 1939 and 1940, Congress appropriated funding to increase the country's armed forces in response to the military aggression by Germany and Japan. Cheyenne's Chamber of Commerce, hoping the city could benefit from the increased appropriations, prepared a proposal titled "Fort Francis E. Warren as Headquarters and Station for a Streamline Division," that would increase the number of troops at Fort Warren by 1,600 men. Wyoming's U.S. Senator Joseph C. O'Mahoney was the city's main advocate with the War Department. It is unclear whether he presented the chamber's proposal to the department, but whether the senator did or did not, it was not enacted.[3] However, after several conferences between the senator and the army, Major General George C. Marshall, the army chief of staff, announced the number of soldiers at the fort would be greatly increased, along with a "$3,000,000 construction program" to include barracks and other buildings for a temporary garrison of 10,000 soldiers. The general also announced that a Quartermaster Replacement Training Center (QMRTC) would be built by the fort.[4]

While many recognized the importance of the Quartermaster Center to the war effort and understood that it would benefit Cheyenne, there was concern about providing enough affordable housing for construction workers and the officers who would be assigned there. The *Wyoming State Tribune* in November 1940 published an article about how city "realty owners" must provide living quarters at "reasonable rent." The newspaper made clear that profiteering in renting property "will not be tolerated." The realtors had to protect Cheyenne's interest. The article concluded that losing the center because of the lack of housing "would be disastrous to Cheyenne's interests, both in the immediate future and possibly in its bearing upon the permanency of Ft. Warren."[5] A month later, the *Tribune* advertised for rental rooms, requesting that any such rooms or apartments be listed with the Cheyenne Chamber of Commerce.[6]

Construction of the QMRTC began in early October. Temporary wooden barracks, mess halls, and other facilities began to appear on the fort grounds. The Quartermaster Center was located south of Crow Creek, which at that time was several hundred acres of open prairie. Several thousand construction workers began work on the Quartermaster Center in November, and by the following month, the number increased to approximately 3,000.[7] Construction work at the training center included 121 barracks, 30 mess halls, a post office, a post exchange, warehouses, repair shops, two recreation centers, a firehouse, 5 administration buildings, 3 guardhouses, quarters, and an infirmary. Also included at the center were three chapels.[8] The center continued to expand, and by the summer of 1941, it included a hospital, commissary, post exchanges, polo grounds, a nine-hole golf course, tennis courts, a gymnasium, skating rink, bowling alleys, a swimming pool, and clubs for NCOs and officers. The QMRTC was not officially a part of Fort Warren. It reported directly to the Quartermaster General in Washington, D.C.[9]

In addition to the number of trainees at the QMRTC, the army added 10,000 troops for infantry training at the fort.[10] An induction center was also added. Draft boards in the area sent draftees to the Fort F.E. Warren Induction Center for a physical exam, creation of their personnel files, and their "swearing in." After a short stay there, the new soldiers went to another base. Many went to Fort Logan, Colorado, to take aptitude tests that determined the type of work and unit in which the soldier would be most qualified to serve. From Logan, they were off for three months of basic training, followed by additional training for combat duty or for service in QMRTC units. The army established twenty-two centers for quartermaster training. Camp Lee in Virginia was the first, and Warren was the second.[11]

The center had five regiments. Regiments one through four taught the soldiers "motor operations, motor maintenance, automotive supply, jungle warfare equipment supply, railhead operation, carpentry, plumbing, painting, drafting, electrical, sheet metal work, steam fitting, and packing and crating." The fifth regiment trained them to operate supply depots, cook and bake, repair shoes and clothing, perform refrigeration and cold storage, and supply motor parts. The training at the QMRTC usually lasted thirteen weeks, but occasionally only eight weeks.[12]

Because of this sudden increase, housing was needed. The federal government, recognizing this, passed the "Defense Housing and Community Facilities Act" that fall, which made federal funds available for housing in affected communities. The act provided funds for housing, recreational facilities, water and sanitation plants, day care centers, and schools.[13]

By January 1941, construction in Cheyenne had broken all records for the month, according to building permits, and it was clear that housing would be an important issue for the city to address. Already, homeowners began to remodel their homes to add sleeping rooms or an apartment to their houses.[14] The *Wyoming Eagle,* in an editorial titled "Homes Wanted" in early 1942, shortly after the war began, wrote about the need for new housing for the new one thousand workers who would be employed at the city's airport. According to the editorial, "The housing situation, therefore, becomes Cheyenne's most pressing problem. Anyone who has attempted to find living quarters in recent months knows that the situation already is acute." It concluded: "So why can't we get on with the building of homes to accommodate the hundreds of new workers and their families?"[15]

The wife of a civilian instructor at Fort Warren also wanted to know why Cheyenne could not provide adequate housing. She wrote to Mayor Ed Warren and asked him if he was aware that "this emergency is simply being used as an opportunity by Cheyennites [sic] to back us into a corner and rob us." "It is impossible to find a decent place to live regardless of one's ability to pay so knowing these owners of these antique old fire traps (I speak advisedly) are demanding exorbitant rent with no concessions." One "filthy" place with no curtains rented for seventy-five dollars and the author was disgusted by the city's sanitation, asking "What in the manner of all that's holy is your sanitation laws if any in this miserable one-horse town." She did apologize for the description of the city as a one-horse town because "I just talked to the street-cleaner!? And he swears there is more than one horse here." The couple found an apartment to rent with three rooms, which she described as a firetrap with no refrigeration, no telephone service, and an old tin washtub. Outside their window was an incinerator next to the sidewalk. Returning to her complaint about renters being taken advantage of, she wrote that the civilian instructors, non-commissioned officers, "and other workmen families are not just prospects for bleeding and robbing but are bona fide humans whose work has unhappily and due solely to this emergency forced us to become residents of this town."[16]

The frustrated letter writer addressed several issues facing Cheyenne's renters at the time, but she did not mention one that the *Wyoming Eagle* considered important enough to address in two editorials. The first column, titled "The Rats Must Go," certainly got right to the point. The first sentence clearly stated that everyone in the city must "burn their rubbish." It continued, "there are said to be literally hundreds, perhaps thousands, of open ash pits, incinerators, garbage cans and other alley containers which attract dogs, cats, rats and mice." The newspaper did not view this as a public health issue that only the county health department or the city needed to deal with, but *everyone* needed to do what was necessary to keep the number of rats down. This editorial received so many positive comments that the *Eagle* followed up with another editorial the following week titled "Rats Versus Bombs." The reference to bombs, based on estimated damage caused by rats nationwide, was more than three and one-half billion dollars, which could be used to build many bombers instead of repairing damage caused by rats. The editorial continued: "Cheyenne is filled to overflowing (with rats)" because of the housing conditions, trailer camps, and temporary residents. It ended with a plea: "Examine your garbage cans and incinerators. Make them rat proof. Do it today."[17]

The construction of the QMRTC and other needs for the troops at Fort Warren were not the only projects that brought workers to the city. The Cheyenne airport already hosted United Air Lines (UAL), Inland Air Lines, and Plains Airways, as well as the Weather Bureau and Civil Aeronautics Authority. By 1941, the payroll for airport employees totaled $1 million dollars. UAL had five hundred workers employed at its repair shop for its Mainliner aircraft, and the company added more employees when it moved its pilot training program to Cheyenne. However, the largest employer for UAL was the Cheyenne Modification Center.[18]

Boeing Aircraft Company needed a facility capable of modifying its bombers with new guns, instruments, and other necessary adjustments. Once those changes were made in Cheyenne, the planes left for Europe. UAL employed many highly trained aviation mechanics who were familiar with Boeing products.[19] Planning for the important facility began in March 1942 when United received a telegram from the Army Air Corps. The telegram concerns the planning by manufacturers and airlines to establish their own modification centers. Lockheed already had such a plant in Dallas. Boeing sought to meet this need of the Air Corps and selected Cheyenne as the site. The new center was titled "Modification Center No. 10."[20] This center modified B-17 bombers.

According to the Air Corps, the duties of these centers were to "modify standard production airplanes to meet certain requirements, which cannot be accomplished during regular production of the aircraft" as well as not disrupting the delivery schedule. The modification centers also had to provide adequate facilities that could meet any needs and to ensure the aircraft could withstand "extreme conditions (ie, weather and fuel)." The centers also had to provide adequate parking for the planes awaiting modification.[21]

To accomplish all these requirements, more hangars at Cheyenne Airport were necessary. The construction estimates for the hangars came to $2,000,000. An important consideration was the location of the center, and several locations were considered, including on the "city's airport golf course and another was north of Pershing Boulevard and just northeast of Olivet Cemetery." The Army Corps of Engineers surveyed the northern portion of the city airfield, and in early May, the federal government signed a lease with Cheyenne for the center on the northwest corner of the airfield. Because of military needs at the time, the city leased 87 acres for $1. The government, Cheyenne, and United agreed to share the cost of maintaining the new airfield.[22]

During the summer of 1942, interested Cheyenneites read about all that

Cheyenne's United Air Lines facilities were doing for the war effort in an article written by W.A. Patterson, the head of the airline. According to Patterson, "Cheyenne this year is seeing more airplanes and more airplane activity than in all its long association with aviation." He emphasized the importance of its Mainliners aircraft, which constantly moved men and materials as needed for the war effort. Those large planes were maintained in Cheyenne and received complete overhauls after every 725 hours of flight. United's passenger service also increased during the war as had the volumes of mail on its airliners.[23] And, of course, the modification center brought many workers to Cheyenne. The airline recruited workers from diverse backgrounds, including farmers, tractor operators, beauticians, stenographers, and others. By the spring of 1943, United had more than 1,600 workers at the modification center, and more than fifty percent were women.[24] Already in July 1942, UAL adopted a ten-hour working shift for all of its employees, done "in the interests of efficiency and closer coordination of United's work as a part of the national war effort." Additionally, for a thirty-day period, all vacation time was eliminated, although workers would receive time-and-a-half for work exceeding eight hours per day and forty hours per week.[25] Just a few months later, the *Wyoming Eagle* reported that the modification center operated twenty-four hours a day with men and women working in shifts to install radar in some of the bombers, or install what was known as the "Cheyenne Turret," which included larger windows for wider visibility, along with many other modifications.[26]

Already by March 1944, the center had modified 3,500 B-17s. To acknowledge achieving that production goal, the airline held a ceremony on March 24. A snowstorm forced the ceremony to be held indoors, but the weather did not temper the event's importance. Head of United, Patterson, spoke at the event, as did Wyoming Governor Lester Hunt. The 3500th bomber was covered by signatures of the center's workers, and on its nose was transcribed "3,500th Headaches for Hitler." Also at the ceremony was the B-17 "Hell's Angels" along with the last crew that flew the aircraft. That plane, which had been modified in Cheyenne in August 1942, had flown forty-eight missions without a single member of its crew being wounded or killed.[27]

By the end of the war, the Cheyenne center's workers had modified 5,736 planes. Most were B-17s, but the workers also made changes to B-24s and some Canadian-built PBY-5 Catalina flying boats. Forty-seven percent of the wartime B-17s had gone through the Cheyenne plant, and for such work, the army awarded the Cheyenne Modification Center two Army-Navy "E" pennants for excellence."[28]

Another government-supported project brought in more than three hundred construction workers, and, when the project was completed, more than two hundred workers remained. This was the 100-octane aviation gas plant. In order to get the best performance from military aircraft, high-octane gasoline was needed. During the 1930s, 75- or 87-octane fuels were commonly used, but Shell Oil Company developed 100-octane gasoline; although more expensive to produce, it provided savings by enabling longer-range aircraft. Because of the importance of petroleum for the war effort, the federal government's Office of Petroleum Coordinator oversaw the production of the fuel. The government believed that plants producing the gasoline should be in the interior of the country, close to oil fields and away from the country's coasts, so as to be less vulnerable to enemy attacks.[29]

Shortly after the war began, Cheyenne businessman M.H. Robineau, the president of Frontier Refining Company in the Capitol City, began to study the possibility of building a 100-octane plant on forty acres of land near his refining company in south Cheyenne, and near the all-important Union Pacific railway lines. The Frontier Refinery had just been upgraded that year to be able to produce "quality petroleum" using oil from Lance Creek oil field to produce what the refinery called "Rarin'-to-Go' Gasoline."[30] Apparently seeking to expand his business, Robineau knew that the construction and operation of such a plant would require government funding. Other communities also proposed building such plants, even Casper, but eventually, the Office of Petroleum Coordinator approved the Cheyenne proposal.[31]

Absolutely necessary for the project was a supply of oil. Robineau contracted with four small independent refineries, "Z&W, Gray, and Albany Oil … and Silver Tip Refinery of Yoder." Standard Oil Company also agreed to sell oil for the plant.[32]

Groundbreaking for the project occurred in August 1942, with completion scheduled for September 1943. All of the aviation fuel was to be sold to the armed forces for the war effort. The new plant, with its workers, would also contribute approximately $900 per day to the city's economy.[33]

Even before the groundbreaking in August, the July 1942 Frontier Days edition of the *Wyoming State Tribune-Leader* and *Wyoming Eagle* carried an article about the soon-to-be-built plant along with a full-page advertisement about the new refinery. The article stated that the plant would cost $4 million. According to Robineau, the addition would increase the capacity of the Frontier Refinery "from 1,600 barrels of crude per day to 3,500 and that it will allow the manufacture of 1,500 barrels of 100-octane gasoline daily, in addition to other products." The ad thanked Wyoming for purchasing Frontier's products "at the rate of more than 15,000,000 gallons a year." It also announced the new 100-octane plant, and stated it would cost $5,000,000. Soon there were to be new tanks, furnaces, towers, and a great modern refinery." The article highlighted what the new refinery would mean for Cheyenne. Many of the construction workers would be from Cheyenne, "Dozens of business firms here will supply construction and operation needs.... When completed, scores more employees will be on steady payroll at Cheyenne."[34]

The plant's completion took longer than expected and cost twice the original estimate. The dedication ceremony was held on April 15, 1944, on the refinery grounds, although the plant had begun producing 100-octane gasoline a few weeks earlier. The *Wyoming State Tribune* and *Wyoming Eagle* published a "Dedication Edition" for the event, featuring photographs and articles about the project. Governor Hunt headlined the dedication, which was attended by city, army, and navy dignitaries. Radio station KFBC broadcast the ceremony. In the joint "Dedication" issue, an article stated the project "helped out Wyoming in the forefront as a major contributor to the war effort." It also said the completion of the refinery was an "inspiring story of American labor, capital, and government working hand-in-hand to achieve" and complete such a project. Some of the newly constructed towers were twelve stories high.[35]

Early on, Robineau realized the need for housing for construction and war workers. Given the work being done by United Air Lines, some workers were bused daily from Greeley and Fort Collins. When Robineau found out about twenty-nine houses for sale at the Lance Creek oil field, about 150 miles from Cheyenne, he applied for a loan from the Defense Plant Corporation to purchase them.[36] A trucking company offered to move the homes and place them on foundations for $14,000. Other expenses included water and sewer hookups, some landscaping, and remodeling. The cost to

Full page ad in the joint July 21-24, 1942 edition of the *Wyoming State Tribune-Leader* and *Wyoming Eagle* sponsored by the Cheyenne Frontier Refining Company thanking the state for its support of the company's new five-million dollar refinery to produce 100-octane aviation gasoline.

purchase a single house was $2,240; the houses were to be located on three city blocks near the refinery. The federal government assisted in other ways to provide housing for Cheyenne's war workers.

Cheyenne experienced a temporary building boom due to a national pre-war defense program in 1940 and 1941. The program resulted in the construction of 500 homes, but after the country's entry into the war, construction of new homes stopped for nearly a year, although some local businesses built new homes in 1942.[37] A November 1942 report stated that people were living in storage buildings, garages, basements, and even former outbuildings.[38] An influx of construction workers and new employees at United Air Lines, the Union Pacific Railroad, Frontier Refining Company, and Fort Warren led the National Housing Agency to authorize new housing for the city

During the first half of 1943, the Federal Public Housing Authority moved 300 trailer homes to Cheyenne. The P.J. Black Company leased 32 acres of land to the federal government, located north of Pershing Boulevard and east of Olivet Cemetery, for $1 per year. The new trailer community had separate laundry and toilet facilities as well as a playground and day nursery. The nursery had a trained attendant to free mothers for their war work.[39] The trailers were intended for war workers and their families and were rented for $6 per week. Occupancy averaged three persons per trailer.[40]

Several housing projects intended for defense industry workers were also sponsored by the Federal Public Housing Authority. The first one, Frontier Park Villa, was located at Frontier Park and included 325 housing units, 125 apartment-like dwellings, and approximately 200 separate units for workers with families, described as "quite livable."[41] These homes were only for the workers at the B-17 modification center. Construction began in January 1943 on the million-dollar building project; it opened to war workers in late June. The *Tribune* reported that the project "is expected to halt the drain of local workers shifting to nearby cities for homes."[42] One resident of the project, Paul Kalisch, described the buildings: "The buildings had flat roofs, and the sides were covered with a kind of tar paper based on siding similar to today's asphalt shingles. They were heated by coal from the bins outside each unit. They were quite warm and comfortable. Rent was $40 to $50 per month." He also added: "When the heavily laden bombers took off to the west, they were extremely low over the two-story units. The buildings shook and no conversations could be heard. As those crews were going to war, this was their farewell salute to the workers."[43]

Two similar housing projects were Careyville Acres and Van Tassell Terrace. Careyville was located on East Pershing Boulevard and had 180 units, from bachelor quarters to three-bedroom apartments. Workers began to move in during January 1944. Van Tassell Terrace, with 200 units, was located on the south side and was built on land owned by Maude Van Tassell. She leased the land to the government for one dollar per year. Each housing project had a well-equipped recreation building with a dance hall, lounge, and a branch of the Laramie County Library, as well as a branch post office, nurseries for children aged two to five, and a grocery store. Rental rates at Careyville range from $28.50 to nearly forty dollars per month.[44] The housing projects were expected to be torn down shortly after the war ended, but Frontier Park Villa and Careyville were not removed until the 1950s. Van Tassell Terrace remains, although it is now known as Pinewood Village. The federal housing projects greatly alleviated the wartime housing emergency faced by Cheyenne.

In September 1943, the *Wyoming State Tribune* printed an article written by Sgt. Bill Davidson, who wrote for the military publication *Yank*. He visited Cheyenne during the spring of 1943 and wrote about his impressions of the city, including Cheyenne Frontier Days. It was titled "How Army Paper Sees City: Yank, Which Is Distributed Only to Men In Service, Describes Wartime Boom."[45] The article was published in September 1943, several months after his visit and it does provide an interesting look at the city during wartime.

> The town has wide-open gambling now with blackjack and poker establishments running full blast behind some of the cafes and pool halls. This is the result of an attempt to make Cheyenne another Reno, the first step in which was a "new 60-day divorce law."

> *The newspaper commented that Sergeant Davidson would have a difficult time trying to find an organized, public-sanctioned gambling game going on in Cheyenne today at the time the article was published. He would find, however, a concerted effort by local law enforcement officials to crack down on gambling games.*

> A tremendous influx of war workers and army families has swollen the population from 22,400 to 35,000. The tiny regular army post at Ft. Warren has mushroomed into a huge quartermaster replacement center. Most of the United Air Lines installation at the airport has been taken over by the army as a modification center where heavy bombers are given their final processing before they are flown overseas.

> Yet little has changed in the basic life of the city. The principal mainstays are still the Union Pacific yards, the federal and state employees always found in a state capital, and the immense sheep and

cattle ranches which encompass nearly the entire state of Wyoming.

Many stores on 16th and 17th streets are bustling with activity and rolling in wealth. The prices are stunning. A good deal of the city's new-found wealth goes into war bond drives and a super USO in the half-million-dollar white Consistory temple on Capitol avenue. This structure is so lavish that one private reverently took off his hat on entering it for the first time. "I thought I was in the capitol building," he said.

The little yellow city buses, which used to chug lazily along the quiet streets less than half-filled are now jammed to capacity with war workers and sport all sorts of messages to the public, such as "Step to the rear—It helps ease the squeeze."

The newly arrived war workers are industrious and quiet and keep mostly to themselves, except when they are called upon to help support such affairs as Cheyenne's renowned rodeo, Frontier Days.

Seventeenth street on Saturday night is a solid wall of khaki and you can't get into the movies, the cocktail lounge of the Frontier hotel or the Wyoming and Oak rooms of the Plains Hotel.

Juvenile delinquency has become a problem. A 13-year-old boy killed another youth with a Sharpe revolver he had stolen from the state museum. A 19-year-old girl rented a house on the corner of 21st and Central and was using it as a "recreation club" in which 28 teen-age girls were providing recreation for free. As a result of such incidents, F.B. McVicar was appointed to the new post of juvenile delinquency officer.

It was decided that an increased sports program was what the town needed to counteract this wave of delinquency, so a new 14-team softball league was set up for the kids, and a four-team industrial league for the adults. In addition, a crack Ft. Warren league, including former minor leaguers, is in full bloom. Accordingly, Pioneer Park—which was closed when the Western league folded and took the famous Cheyenne Indians off the active list in 1941—now has baseball seven nights a week for the first time in its history. The two golf courses play 500 golfers on a Sunday and the 11 bad tennis courts are always jammed.

There are still the old standard gags about Frontier Days, which generally go as follows: "There are only two seasons in Cheyenne—

winter and Frontier Days," or "In Cheyenne, the groundhog comes up on Feb. 2 looks around and says, 'I'm going back to sleep. Don't wake me up again until the opening day of Frontier Days."

Because of the influx of war workers, there was no decrease in attendance this year. Nearly all the performers were back, including Buck Sorrells, Carl Arnold, Bob Crosby and the local favorite, King Merritt. It seems that the bulldoggers and ropers are too old for the army, and the bronco-riders have so many broken bones that they are invariably rejected. The old show was the same, with the citizenry wearing cowboy clothes, Chief Red Cloud and his Sioux Indians indulging in squaw dances and buck races, and the city enjoying the usual profits.

And so life goes on in Cheyenne. The men hunt moose and elk in the Snowy Range; the women play cards; the kids go to Roedels' and the Owl inn, swim in Sloan's lake and neck in Lions park. The ranches are short of cowpunchers, but old-timers like Ernie King are still around. And with women replacing men as shearers, sheep raising is more profitable than ever at a new high price of 43½ cents a pound for wool. Actual war still seems far away.

The war may have seemed far away, but the many changes it brought to the city, such as the many new war workers, the great need for adequate housing, the non-stop activity in Cheyenne and the fort were very apparent to the city's residents. Another change brought about by the army must have surprised and, likely, concerned many in the Capitol City. The change related to some of the soldiers who were trained at the QMRTC, specifically those in the Fourth Regiment.

CHAPTER I ENDNOTES

1   Larson, T.A., *Wyoming's War Years: 1941-1945*, reprint edition, Cheyenne: Wyoming Historical Foundation, 1993, 134.

2   Historian Gerald D. Nash compared the World War II boom in western cities to the nineteenth century mining and railroad booms in the West. Wartime mobilization created millions of new jobs in the West. Nash, Gerald D., *The American West Transformed: The Impact of the Second World War*, Lincoln and London, University of Nebraska Press, 1985, 57.

3   Adams, Gerald M. "Fort Francis E. Warren and the Quartermaster Corps in World War II, 1940-1946," Fort Collins, Colorado, Citizen Printing, 8-9.

4   "$3,000,000 Construction Program Slated For Post: 10,000 Troops To Be Trained At Ft. Warren," *Wyoming State Tribune*, October 9, 1940, 1 and 10.

5   "Cantonment Threatened Unless City Offers Reasonable Housing: Renters Asked to List Property Immediately," *Wyoming State Tribune*, November 20, 1940, 1 and 10.

6   "Rooms Are Needed," *Wyoming State Tribune*, December 20, 1940, 1.

7   Adams, "Fort Francis E. Warren and the Quartermaster Corps," 9-13. The number of workers involved in QMRTC construction totaled 4,546 on February 1, 1941. The number included fourteen hundred carpenters. Many of the workers were from Wyoming, but since the state only had two hundred carpenters many were recruited from other states. Larson, 204.

8   Ibid., 12, 14.

9   Ibid., 8, 16; "215 Structures at Cantonment Finished," *Wyoming State Tribune*, March 16, 1941, 1.

10   *Wyoming Eagle*, February 5, 1941, 2.

11   Adams, 10-11; "Quartermaster Training Center Planned at Post," *Wyoming Eagle*, January 23, 1941, 7.

12   Ibid., 20-21.

13   Robert F. Gish, *Cheyenne, Wyoming 1940-1955: History-WWII Industries-Schools, Living in Government Housing Projects,* privately printed, 2016, 3-4.

14   "Construction Here in January Breaks All Construction Records," *Wyoming State Tribune*, January 31, 1941, 1 and 12.

15   Editorial, "Homes Wanted," *Wyoming Eagle*, May 13, 1942, 6.

16   RG3001, City of Cheyenne, Cheyenne Mayor Records, Administrative Files, Cheyenne City Records, Complaints, Anonymous, box 4, Wyoming State Archives. The letter was not anonymous but signed by Mrs. Roy Picket. She referenced the race for Cheyenne mayor Warren was running in, so this may have been during the 1943 mayoral election.

17   "The Rats Must Go," *Wyoming Eagle*, June 9, 1943, 6; "Rats Versus Bombs," *Wyoming Eagle*, June 15, 1943, 6.

18   Larson, 247.

19   Ibid..; Kassel, Michael B, "Thunder on High Cheyenne, Denver and Aviation Supremacy on the Rocky Mountain Front Range" (M.A. Thesis), History Department, University of Wyoming, 2007, 172-173.

20   Ibid., 181.

21   Ibid., 181-182.

22   Ibid., 183. The new construction included two new hangars, a cafeteria, and a concrete parking lot for the aircraft although once completed it contained more buildings as well as operating equipment and needed tools. Kassel, 186.

23   "U.A.L. Facilities: City Is Center of Vital Activities," *Wyoming State Tribune-Leader and The Wyoming Eagle*, July 21-24, 1942, p. 7.

24   Kassel, 189.

25   "UAL Employees Adopt 10-Hour Working Shift," *Wyoming Eagle*, July 16, 1942, 4.

26   "Modification Center Here Working 24 Hours Daily on Big Flying Fortresses," *Wyoming Eagle*, October 24, 1942, 1 and 10; Kassel, 192.

27   "3500th Bomber Rolls Out of Airport Plant: Dignitaries Take Part in Public Program in Observance of Production Mark Here," *Wyoming State Tribune*, March 24, 1944, 1; "Hell's Angels Will Return to Cheyenne: Famous Bomber and Crew Will Visit City on March 24, B-17 Modified at U.A. L. Plant," *Wyoming State Tribune*, March 19, 1944, 1 and 8. The crew of Hell's Angels was touring the country.

28   Kassel, 203.

29   Mackey, Mike, "Cheyenne's 100-Octane Plant," *Readings in Wyoming History: Issues in the History of the Equality State*, edited by Phil Roberts, Laramie, Skyline West Press, 2004, 123.

30   "New Frontier Refinery In Operation: $500,000 Plant Producing 'Rarin'-to-Go Gasoline," *Wyoming State Tribune*, August 2, 1941, 1.

31   Mackey, 126-127.

32   Ibid.

33   Ibid.

34   "Frontier Refinery to Turn Out Fuel for Nation's War Planes: $4,000,000 Addition to Cheyenne Plant Started; Plays Vital Role in Region," *Wyoming State Tribune-Leader and Wyoming Eagle*, July 21-24, 1942, 2; "Thanks, Wyoming: You've Sure Done Right By Us!" *Wyoming State Tribune-Leader and Wyoming Eagle*, 3.

35   "Key Role in War Set for Octane 'Gas' Plant: Frontier Gasoline Plant Dedication Set April 15," Frontier Refinery 100-Octane Plant Dedication Edition, April 14, 1944, 3; $8,000,000 Plant Is Operating Here," Frontier Refinery 100-Octane Plant Dedication Edition, April 14, 1944. One of the articles in the special edition was a short biography of M.H. Robineau, "The Success Story of M.H. (Bud) Robineau: Completion of 100-Octane Plant Features His 20-Year Career in Oil," Frontier Refinery 100-Octane Plant Dedication Edition, April 14, 1944, 3 and ll.

36   Mackey, 128-129.

37   "Project Awaiting Approval of FHA," *Wyoming State Tribune*, August 3, 1942, 1 and 7; "Construction of 28 Houses Is Authorized," *Wyoming Eagle*, September 16, 1942, 2; "Work Well Advance Here On War Workers' Houses," *Wyoming Eagle*, September 10, 1942, 1 and 28.

38   Larson, 137.

39   "300 Trailer Houses to Be Brought To Cheyenne," *Wyoming Eagle*, March 20, 1943, 1 and 8; "$1-a-Year Lease for Trailer House Community Site Is Executed Here," *Wyoming Eagle*, April 1, 1943, 1 and 6; "Cheyenne's Trailer Community," *Wyoming Eagle*, June 8, 1943, 8.

40   "142 of 300 Trailers Being Used," *Wyoming State Tribune*, November 16 1943, 1.

41   "Housing Project Won't Hinder Frontier Show, Official Says," *Wyoming Eagle*, October 16, 1942, 1 and 3.

42   "Work Started on $1,500,000 Frontier Park Housing Setup," *Wyoming State Tribune*, January 29, 1943, 1; "Frontier Park Villa Will Be Occupied Soon," *Wyoming State Tribune*, June 14, 1943, 1 and 8.

43   Paul Kalish Papers, Wyoming State Archives.

44   "First Careyville Unites [sic] Slated for Occupancy Today, *Wyoming Eagle*, January 22, 1944, 19; "Housing Units To Be Erected On South Side, *Wyoming Eagle*, August 27, 1943, 12; "978 Housing Units Built," *Wyoming State Tribune*, April 16, 1944, 1 and back page.

45   "How Army Paper Sees City: Yank, Which Is Distributed Only to Men In Service, Describes Wartime Boom," *Wyoming State Tribune*, September 13, 1943, 6. The editor of the *Wyoming State Tribune* corrected the statement about hunting. "There are no moose and few, if any, elk in Snowy Range."

Only Six Square Blocks

The United States Army was segregated during World War II. On October 9, 1940, the White House announced: "The policy of the War Department is not to intermingle Colored and White enlisted personnel in the same regimental organizations." This apparently was the first time the government made an official statement "setting segregation and discrimination as the policy for the United States Army."[1] Some leaders in the army certainly supported this policy. General George C. Marshall feared morale could be weakened if African American troops were not segregated, and Secretary of War Henry L. Stimson believed Black troops were inferior, writing in his diary: "Leadership is not embedded in the negro race yet."[2] A survey conducted by the Office of War Information in 1943 reported that 96 percent of White Southerners and 85 percent of White Northerners wanted military segregation. Conversely, 90 percent of northern Blacks and 67 percent of Blacks from the South wanted integrated units.[3]

Black servicemen had served in every war fought by the United States, but "military leaders actively discouraged Black people from enlisting in the two decades after World War I." Several years after the end of the First World War, the Army War College wrote and published a report about Black soldiers titled "The Use of Negro Manpower in War." It evaluated how Black soldiers performed in the war. Written by White officers, the report had a negative opinion of the usefulness of Black servicemen, and it concluded that "Black people lacked the intelligence, courage, and moral character to thrive as military leaders or soldiers." Some of the report's claims included: The Black soldier "is mentally inferior to the White man…." Also stated was that the "Negro is profoundly superstitious. He is by nature sub-servient and naturally believes himself inferior to the White." Two other conclusions were that the "Negro is unmoral" and "An opinion held in common by practically all officers is that the negro is a rank coward in the dark." Such was how the leaders of the U.S. Army perceived the value of African American soldiers.[4] Still, with the war approaching, Black soldiers were recruited and drafted by the military, and soon some were to be posted outside Cheyenne at the Quartermaster Training Replacement Center in the 4th Regiment.

At the time, Cheyenne had a small population of African American citizens. The 1940 federal census reported 262 in the city. It was not uncommon for cities with small Black populations to protest the inclusion of Black soldiers at nearly all military installations, explaining that the city did not have the necessary recreational facilities for the Black soldiers. In early 1941, one of Wyoming's United States Senators, Harry Schwartz, asked the army to reduce the number of African Americans scheduled for the fort. This did result in five hundred soldiers being redirected from Warren to Camp Lee. However, the substitution of White soldiers at the fort created local housing issues in Cheyenne, and the army "declared that the reduction of Negroes and the substitution of White men could not be accomplished if strict segregation was to be held to."[5] Black troops did arrive at the QMRTC in 1941, and the army segregated them.

Planning began in 1940 for the housing and other buildings for the troops to be trained at the cantonment, a word often used to describe the training center. Eighty-eight barracks were expected for the White troops and were to be located west of the Colorado and Southern railroad tracks and north of Happy Jack Road. Barracks for the Black troops, which would be separated from the White barracks, totaled twenty-five. Each unit was built to be "self-sustaining, with mess halls, recreation centers, post offices, officers' quarters, motor repair shops, classrooms, fire stations, infirmaries, guard houses, and company storehouses.[6] A drawing of the area for the QMRTC was included in the December 27, 1940, edition of the *Wyoming Eagle*. "One 'suburb' is for White conscriptees due here March 15 and other for the Colored."[7] The first seventy-five Black troops arrived in February 1941. The plans at that point were to station about fifteen hundred Black troops at a time at the QMRTC.[8] The expectation was that not more than twenty-four hundred would ever be trained at one time.

The training centers were like small cities and needed street names. Colonel George Blair, who was the executive officer at Fort F.E. Warren, with approval from Brig. Gen. F.E. Uhl, the post commander, named the streets. The streets in the White section received the names of various states, includ-

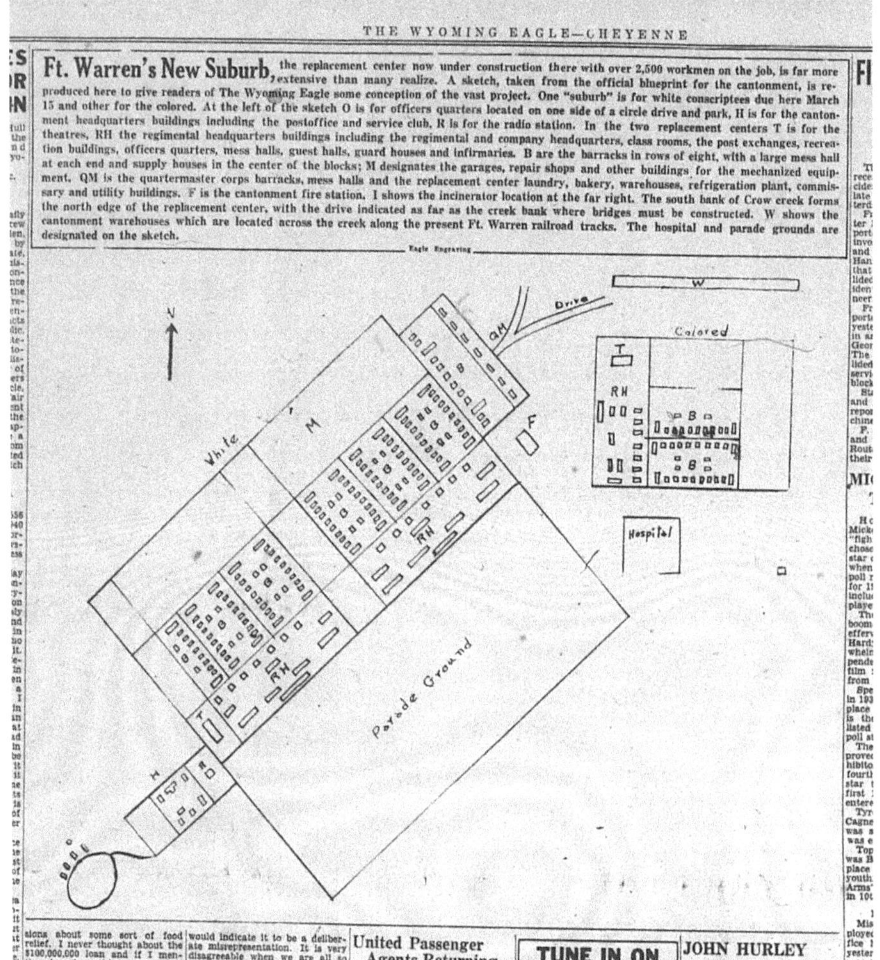

THE WYOMING EAGLE—CHEYENNE

Ft. Warren's New Suburb, the replacement center now under construction there with over 2,500 workmen on the job, is far more extensive than many realize. A sketch, taken from the official blueprint for the cantonment, is reproduced here to give readers of The Wyoming Eagle some conception of the vast project. One "suburb" is for white conscriptees due here March 15 and other for the colored. At the left of the sketch O is for officers quarters located on one side of a circle drive and park, H is for the cantonment headquarters buildings including the postoffice and service club. R is for the radio station. In the two replacement centers T is for the theatres, RH the regimental headquarters buildings including the regimental and company headquarters, class rooms, the post exchanges, recreation buildings, officers quarters, mess halls, guest halls, guard houses and infirmaries. B are the barracks in rows of eight, with a large mess hall at each end and supply houses in the center of the blocks; M designates the garages, repair shops and other buildings for the mechanized equipment. QM is the quartermaster corps barracks, mess halls and the replacement center laundry, bakery, warehouses, refrigeration plant, commissary and utility buildings. F is the cantonment fire station. I shows the incinerator location at the far right. The south bank of Crow creek forms the north edge of the replacement center, with the drive indicated as far as the creek bank where bridges must be constructed. W shows the cantonment warehouses which are located across the creek along the present Ft. Warren railroad tracks. The hospital and parade grounds are designated on the sketch.

———— Eagle Engraving ————

The *Wyoming Eagle*, December 17, 1940, included this drawing of the future buildings of the Quartermaster Training Replacement Center. It was drawn from the official blueprint for the center. The accompanying article about the center was titled "Ft. Warren's New Suburb," one suburb for the White soldiers and the other for the Black soldiers. The larger section with the Parade Ground was for the White "conscriptees" and "other for the Colored."

ing South Dakota and North Dakota, Iowa, Nebraska, Minnesota, Arkansas, Missouri, Kansas, and Wyoming. The streets in the Black section received names of "prominent men of the Colored race." Among the streets were "Booker Avenue, Douglas Street, Young Street, Laramie Loop, and Cheyenne Road." Booker Avenue was named for Booker T. Washington, "famous Negro educator," and Douglas Street for Frederick Douglass, a noted abolitionist. Young street named after the first "Negro officer to serve in the U.S. army."[9]

In March 1941, the army announced two movie theaters had been opened in the camp. The theater for the 1ˢᵗ and 2ⁿᵈ regiments had a forty-foot stage and dressing rooms, so it could provide stage presentations. The Black troops were assigned to the 4ᵗʰ Quartermaster Training Regiment, and they had their own theater. The army also built a hospital to be used by both White and "Colored" troops, although in separate wards.[10] In April 1941, General Uhl announced that five chapels would be built at the fort and QMRTC. Two were for the main post and three for the Quartermaster Center, two for the White soldiers, and one for the Black soldiers. Money had also been allotted for a service club and guest house for the 4ᵗʰ Regiment.[11]

During the summer of 1941, some concern was apparently raised about whether the Black soldiers would be able to swim in the city's Sloans Lake. The city responded by announcing the plan to recondition Kiwanis Lake beach and "turn it over to the Colored soldiers and Colored residents of Cheyenne and Ft. Warren." The lake, which had been used in previous years, had been cleaned, and the dressing rooms and toilets were being prepared for use.[12] However, the city council's City Park Commissioner, Al Kay, said the city would not be able to provide lifeguards for Kiwanis Lake. Kay also said the army should provide lifeguards and military police "for the protection of lives at Kiwanis Beach." He said the city had done everything to prepare the lake for use and that it would be difficult for the city to provide the guards. The parks program made it clear in the newspaper that it would provide lifeguards at Sloans Lake, but it would not take any responsibility at Kiwanis Beach. This seems somewhat odd since the fort agreed to provide two lifeguards at Sloans Lake.[13] The U.S. Army clearly was segregated, as was the city of Cheyenne.

In 1943, Harvey Jackson, the Chief of Police for the Cheyenne Police Department, described the living conditions for African Americans in the city. Writing to Cheyenne Mayor Ed Warren, he stated: "As you know, our housing facilities here already are being taxed to the limit. We have an area of only six blocks square to house the Colored people and most of that, of course, is taken up by Mexicans. The majority of these houses are small and at the present time some of these small houses have as many as twelve to fifteen people living in four rooms. This also is a bad situation due to the lack of sanitation facilities." The letter continued: "Before the war, the negro population of Cheyenne was less than two hundred. One can readily understand that we are unable to absorb many more Colored people at the present time…. We have only one Colored saloon in town and now, as you know, it is almost impossible to get the State to grant another license."[14] The "Colored saloon" referenced in the letter was Baker's Place. It was not owned by African Americans, but by Bill Miyamoto and Johnny Baker, who was half Native American and half Black. The bar was on the West Side at 418 West 17th Street.[15] The Cheyenne City Ordinances did not preclude any bar or restaurant from receiving a liquor license, but at that time, none of the Black-owned businesses applied for a liquor license.

The area where the African Americans lived was known as the West Side. Unfortunately, Jackson did not describe the exact area of the six square blocks. However, looking at the 1940 federal census, the West Side was larger than his idea of six square blocks. According to addresses for the Black population in the census, the south boundary of the West Side was West Fifteenth Street. The east boundary was Thomes Avenue, and the north boundary was West 27th Street. West 18th Street to the 1700 block had more Black residents than any other street. Two African American women lived on Carey Avenue, one at 3003 Carey and the other at 2312. One was listed as a servant for a White family and the other as a maid for a White family. Also, a few Blacks lived on the city's South Side. The census listed 262 African Americans in Cheyenne, compared to 22,087 White residents, and other races totaled 125. For the entire state, there were 246,597 Whites and 956 "Negro" along with 2,349 "Indian," 102 Chinese, and 648 Japanese.[16]

If an African American family was traveling through Cheyenne and Wyoming and needed a place to stay for a night in 1941, they probably would have looked at *The Negro Motorist Green-Book*. The 1941 edition of that book listed three places where they could have spent the night in Cheyenne. The only hotel listed was the Barbeque Inn at 622 West 20th Street. There were two other places listed as "Tourist Homes." They were Mrs. I. Randall at 612 West 18th Street and Mrs. M. Herman at 621 West 18th Street. All three were on the West Side.[17]

Before the war, two Black teams were able to participate in Cheyenne's sporting leagues. During the 1939 softball league in the city, "for the first time in a number of years will be an all-Colored team." The team played in the B league and was sponsored by the Black and Tan Café at 901 West 18th Street, owned by Lola West. The newspaper articles about the league and the teams often described the players on the Black and Tan club as the "Colored boys."[18] Cheyenne also had a men's basketball league, and in 1940, an African American team joined the league. The team name was the "Colored Cobras." Buck Rhone was the captain of the team. Besides the sports teams, Blacks from the city also started their own groups, such as the "Colored Masons," Masonic Lodge No. 290 for "Colored members." During August 1940, the lodge had "their emancipation celebration at the community house."[19] However, at times, racial tensions in Cheyenne did arise.

One such incident occurred at the Black and Tan Café in August 1939. The headline of the newspaper article about the occurrence was titled "Mixed Parties at Negro Night Club Denounced." According to the story, Chief of Police T. Joe Cahill described the raid on the "Negro night club" as involving "mixed parties." He said: "The police department is absolutely determined to break up mixed parties." The police arrested thirteen individuals, some White, some Black. Cahill continued: "When White folks mix with Colored folks, dance together and eat together, it generally results in very serious trouble. We know from experience that most anything can happen, even the most serious crimes, when these two unmixable elements get together. The color line must be drawn in Cheyenne … if we are to avoid disturbances." The police chief used the arrest as a warning to young White couples not to "frequent Negro establishments." One of the charges was "frequenting a disorderly house." That term is listed in the city ordinances and is described as a house of prostitution. Seven of those arrested had their charges dismissed, three forfeited bonds totaling $120, and three were fined a total of $55. Lola West was charged with "selling liquor and running a dance hall after midnight," which was against city ordinances. The ones who had their charges dismissed were boarders at the Black and Tan Club.[20] However, the arrest of the thirteen and the remarks by Cahill, did lead to some pointed comments about the incident.

At the time, the *Wyoming Eagle* allowed Cheyenneites to write comments in a column the newspaper titled "Voice of the People." In the August 10, 1939, edition, Samuel Jones wrote a column titled "Takes Exception" in response to the mixing comments. He wrote, referring to an article of a few days before: "It was an article of far reaching importance because it has to do with mixing of White and Colored people. This night club was raided. A White woman and her White escort were taken along with the others,

Negroes and White men. Is that mixing? If Negroes go into a clothing store, grocery store, motion picture theatre or a White church, is that mixing? No, it is not." Jones went on to describe the article as "conducive to racial discrimination." He said just because there was a White woman there that was the justification for the publicity, also stating that when "Negro women and Negro men and White men" were involved in similar situations, there was nothing newsworthy. He continued: "The Negroes of Cheyenne are very active in doing their part as citizens. We have many fair-minded White people in Cheyenne who will readily patronize Negro activities, and we in turn will patronize White activities (provided there is no discrimination)." Jones believed that it was regrettable that the press covered the story. "The Negro is a citizen of the United States. They have died for Old Glory." He concluded by stating he was a friend of Cahill, but he did not approve "of his public declaration in this case. It will lead into many difficulties."[21]

Not quite two weeks later, another African American responded to Cahill and his comments on mixing. This one wanted to defend the club. The writer described herself as a "free-born American Negro and I attended Cheyenne schools."[22] She wrote: "I feel I should have a word to say." She supported the owner of the Black and Tan Club, saying she is a citizen and taxpayer and that the club was there for everyone. "There was no segregation." According to her, "all races patronized it" and it had "clean entertainment." "There was no mixing of races. Each race brought his own party and was served and highly respected. If that was mixing, then what were we doing at Pioneer Park Friday evening when 1,500 White and Black cheered the White and Black teams on the softball field? American race prejudice must be destroyed." The writer was identified as Berice West. It should have been Bernice West. She was the daughter of Lola West.[23]

Similar comments about race in Cheyenne were presented in another Voice of the People column in December 1940. This one was titled "Colored People Want Change." The author was L.R. Chumley of Cheyenne. He wrote: "We Negro Americans love America as well as any White American. And as yet there has been no real steps taken toward the training of our boys in this modern 'blitzkrieg' type of warfare. Nor has there been any exceptions made for the training of our men to serve in this vast defense program not under way for the White Americans. Why make the difference? We are Americans, aren't we all? We have been educated in your public school systems, many of us are college graduates. But where do we stand in the schools of national defense?" He went on to say that Black Americans "want to do our bit as defenders of our country, but in these modern times we must also be trained and taught in the modern ways of fighting…. Yes, we are fighters, our race of people are heroes on all fields of battle as history marks from ancient times. Our forefathers fought for freedom from slavery, and we will if necessary fight for freedom from totalitarianism. But first we must be prepared." Chumley concluded if they were trained and joined in the defense of the country "you would before many years regard us, the Colored race, as a solid group and would be a concrete step to the unity of this great nation, and would make a democracy against which no totalitarian dictatorship could ever prevail."[24]

Chumley wrote his letter just before Black soldiers arrived at the QMRTC in February 1941. Once they were at the cantonment, they, like the White soldiers, would take the bus from the Quartermaster Center and fort to go downtown for entertainment. The Black soldiers probably visited Baker's Place, some of the businesses downtown, the Black and Tan Club, and the Porters and Waiters Club on the West Side.

One of the major concerns of the mayor and others was whether the city had enough recreation for the Black troops. In mid-December 1940, the Cheyenne Coordinating Council hosted a meeting to discuss recreational facilities for the soldiers at the fort and Quartermaster Center. The council was originally created for child welfare and recreational purposes, and it realized the need to provide recreational centers for incoming troops. Representatives from thirty-eight city civic organizations attended the meeting, as did General F.E. Uhl, the fort's commanding officer. The general spoke about creating what he described as a "great citizen army," as well as the importance of providing recreation for the thousands of soldiers soon coming to the QMRTC and the fort. He went on: "I know that you do not favor having the soldier spend all his money on wine, song and the wrong kind of women." "You will want to protect them from the exploitation of racketeers." Uhl's description of a typical center was with "small games, chairs and writing tables and a counter or coffee shop." The council determined it would be up to a chamber of commerce committee to select a location for such a center. Discussions had been held about providing one center, but the general "also stressed that cooperation should include the Colored troops" assigned to the QMRTC. Mention was made at the meeting that the "300 Colored citizens" in Cheyenne would assist with the creation of a recreation center for the Black soldiers.[25] S.E. James, who was the district deputy of the local African American Elk organization, in January stated his lodge "would cooperate whole heartedly in the problem of recreational activities for the more than 1,500 Colored trainees who will be stationed at Ft. Warren."[26]

By late February, the chamber of commerce had selected the buildings for recreation centers for both White and Black soldiers. The White center would be at the Cheyenne Consistory temple, located at 21st and Capitol Avenue. The plans called for the basement to be used for the center, but eventually the entire building was used. The chamber chose the former Cheyenne Creamery building as the site for the Black recreation center. It was located at 421 West 18th Street on the West Side and was owned by John Howard. The business had not been in operation for several years, and the building needed extensive renovation to be ready for the soldiers. The chamber, the city, and Laramie County cooperated in bringing the recreation plans to fruition.[27]

Only weeks later, both buildings opened on March 28. Official ceremonies were held that evening, with Mayor Warren presenting the center on Thomes Avenue to General Uhl and John Pickett, the president of the city's chamber of commerce, presenting the center at the Consistory temple to Uhl. The *Wyoming Eagle* described it: "Cheyenne's doors to relaxation and entertainment will open tonight at 7 o'clock for the draftees at Ft. Warren." A week before they opened, Mrs. James Greenwood announced that she had organized a group of four hundred Cheyenne women, voluntarily conscripted, to provide entertainment for the recreational center's attendees. This referred entirely to the White center, not the center for the Black soldiers.[28] By the end of the year, a third USO center opened in Cheyenne. That was the Catholic USO center sponsored by the National Catholic Community Service and was located in Cathedral Hall at 20th and Capitol Avenue. This one was also only for White soldiers.[29]

At the national level, in early 1941, six national service organizations created the United Service Organization (USO). The six were the Young Men's Christian Association (YMCA), the Young Women's Christian Association (YWCA), the Jewish Welfare Board (JWB), the Salvation Army, the National Travelers Aid Association, and the National Catholic Community Services (NCCS). The new organization was determined to provide morale and recreational services for the country's military. The organization's founding documents did not approve of discrimination based on creed or race in the centers. All were expected to be open to all servicemen. However, the organization's leaders did understand "that the USO was in no position to solve the question of segregation." It was not uncommon for some of the USO centers to be segregated, "either because of local regulations or by the request of African Americans who deplored the tensions that arose when they entered the USO Center." By 1943, more than 180 of 1,326 USO operations were designated for African Americans.[30] The first two Cheyenne centers were under the USO and were sponsored by the YMCA. However, the city had determined to have two centers, one Black and one White, before the involvement of the USO. It is unclear who or what organization determined that Cheyenne would have two recreation centers.

The three USOs held Open Houses in March 1942. This event was part of a nationwide effort sponsored by the USO. It is also tied to the first-year anniversary of the two centers in the Consistory building and the Cheyenne Creamery building. Several officials presented short addresses, including Colonel George Blair from the fort, Wyoming Secretary of State Lester Hunt, and Cheyenne Mayor Ed Warren at an event held Saturday evening. Public tours took place the following Sunday. The facilities in the Consistory consisted of a photographic darkroom, radio club, ballroom, library, writing room, billiard room, kitchen, and canteen, as well as an army wives club.[31]

Both city newspapers published the same article about the Black USO,

The USO for the Black soldiers was located at 421 West 18th Street. The building formerly had been the Cheyenne Creamery business. Photo courtesy of the Wyoming State Archives.

mentioning that Cheyenne's "Colored USO Center" was the first recreational center just for African American troops in the entire nation. The article acknowledged the exterior of the former creamery had not changed much, but the interior had been completely renovated. The soldiers of the Fourth Regiment at the QMRTC enjoyed a canteen that supplied sandwiches, coffee, and soft drinks, a lounge, a library, a reading room, billiard tables provided by various Cheyenne businesses, and an area for weightlifting. Downstairs, the USO included two discarded and salvaged bowling alleys. Also included was a dance floor. When the center held dances for the Black soldiers, USO recreation centers in Denver brought several busloads of women for the events.[32]

A year after the open houses during the spring of 1942, the Black USO celebrated the second anniversary of the recreation center. A special program was held for the event, and the invited guests included Governor Lester Hunt, Mayor Warren, General H.L. Whittaker, and others. An article about the event described the center's activities, which included card tournaments, musical programs, and evening movies. It also made the point that women, servicewomen, wives, and families of the soldiers were all welcome.[33]

One of the soldiers from the Fourth Regiment who used the Black USO described it later in an oral history interview. Jim Byrd noted the center was

The USO for the White soldiers was located in the Cheyenne Consistory Temple at 21st and Capitol Avenue. Photo courtesy of the Wyoming State Archives.

on the southeast corner of 18th and Thomes. He mentioned the two bowling alleys, three pool tables, and "they had a room that they had turned into a dark room with the various things you need to develop pictures if you had the skill to do that." He also mentioned: "And Blacks had a difficult time getting into Plains Hotel and some of the other places. Restaurants, those kinds of things."[34]

Some Cheyenne businesses did not accept business from the African American soldiers trained at the QMRTC. When newspapers advertised several bars for troops to visit, only Baker's Place made it clear it was open to everyone. Its advertisement read: "Always A Hearty Welcome for Ft. Warren's Colored Troops at Baker's Place, 418 W. 17th."[35]

In an undated letter, the local branch of the National Association for the Advancement of Colored People (NAACP) wrote to Cheyenne's mayor to contest a sign placed at the Texas Café. The business was located near Thomes and 18th, and the "insulting" sign said: "No Colored Trade Solicited." The letter stated: "These signs are provocative and UNAMERICAN. They are contrary to the spirit of the Constitution of the United States. We beg you to use your office to see that the citizens of Cheyenne and the state of Wyoming are respected."[36] Other letters came from Fort Francis E. Warren.

Isaiah H. Hunt served as a U.S. Army chaplain at Fort Warren in 1943. In August of that year, he wrote a letter to Cheyenne's mayor, Ed Warren, and the president of the Cheyenne Chamber of Commerce. Hunt served as chaplain to the "Negro troops" at the fort, and he felt "by the virtue of my office, I must share the responsibility and the sacrifices and various insults, with the men whom I serve." He was the only Black commissioned officer at the fort and in his position "the men feel free to bring me there (sic) problems and it is, but natural that they must have some one to carry there (sic) problems too, and I assure you that they are many." Hunt listed several incidents that some African American troops encountered in Cheyenne at that time. At a restaurant near Union Station, a Black soldier entered the business and sat at the counter. The proprietor of the business directly told him "We don't serve ______ in here." Another soldier purchased a ticket at a downtown theater and an "Usherette" told him, "______ can't sit here, you will have to go upstairs."[37]

Chaplain Hunt offered more examples. At a downtown drugstore, one Black soldier who had purchased several items elsewhere wanted to buy a sundae. The girl at the fountain told him, "No negroes are allowed to be served at this counter." Another of the city's drugstores "refused to serve the Negro soldiers of the Post." At a "Ten Cent Store," there had been "numerous complaints about the treatments and insults that the Colored troops have incontered (sic) while trading at the store." At a Cheyenne dry goods store, one of the Black soldiers had purchased a soldier suit for his son and a summer dress for his daughter. The store altered clothing for free, but when the soldier requested that service, the clerk told him, "Colored soldiers had nothing to do but wait until she had waited upon her regular customers. Ther (sic) period of waiting was three hours." The chaplain ended his letter: "Other similar incidents have taken place in restaurants and drugstores, and most of the Statements refer to were given in the most insulting manner. We submit this letter for your record and consideration."[38] The file did not include any response to the chaplain.

The day before Chaplain Hunt mailed his letter to the mayor and chamber of commerce, another chaplain at the fort, Rolland D. Smuffer, Chief, Chaplain Branch, sent a memo to Fort Warren's commanding officer. The subject was: "Relationship of City of Cheyenne to Colored Troops." Smuffer related several examples Hunt had used in his letter to the mayor. At the end of the memo, however, he suggested "a meeting with officials of civic organizations and city and state officer, together with members of the post official group to determine policies to be established that this problem not become a menace." He also suggested several policies. "A method of courteous information transmitted to the Colored soldier by means of either a printed small card to be handed to the soldier, or a displayed poster at the entrance." Language for such a poster was not included in the memo. Other suggestions included were more activities at the USO and "the Colored churches of the community," as well as a "Colored picture show and a good Colored restaurant," and finally "An orientation talk by the Chaplain to all new troops," which would include explaining the attitude of managers, certainly referring to the managers of Cheyenne businesses. Smuffer asked for another Black chaplain if more Black troops were to come to the fort.[39]

The Cheyenne Police Department took great interest in the arrests of African American soldiers between 1941 and 1943. The department compiled two lists of "Arrests of Colored Soldiers From January 1941 to September 2, 1943." These lists are of arrests and not trials. One of the lists had three columns: Name, Charge, and Disposition. Under Names, two of the men also had their ranks listed; both were staff sergeants. In 1942 and 1943, most offenses were drunk as well as drunk and disturbance. Other charges in all three years included peeping tom, fighting, gambling, prowling cars, breaking and entering, immorality, grand larceny, slugging, and robbery of a person, reckless driving, purse snatching, and assault with a deadly weapon. There was one statutory rape listed, and that person was turned over to the county sheriff. Most of the violators were referred to the Military Police or Military Authorities, with a few more to the sheriff's office.[40]

The second list included more information about some of the arrests. Titled "Briefs From Daily Record Book Involving Colored Soldiers, January 1941 to September 2, 1943," it included such descriptions as a "breakin" at United Auto Supply. A report that two Black soldiers were in a car with a White man, all drunk, and the two soldiers apparently hit Peter Sturick "with some kind of instrument." The injured man was taken to the hospital. Another man was robbed of forty or fifty dollars by two soldiers at 1709 Bent Avenue. In another incident, at 1720 Bent Avenue, there was a disturbance with "15 to 20 Colored people, civilians and soldiers arguing." One of the men had a head injury, and a woman was injured as well. The Black soldiers involved were taken to the military police at the fort. The majority were robberies and attempted robberies, although there was a report of one attempted rape and one rape. There was another one of a woman who claimed she was molested by a soldier, "probably Italian, Mexican, or Negro." This four-page list was compiled by Chief of Police Jackson.[41] Cheyenne police did not compile lists of the "arrests" of White soldiers during the war.

In Chief of Police Jackson's letter to Mayor Warren, in which he referred to the six square blocks where the city's African American population lived, he also included information about Black soldiers related to "Attempted Rape cases on White women, also Malicious Trespassing, Peeping Toms, House Burglaries, and Cutting Scrapes. We had one White woman beaten, robbed, and raped by a negro and one near riot between the Blacks and Whites." He also mentioned three African Americans had been sentenced to the Wyoming State Penitentiary for "attacking White women." Jackson told the mayor that he was unable to hire any more police, since the "Army and Defense Plants have taken most able-bodied men." He stated that if more Black troops were to come to the fort, "we will have trouble between the Blacks and Whites."[42] A month before Jackson wrote to the mayor expressing his concern about the number of African American troops, the army announced it would close the QMRTC, which apparently would have eased any concerns Jackson may have had.

The headline in the *Wyoming Eagle* on July 2, 1943, stated: "Army Says QM Center Will Be Replaced Here in About 6 Weeks." The War Department decided to close one of the Quartermaster training centers, and the one at Fort Warren was selected for closure rather than the center at Camp Lee, Virginia. At the time, the QMRTC had six regiments: the 1st, 2nd, 3rd, 4th, 5th, and 16th. The newspaper article included the information that more troops would be sent to Fort Warren for training but did not specify whether training for infantry and artillery troops would continue.[43] However, the planning for the closure of the QMRTC changed quickly: in September, Cheyenne's mayor wrote to Henry L. Stimson, the Secretary of War, with concerns about the War Department's new plan.

The new plan was to keep the Quartermaster Center open and station approximately 8,000 to 10,000 more "Negro troops" at the post. Warren's letter stated that the proposed number of Black troops, 8,800, or possibly up to 10,000 or 15,000, was too many since at that time the city only had an African American population of 350. He wrote: "In offering my suggestions as to the inadviseability of this move because of the dangerous condition it would create, I wish you to understand that I am putting this matter up to you for your consideration in the manner of a plea, and regardless of how this important matter is settled I would want you to know that Cheyenne will, as in the past, cooperate with the War Department to its fullest ability." The letter continued: "I am extremely alarmed and fearful that a serious situation will arise if great numbers of Negro troops are sent to our post. I am appreciative of the fact that these grand Negro troops are a part of our great army, and while I personally respect and honor them, both as soldiers and American citizens, I feel certain that I am in no sense being an alarmist when I tell you frankly that I feel absolutely certain that Cheyenne, with her less than 350 Colored people, one Negro saloon and one or two small and not good restaurants for Negroes, will be entirely unable to provide properly for the large contingent it is planned to send here." Warren also requested that if more Black troops were sent to the QMRTC the total contingent would not number more than three thousand, "and that at all times our White troops outnumber them from two to three to one."[44]

Secretary of War Stimson responded in a letter more than a week later. He told Warren that the issue of sending more Black troops to the QMRTC had been studied carefully and that the center had the best facilities and equipment necessary to train more Quartermaster troops. The secretary assured the mayor that the total number of Black troops would not exceed ten thousand and that they would not need an extended period to train. He also wrote: "Fully adequate recreational facilities for Colored troops will be provided at the center and in the vicinity. The morale and discipline of the troops assigned to the center will receive close supervision from higher commanders, and no unpleasant situation will be permitted to develop." The letter concluded that the War Department was aware of problems and that he was confident Cheyenne's citizens would cooperate, and he added "that communities throughout the nation are being called upon to make a great variety of sacrifices to the end that our cause may eventually prevail."[45]

Still concerned about the possible consequences of increasing the number of African American soldiers at the QMRTC, Warren contacted Ames K. Bagley of the Organization and Civilian War Services in the Office of Civilian Defense. The Office was charged with the "principal responsibility for safeguarding a community from undue and unreasonable shocks and stresses." In response, Bagley met with a variety of Cheyenne and state leaders including Senator Joseph O'Mahoney and then attended a meeting of Cheyenne's Defense Council, made up of the mayor, R.J. Hofman, the chairman of the council, Robert D. Hanesworth, a member of the council and secretary of the chamber of commerce, and Col. Randolph L. Esmy, executive vice-chairman of the council, and others. Bagley presented ideas about how to deal with the influx of more Black soldiers when Esmy remarked, "All of this planning of programs is futile if the army brings those Colored troops to Cheyenne." Members then expressed their "resentment" to the plan to bring those troops to the QMRTC, stating it was "unwarranted and unreasonable to impose such a problem upon the city." One council member said, "It will set Cheyenne back ten years." Warren continued to hope the number of African American troops could at least be reduced by half and he and others continued to look to Bagley and his office to assist the city in dealing with the issue.[46]

A few days after the Defense Council meeting, Warren wrote to the Federal Works Agency requesting assistance with housing for the expected increase in the Black civilian population resulting from the influx of thousands of additional African American troops, as well as with alterations to the Black USO. The mayor explained in his letter that the area in Cheyenne to be selected for the new housing would be "remote from the center of the White population, for the installation of the housing development and thus reduce any possible friction that might occur between the races." The Federal Works Agency leased and operated the USO, and Warren requested $10,150 in financial assistance for general construction, heating and plumbing work, equipment, and contingencies. The USO had been designed for up to 2,400 Black troops, but with the anticipated increase in their number, alterations were needed. Warren's letter included a formal request for additional funds.[47]

Bagley and his colleagues in the Office of Civilian Defense apparently were able to resolve the matter in Cheyenne's favor. On October 12, he wrote to Warren: "While we cannot make any authoritative statement at this time, it is the belief of our Washington headquarters that we will get appropriate action. We are not unmindful of the great problem of the army in the placement of Colored troops, nevertheless we are assured that the War Department is endeavoring to make every proper adjustment in full cognizance of Cheyenne's community problems." The increase in the number of Black troops at the QMRTC never occurred. The mayor and the others involved in the efforts to reverse the proposed army plan were successful.

CHAPTER 2 ENDNOTES

1   Guglielmo, Thomas, A., *History of Racism and Resistance in America's World War II Military*, Oxford University Press, New York, 2021, 108.

2   "A Matter of Color: African Americans Face Discrimination," State of Oregon: World War II, Official web site of Oregon Secretary of State.

3   Delmont, Matthew F., *Half American: The Epic Story of African Americans Fighting World War II At Home And Abroad*, Viking, an imprint of Penguin Random House, 2022, 165.

4   Delmont, 26-27.

5   Lee, Ulysses, *The Employment of Negro Troops*, Office of the Chief of Military History, Department of the Army, Washington, D.C., 1966, 101-102.

6   "88 Barracks To Be Built At Ft. Warren," *Wyoming State Tribune*, November 15, 1940, 2; "Blueprints Of New Buildings At Post Okayed," *Wyoming Eagle*, November 16, 1940, 14.

7   "Fort Warren's New Suburb," *Wyoming Eagle*, December 27, 1940, 2.

8   "First Colored Troops Arrive at Ft. Warren," *Wyoming State Tribune*, February 13, 1941, 10.

9   "Cantonment Streets Are Assigned Names," *Wyoming State Tribune*, January 3, 1941, 2.

10   "Two Theaters Opened at Cantonment," *Wyoming State Tribune*, March 27, 1941, p. 4; "New Cantonment Hospital Will Cost $311,500," *Wyoming Eagle*, June 8, 1941, 14.

11   "New Buildings Will Be Erected at Cantonment," *Wyoming State Tribune*, April 17, 1941, 2.

12   "Kiwanis Beach To Be Prepared For Swimmers," *Wyoming Eagle*, June 11, 1941, 1 and 9.

13   "Post To Supply Two Lifeguards At Sloans Lake," *Wyoming State Tribune*, June 6, 1941, 3; "Army Asked To Provide Life Guards At Lake," *Wyoming State Tribune*, June 11, 1941, 2; "Kiwanis Beach Not Guarded In Parks Program," *Wyoming Eagle*, June 20, 1941, 8.

14   RG3001, City of Cheyenne, Cheyenne City Records, Administrative Files, Cheyenne Mayor, Police Dept., Jan. 1943-Nov. 1945, letter, Chief of Police Harvey Jackson to Cheyenne Mayor Ed Warren, August 31, 1943, box 4, Wyoming State Archives.

15   Field, Sharon, Lass, ed., *History of Cheyenne, Wyoming, Laramie County, Vol. 2*, Dallas, Texas: Curtis Media Corporation, 1989, 473. Also mentioned is the fact that celebrity Sammy Davis, Jr. frequented Baker's Place. For more information about Davis and his time in the army during World War II at Fort Francis E. Warren, see Davis, Sammy, Jr., and Jane and Bury Boyar, *Why Me? The Sammy Davis, Jr. Story*, New York: Farrar, Straus and Giroux, 1989, 8-27; Jacobson, Matthew Frye, *Sammy Davis, Jr. and the Long Civil Rights Era: A Cultural History*, Oakland, California: University of California Press, 2023, 35-63. Davis was not stationed at the QMRTC, but at Fort Francis E. Warren. The author started the chapter on Davis stating this: "By His Own Account, Davis was first introduced to the full hostility and the violent undercurrents of American racism at the very moment he had been conscripted to defend American democracy."

16   United State Federal Census, Cheyenne, Wyoming, 1940.

17   *The Negro Motorist Green Book*, New York City, Victor H. Green, Publisher, 1941, 48. The three places were also listed in the 1939 edition of *The Negro Motorist Green Book*, New York City, Victor H. Green, Publisher, 45.

18   "New Team in Softball League," *Wyoming State Tribune*, May 4, 1939, 4; "Sports Wrangler by Harold Davis," *Wyoming State Tribune*, May 9, 1934, 4; "Cafemen Upset Bowlers," *Wyoming State Tribune*, August 23, 1939, 2. Cafemen referred to the players sponsored by the Black and Tan Café.

19   "Colored Masons To Have Fete Here Monday," *Wyoming Eagle*, August 3, 1940, 15.

20   "Mixed Parties at Negro Night Club Denounced," *Wyoming State Tribune*, August 8, 1939, 1 and 8; "Negro Night Club Raid Jails 13," *Wyoming State Tribune*, August 7, 1939, 1; "7 of 13 Held In Raid Are Freed Here," *Wyoming Eagle*, August 8, 1939, 17.

21   "Voice of the People," *Wyoming Eagle*, August 10, 1939, 5.

22   Cheyenne schools were not segregated.

23   "Voice of the People," *Wyoming Eagle*, August 22, 1939, 8.

24   "Voice of the People," *Wyoming Eagle*, December 21, 1940, 22.

25   "Downtown Recreation Center Planned for Post Conscriptees: 38 Organizations Pool Efforts to Meet Problem," *Wyoming Eagle*, December 19, 1940, 1 and 8.

26   "Christensen Is Re-elected Council Head," *Wyoming Eagle*, January 10, 1941, 3.

27   "Recreational Hall for Colored Draftees Planned: Old Creamery Plant May Be Used by Chamber of Commerce," *Wyoming State Tribune*, February 26, 1941, 7; "Plans Being Made for Two Troop Centers," *Wyoming Eagle*, February 27, 1941, 3.

28   "Draftee Centers To Open," *Wyoming State Tribune*, March 9, 1941, 1; "Recreational Center Work Moves Rapidly," *Wyoming Eagle*, March 12, 1941, 8; "Two Recreation Centers To Be Opened Tonight," *Wyoming Eagle*, March 28, 1941, 7. "Hostesses For Draftee Center 'Conscripted' Here: 400 Women Volunteer for New Organization," *Wyoming State* Tribune, March 17, 1941, 2. Earlier in March the Laramie County Board of Commissioners requested the Cheyenne City Attorney determine if the "county's financial responsibility in a civic project to provide recreational facilities for Colored troops at the replacement center at Ft. Warren." The attorney found it was allowed. The request only was about the African American center. "Starnes To Determine If County Can Give Aid to Draftee Center," *Wyoming State Tribune*, March 6, 1941, 2.

29   "Catholic USO Center Opens," *Wyoming Eagle*, December 23, 1941, 11; "Catholic USO Will Join in Open House," *Wyoming State Tribune*, March 15, 1942, 6.

30   "How the USO Served a Racially Segregated Military Throughout World War II," United Service Organization website, accessed February 7, 2022; Gretchen Knapp, "Experimental Social Policymaking During World War II: The United Service Organizations (USO) and American War-Community Services (AWCS)," *Journal of Policy History*, 2009-04, Vol. 12 (3), 327.

31   "Dedication, Open House Planned For USO Centers This Weekend," *Wyoming Eagle*, March 10, 1942, 1 and 8.

32   "Colored USO Center Was First in Nation: Ex-factory Building Remodeled Into Fine Unit," *Wyoming Eagle*, March 14, 1942, 14; "USO Center For Colored Troops Is First In Nation," *Wyoming State Tribune*, March 15, 1942, 6.

33   "Weekend Programs to Mark 2nd Anniversary of 18th Street USO," *Wyoming Eagle*, March 20, 1943, 9.

34   Jim Byrd oral history interview, Wyoming State Archives.

35   "Always a Hearty Welcome," *Wyoming Eagle*, July 1, 1943, 13. This ad can be found in many editions of the Cheyenne newspapers.

36   Undated letter, The N.A.A.C.P. Committee, Local Branch, to His Honor the Mayor, RG 3001, City of Cheyenne, Cheyenne Mayor Records, Administrative Files, Petitions from Citizens, Oct. 1940-Aug. 1942, box 4, Wyoming State Archives. Since it was filed in this folder the mayor would have been Ed Warren, who served in that office until January 1944.

37   Letter, from Isaiah H. Hunt, Chaplain U.S. Army, to Mayor of the City of Cheyenne and the president of the Chamber of Commerce of the city of Cheyenne, 31 August 1943, RG 3001, City of Cheyenne, Cheyenne Mayor Records, Administrative Files, Cheyenne Mayor-Misc. Correspondence, Feb. 1943-Dec. 1943, box 4, Wyoming State Archives.

38   Letter, from Isaiah H. Hunt, Chaplain U.S. Army, to Mayor of the City of Cheyenne and the president of the Chamber of Commerce of the city of Cheyenne, 31 August 1943, RG 3001, City of Cheyenne, Cheyenne Mayor Records, Administrative Files, Cheyenne Mayor-Misc. Correspondence, Feb. 1943-Dec. 1943, box 4, Wyoming State Archives.

39 Memo, from Rolland D. Smuffer, Chief, Chaplain Branch, to Commanding Officer, Ft. F.E. Warren, Wyoming, 30 August 1943, City of Cheyenne, Cheyenne Mayor Records, Administrative Files, Cheyenne Mayor-Misc. Correspondence, Feb. 1943-Dec. 1943, box 4, Wyoming State Archives.

40 "Arrests of Colored Soldiers From January 1941 to September 2, 1943," RG 3001, City of Cheyenne, Mayor Records, Administrative Files, Cheyenne Mayor, Police Dept., Jan. 1943-Nov.1945, box 4, Wyoming State Archives.

41 "Briefs From Daily Record Book Involving Colored Soldiers, January 1941 to September 2, 1943," City of Cheyenne, Cheyenne Mayor Records, Administrative Files, Cheyenne Mayor, Police Dept. Jan. 1943-Nov. 1945, box 4, Wyoming State Archives.

42 Letter, Chief of Police Harvey Jackson, to Mayor Warren, August 31, 1943, RG 3001, City of Cheyenne, Cheyenne Mayor Records, Administrative Files, Cheyenne Mayor, Police Dept., Jan. 1943-Nov. 1945, box 4, Wyoming State Archives.

43 "Army Says QM Center Will Be Replaced Here in About 6 Weeks," *Wyoming Eagle*, July 2, 1943, 1 and 4.

44 Letter, Mayor Ed Warren to Henry L. Stimson, Secretary of War, September 9, 1943, RG 3001, City of Cheyenne, Cheyenne Mayor Records, Administrative Files, Cheyenne Mayor to Fort Francis E. Warren, Sep. 1943-Dec. 1945, box 4, Wyoming State Archives.

45 Letter, Henry L. Stimson, Secretary of War, to Mayor Ed Warren, September 20, 1943, RG 3001, City of Cheyenne, Cheyenne Mayor Records, Administrative Files, Cheyenne Mayor-Fort Francis E. Warren, Sep. 1943-Dec. 1945, box 4, Wyoming State Archives.

46 Memorandum, from Ames K. Bagley, Eastern Sector, Organization & War Services, to Frank S. Gaines, Asst. Director, Ninth Civilian Defense Region, Subject "Cheyenne—Colored Troops," September 26, 1943, RG 3001, City of Cheyenne, Cheyenne Mayor Records, Administrative Files, Cheyenne Mayor-Fort Francis E. Warren, Sep. 1943-Dec. 1943, box 4, Wyoming State Archives; Letter, from Ames K. Bagley, Organization and Civilian War Services, to Cheyenne Mayor Ed Warren, September 28, 1943, RG 3001, City of Cheyenne, Cheyenne Mayor Records, Administrative Files, Cheyenne Mayor-Fort Francis E. Warren, Sep. 1943-Dec. 1943, box 4, Wyoming State Archives.

47 Letter, to the Federal Works Agency, from Cheyenne Mayor Ed Warren, October 1, 1943, RG 3001, City of Cheyenne, Cheyenne Mayor Records, Administrative Files, Cheyenne Mayor-Fort Francis E. Warren, Sep. 1943-Dec. 1945, box 4, Wyoming State Archives; Memorandum to E.C. Tilley, Community War Services and Howard C. Beresford, Community War Services, "Recommendations: Cheyenne Negro Recreation Facilities," RG 3001, City of Cheyenne, Cheyenne Mayor Records, Administrative Files, Cheyenne Mayor-Fort Francis E. Warren, Sep. 1943-Dec. 1945, box 4, Wyoming State Archives.

Unsavory Moral Conditions Created by the War

In 1942, Cheyenne attorney Edward Byron Hirst decided to run as a Republican for the office of County and Prosecuting Attorney for Laramie County. His father, Ed Hirst, had served the public as Laramie County Treasurer until his death in 1940. The son was born in Grand Island, Nebraska, in 1912. After three years in Rock Island, Illinois, the family moved to Cheyenne in 1927. Hirst graduated from high school in 1929 and from the University of Nebraska in 1933. Following graduation, he moved to Washington D.C., where he worked for Wyoming Senator Joseph O'Mahoney, graduated from George Washington Law School, and was admitted to practice law in the District of Columbia. Hirst also received a degree from Harvard Law School. Upon returning to Cheyenne, he practiced law for five years before running for public office as the county attorney.[1]

Hirst's opponent for the office of prosecuting attorney was Democrat Ken Starnes, who had served one term in the office. In 1938, in his initial campaign for office, Starnes promoted himself as a twenty-year resident of Cheyenne, a juvenile court judge, and added he also was a taxpayer. He pledged "Justice to All."[2] In his run for re-election, he cited his experience in the office. His advertisement stated, "Qualified through Proven Experience."[3] An article in the *Eagle*, "Experience Fits Starnes To Be County Attorney," also cited his knowledge of judicial procedure because of his time on the juvenile court and that he was "especially interested in Laramie County problems," such as the need for ambulance service.[4]

Hirst certainly had strong qualifications to serve as County and Prosecuting Attorney for Laramie County. The *Wyoming State Tribune* ran an article, "Hirst Well Trained for Public Post." It discussed his qualifications and his record of public service, which included serving as the Chief Air Raid Warden for Cheyenne, among other duties. He was also the special attorney for the city of Cheyenne. However, his newspaper advertisement only states

Byron Hirst ad in his campaign to become Laramie County's County and Prosecuting Attorney, featured in the *Wyoming Eagle,* October 31, 1942.

his name, Edward Byron Hirst, and that he is a candidate for the office of County and Prosecuting Attorney, ending with "Your Support Appreciated."[5]

The election results showed that a majority of Laramie County offices were won by Republicans. Hirst defeated Starnes with a vote of an even five thousand, while Starnes received 4,084.[6] The *Wyoming Eagle* expressed surprise that Hirst was able to defeat an incumbent, noting his newness on the political scene. Also a surprise to the Democratic newspaper was the victory of Norbert Tuck, a former police chief for the Cheyenne Police Department, as Laramie County Sheriff over Sheriff George J. Carroll, who had served as sheriff for 20 years.[7] Both Hirst and Tuck thanked the county voters and said they would show, by their actions over the next four years, that the voters' confidence in them was justified.[8] Another noteworthy election was Ira Hanna's commanding victory over John Schepp with 6,747 votes to 2,221, for the office of Laramie County Assessor.[9] Although during the election,

Hirst did not specify what his goals were, his actions in the coming years showed exactly what he wanted to accomplish as county attorney. Both Tuck and Hirst would play important, but different, roles in what would soon take place in the capital city

Before Tuck ran for the office of county sheriff, he had served as Cheyenne's Chief of Police. However, his tenure in that position ended in December 1940. Several months before, in June of that year, Mayor Ed Warren sent a letter to Chief Tuck that can only be seen as a disciplinary one. The mayor wrote the police should set an example to all the other departments in the city, yet he had learned "from the proper authority that three or four of the men have women in the sporting districts. This will have to be discontinued. In the future, the men of this department will not be allowed to visit sporting houses." He went on to say he will have special officers "checking the girls in these places" and that officers will not be allowed to wear their uniforms in bars unless called. Warren also clearly stated men on duty will not be allowed to haul women around in their "prowl cars" and that gambling and card playing was not allowed in the police department. He also said the behavior of the officers testifying in court must improve, including "standing in an erect posture and addressing the court as His Honor." The mayor also received many complaints about the lack of regard for traffic regulations, such as speeding, reckless driving, and double parking, which were being abused. Warren made it clear he was not satisfied with the police department's performance, so he took what he considered a "drastic measure" by sending this letter, warning that this would only be the beginning if his concerns were not corrected.[10] Apparently, things did not improve.

During a December 1940 meeting of the Cheyenne City Council, Warren approached the other two city commissioners, Al Kay and J.A. "Buck" Buchanan, and asked their approval to remove Tuck as chief of police for "inefficiency." A motion was made, and the three approved the motion to remove Tuck from that position. Warren then asked for approval to appoint Detective Captain Harvey Jackson as the new chief of police. It was approved, and he was sworn into office. According to an article in the *Wyoming State Tribune*, it was Warren who was inefficient, not Tuck. However, Tuck refused to resign from the office even though Jackson had been sworn in, which led to the *Wyoming Eagle* story titled "Cheyenne Has Two Chiefs of Police." In the end, Tuck became the Captain of Police, a position he had held before becoming chief, a position supervised by the chief of police.[11]

Although apparently not made public, the mayor's records list a "few reasons" why Tuck was dismissed as chief of police. These included not being in his office during office hours; using a patrol car for personal use; not enough discipline in the police department; "Patrolmen visiting upstairs on Pioneer Avenue; unpleasant demeanor toward public; traffic and parking conditions; speeding and reckless driving; failure to attend Police Court regularly; and Complete disregard of warning given in letter of June 28 1940."[12] A year and a half later, Tuck resigned from the Cheyenne Police Department after twelve years of service in order to run for the office of Laramie County Sheriff.[13] He won that election in November 1942. He and Hirst worked well together in the upcoming months and years.

The city of Cheyenne faced many legal challenges during the war years. Certainly, these were not that different than many cities across the country at that time. Perhaps because of the location of Fort Francis E. Warren next to Cheyenne, there were other issues for the community, as we will see, but overall, many cities at that time dealt with illegal gambling, illegal sale of alcohol, drunkenness, and perhaps prostitution. These problems were present before and after Hirst took office in January 1943, and not only did the office of county attorney attempt to deal with them, but so did local law enforcement and the Cheyenne City Council.

Hirst only served one term as county attorney, but during those years, he prosecuted a variety of cases. Surprisingly, he represented several women in divorce cases during his first year in office. According to the newspaper reports, the women claimed, "intolerable indignities."[14] Perhaps he had committed to represent those clients before he took office. As one would expect, he prosecuted murder cases in his first year as county attorney, and his first time in court as the county attorney was for a preliminary hearing for a case of a husband murdering his wife.[15]

"Albert (Coon Can Sam) Perkins," an African American, was charged with first-degree murder for shooting and killing his wife, Jean, on December 7, 1942. His trial began in early March 1943. Hirst and Perkins' defense attorney, Clyde Zachman, questioned the jurors at the beginning of the trial. Zachman included such questions as "Do you know what a prostitute is?" "Do you believe a prostitute can be pretty mean?" "Have you any prejudice against Negroes?" After the jury was selected, Hirst, in his opening statement, clearly stated he would prove Perkins and his wife were alone in the apartment when his wife was shot by a gun purchased by Perkins, and that sometime before the shooting, Perkins told someone he had contemplated killing his wife. Zachman declined to provide the jurors with an opening statement.

One of the first witnesses for the prosecution was Mrs. Stowers, who had rented a room in the boarding house to the Perkins. She testified that the evening of the shooting, she heard Mrs. Perkins scream, and she went across the hall and knocked on their door. Mr. Perkins answered and told her he "had slapped Jean, and that wasn't all he intended to do." Stowers went back to her apartment and then heard shots fired. She opened her door and saw Perkins back out of his apartment, then run out the front door with a gun in his hand. Mrs. Stowers found Jean had been shot and called the police. She and two other women in the house placed Jean on her bed. Sheriff Tuck investigated and spoke to Mrs. Perkins, who told him, "We were just arguing. He had no right to shoot me." She was taken to the Cheyenne hospital, where she died a few days later.[16]

Upon cross-examination, Perkins' attorney attempted to implicate Mrs. Stowers by asking if she ran a house of prostitution. Stowers denied the accusation, and when asked if she knew how Mrs. Perkins "made her living," she answered no. However, Zachman then referred to her testimony at the coroner's inquest when Stowers was asked if Mrs. Perkins entertained men for money, she answered, "That's right." In response, she said she did not remember making that statement. The attorney also brought race into the trial when he asked her, "Hasn't Sam had something on you since September? Didn't you then sleep with a white man?" Stowers denied that accusation.[17]

Perkins claimed self-defense. He testified he and Jean had been married for three and one-half years and that she earned her living as a prostitute, and he went on to describe what life was like living in a house of prostitution. He described her as a "sporting woman." He also stated on the stand that she had threatened to kill him during the past fall. According to Perkins, what happened the day of the shooting was that his wife began drinking at 11 in the morning and continued all day. At one point, Jean hit him, and when he tried to leave, she pulled him back in and grabbed the pistol, which was under a pillow. He realized she might shoot him, so he "grabbed her around the waist with one hand, the gun in the other hand, and I was holding one part of the gun, the barrel, and she the other, the handle, when the shooting occurred."

He said his wife told him, "I'm shot. I want a doctor. Don't let the policemen catch the gun in here or you either." Continuing his testimony, Perkins said he wasn't sure she had been shot, so he disposed of the gun and went to Omaha. While there, he learned Jean indeed had been shot, so he turned himself in to the Omaha police.[18] His testimony apparently was not convincing, as the jury found Perkins guilty, and District Judge Sam Thompson sentenced him to life in prison at the Wyoming State Penitentiary.[19]

Another case prosecuted by Hirst in late 1943, according to the *Wyoming Eagle,* garnered statewide interest. Cheyenne residents were certainly watching the results, since the person charged with second-degree murder and manslaughter was a former member of the county's law enforcement. George J. Carroll, who had served as Laramie County's sheriff for two decades until his defeat by Tuck in the 1942 election, shot sixteen-year-old Charles Bowershock on July 25, 1943. Hirst did not charge the former sheriff until October, after the boy died in the hospital on October 12.[20]

The shooting took place at the Mission Auto Court, a tourist camp owned by Carroll, located on East Lincolnway. According to reports, Bowersock had been seen "prowling" around the camp. Mrs. H.L. Schroeder, who lived at 1615 House, reported there had been a prowler in the neighborhood for several weeks, and she claimed she had seen a "window peeker," according to the *Wyoming Eagle.* In Carroll's statement to Hirst on August 7, he said he thought Mrs. Schroeder may have been molested, so he grabbed his gun and went to investigate.

He found the youth in the alley behind the court and grabbed him by the arm to take him to the office. Bowersock broke free and started to run. Carroll yelled for him to stop. When the teen ignored the order and continued to run, the former sheriff fired two shots into the ground. One of the shots ricocheted and the bullet entered the youth's back, traveled through his body, and exited from his chest. A Cheyenne police officer and a military police officer traveling with the Cheyenne officer in a "prowl car" responded to the shots, found Carroll and Bowersock, and took the boy to the hospital.[21]

After Bowersock died, an inquest was held, and the officials who testified determined that the gunshot was not the only cause of death. Carroll did not testify, but his statement was read during the proceeding. The attending physician, Dr. George F. Johnston, and the pathologist who performed the autopsy, Marjorie Andersen, both testified. According to Dr. Johnston,

Bowersock developed pneumonia after a surgery to repair the damage to his stomach caused by the bullet, which was then followed by emphysema, and then meningitis occurred in the brain stem, leading to his death. At the inquest, Hirst asked the doctor: "Would the conditions leading up to the boy's death have arisen if he hadn't been shot?" Johnston responded, "Only the Lord knows." Dr. Anderson stated: "I couldn't say the bullet wound was the primary cause of death, but I could say that the wound probably contributed to the death." She also stated, "It's possible the conditions present would have arisen without the bullet wound." The inquest determined that Bowersock, on October 12, died "from complications resulting from a bullet wound received by the deceased on July 25." One might think this would be the end of the investigation and possible charges, but it was not.[22]

County Attorney Hirst twice brought charges of second-degree murder, manslaughter, and aggravated assault and battery against the former county sheriff. After Bowersock died, his father, Herman, filed a complaint against Carroll and Hirst, presenting the charges in a preliminary hearing in the court of Justice of the Peace H.A. Brookhart. Throughout the hearing, Hirst contended that Bowersock had not committed any crime that Carroll was aware of, and therefore, he should not have fired. Prosecution witnesses included the boy's father and several witnesses from the court and nearby neighborhood. When Carroll testified, his attorney, John Pickett, asked him if he intended to shoot the young man. Carroll responded: "Certainly not—and I'm sorry I did. Half the time when I was performing duty as sheriff, I didn't carry a gun." Upon being asked if he had ever shot anyone, Carroll said: "No, sir, I never drew blood on a man before." After the testimony, Brookhart dismissed the charges. He based the dismissal on the fact that Carroll was an authorized deputy sheriff and, at the time, performing his duty. According to his ruling, Bowersock was in the wrong, by running from Carroll. The justice said the shooting was "accidental but justifiable."[23] However, a second preliminary hearing soon took place.

Harvey Bowersock filed another complaint, and Hirst refiled the charges. This time, however, since Brookhart, the Cheyenne Justice of the Peace, had dismissed the charges, he filed the charges in Burns, a small town near Cheyenne. Justice of the Peace Charles Lyon oversaw the hearing. Hirst told the *Wyoming Tribune* that he had received a petition with 150 names urging that the Carroll case be tried in district court. The newspaper also reported that some of Carroll's supporters might submit a larger petition against a district court trial.[24]

Carroll's second preliminary hearing began the morning of November 5. John Pickett, Carroll's attorney, stated that since the prosecution had not provided enough evidence to sustain the charges, he requested that the charges be dismissed. Even with this request, Justice Lyon heard some of the same witnesses from the first hearing, such as Herman Bowersock and Dr. Johnston, among others. However, later in the hearing, after Hirst had rested his case, Lyon said Pickett's motion "was well taken" and, from what he had heard, agreed sufficient evidence had not been presented by the prosecution. He found no crime had been committed. Lyon gave Hirst another chance to provide more information, but nothing was forthcoming, and Lyon dismissed the charges for a second time. He said the evidence "is wholly insufficient to establish that an offense had been committed or that there is probable cause to hold the defendant for trial." The *Wyoming Eagle* stated Hirst had provided a "vigorous prosecution," and the county attorney expressed his opinion. "The issue of this case might have been determined by a jury trial in district court. To bring a defendant in district court he must first be bound over for trial by a justice of peace. However, since all available evidence has been presented to two duly-elected justices of the peace of Laramie County who have determined, that, in their opinion the defendant should not be bound over for trial, I shall not institute any further criminal proceedings." At the end of the *Eagle's* article about the second hearing, the newspaper included mention of some of Carroll's well-known successes as county sheriff.[25]

Apparently, Hirst and Tuck, along with the city of Cheyenne and the Laramie County Board of Commissioners, realized the need for more assistance to address the crime and vice that were then engulfing the city. In April 1943, after meeting with businessmen and police officials, Cheyenne Mayor Ed Warren appointed F.B. McVicar, a "local investment man," as the city's juvenile officer to address the increase in juvenile delinquency.[26]

Several months later, the board of county commissioners appointed George E. (Red) Smith to the positions of special investigator and deputy sheriff. Smith had extensive law enforcement experience. During the early 1930s, he organized the Wyoming Highway Patrol and served as its head for six years. He was also a deputy sheriff under Sheriff Carroll. Hirst and Tuck announced that his duties involved eradicating vice conditions in the city.[27]

According to Tuck: "The duties of the deputy will be to investigate all vice conditions and take proper steps toward the abolishment of them." He and Hirst expected Smith to "investigate all gambling, slot machines and other forms of vice with special attention given to the sale of liquor to juveniles."[28]

The *Wyoming Eagle*, in an editorial after Smith's appointment, expressed support for both additions to law enforcement. It stated: "Every American city whose population has been inflated by reason of military activities or the presence of war industries has inherited a number of aggravating problems. Included in the list are gambling, prostitution, and juvenile delinquency, along with an increase in what might be termed general criminal activities." Another problem noted was that the current Cheyenne police department was about the same size as it had been before the war. The city's population had grown to about thirty thousand, compared with the 1940 figure of twenty-two thousand. The editors determined that the hiring of McVicar as a juvenile officer was the first step to dealing with the many issues ongoing in the city, and Smith's hiring as the second essential step to begin to address the "unsavory moral conditions created by the war." However, the editorial writers realized more actions would be necessary, and that cooperation from civic groups, parents, and public-spirited individuals would aid the effort.[29]

Gambling in Cheyenne was "Forbidden," and the city ordinances listed many forms, including roulette, keno, craps, poker, faro, card games, various devices, and even shuffleboard. The penalty for gambling was a possible fine of ten to one hundred dollars and possibly ten days to three months in jail.[30] On August 17, 1943, Hirst announced that all gambling houses in Cheyenne had been closed. He said, "In cooperation with local city and county police authorities and special investigator George Smith, he had personally seen to it that no gambling houses in the city were open."[31] Staff of the military publication, *Yank*, toured Cheyenne in September and commented that it would be difficult to find a public-sanctioned game in the city because of "a concerted effort by local law enforcement officials to crack down on gambling games."[32] To aid in the campaign against gambling in the city, Hirst "warned" that those who participate in gambling are also liable for prosecution, just like the operators of any illegal games. This included activities such as baseball pools and slot machines, regardless of where they were operated.[33]

Slot machines continued to be a problem into 1944, and the newspapers included stories about the machines being confiscated and then destroyed.

Both the *Wyoming State Tribune* and *Wyoming Eagle* reported on slot machines confiscated at four establishments in early January. Hirst filed the complaints in Judge Brookhart's court and the race-horse type machines were confiscated from the Cheyenne Novelty Co. (1514 Carey Ave.), the Victory Cigar Store (517 Carey Ave.), one machine from the Havenor Recreation Alley (418 W. 18th St.), and a "Jumbo" machine from the Recreation Bowling Alley (211 W. 18th St.) under the direction of Tuck. Hirst made it clear that the businesses had received adequate warning that the possession and operation of the machines was illegal. At one of the establishments, one of the gambling soldiers asked if law enforcement could hold off until he earned back some of his losses. At another of the businesses, the owner said he was only running a repair shop and was not allowing the machines to be operated. One of the officers "asked a woman employee if the slot machine in the establishment was working alright, to which she replied, 'No, we had a little trouble with it last week, it didn't pay off right.'" The judge ruled the machines could be destroyed.[34] After a few days, the machines were destroyed in the employee lot on 18th and Pioneer. Governor Lester Hunt commended Hirst on confiscating and destroying the machines. "May I offer my congratulations to you on this prompt, vigorous action. You are rendering the public a fine service, and I congratulate you on this latest accomplishment."[35]

Hirst and Tuck even participated in the destruction of some of the slot machines confiscated at that time. The *Wyoming Eagle*, in its January 12, 1944, edition, on page 1, included a picture of the two in a vacant lot at 19th and Capitol surrounded by pieces of the former gambling devices. The article stated several witnesses were on hand to watch Tuck and Hirst "wield a heavy hammer until all that remained of the intricate devices, some of which were estimated to cost as much as $600, was broken glass and wooden splinters." Not all went to waste, however, because the sheriff "gave the signal corps at Ft. Warren permission to remove any valuable parts of the machines which the army could use." The two soldiers assigned to this duty said the electrical equipment from the machines could no longer be purchased and could be used in the construction of "walkie-talkie" radios.[36]

As mentioned, one of the issues that received considerable attention in 1943 was juvenile delinquency. The year before, the Cheyenne city council heard complaints about motorists speeding and running stop signs. Mayor Warren dealt with the issue, stating the police department would be

In early January 1944, the city was still confiscating slot machines. Shown here in the January 12, 1944, issue of the *Wyoming Eagle*, are County Attorney Hirst and Sheriff Tuck destroying some of those machines at the scrap metal junk area at 19th and Capitol Avenue.

responsible for apprehending those violators and taking them to police court.[37] However, the issue of juvenile delinquency would need a wider range of actions to deal with the growing problem.

The issue of juvenile delinquency made the front page of the *Wyoming State Tribune* on February 23, 1943, and throughout the rest of the year, ways to reduce the problem were discussed in both city newspapers. Cheyenne Chief of Police Harvey Jackson was quoted as saying delinquency threatened to "break all bounds" and warned "a very serious situation is developing."[38] Nearly two weeks earlier, Jackson announced that children on the streets after midnight would be picked up by police. In early March, city officials adopted a 10 p.m. curfew for children under sixteen.[39] At the same time, the Junior Chamber of Commerce was presenting a series of radio programs on the problems of delinquency. Some of the titles were "The Citizen's Viewpoint on Juvenile Delinquency" and "Juvenile Delinquency in Cheyenne and Its Problems."[40] During a meeting in early April discussing Cheyenne's delinquency problems, Jackson said that while there had been an increase in "robbery by children there has been no appreciable increase in vandalism." He also stated that country girls between fourteen and eighteen who arrive in the city looking for employment, but do not find any, "are among the largest group of female delinquents...." The chief of police also mentioned children of the city's itinerant workers were the most likely to be delinquents.[41] Juvenile Officer McVicar believed recreation and employment were important elements of reducing delinquency. Cheyenne had a city recreation program sponsored by the Cheyenne Recreation Council. McVicar requested assistance from the city's businessmen, explaining that providing employment would be helpful. By June, the city was witnessing some improvement in the issue. The creation of McVicar's position and his "close cooperation" with law enforcement, along with recreation opportunities and some jobs, improved the situation. Hirst reported that month that most cases being prosecuted at the time involved "habitual offenders."[42] However, attempts to reduce delinquency continued throughout the rest of the year, including the establishment of an independent athletic league and other ideas, such as possible involvement in small theater groups.[43]

One of the first charges given to Smith was to investigate the sale of alcohol to minors. Shortly after his appointment, Hirst stated in an article in the *Wyoming State Tribune*, dated August 16, 1943, that he intended to enforce the liquor laws. He announced "an intensive campaign" to prevent the sale of liquor to minors. At the time, the law was that anyone under the age of twenty-one would not be served "alcoholic liquors or malt beverages in bars." Smith's plan to ensure the law was followed was that "girls" would be compelled to show their ration books to determine their ages, "boys" would be asked for their draft cards, and servicemen would need to show their identification cards. If the boys did not have a draft card, it would verify they were not eighteen, since all men that age and older had draft cards. Hirst said he realized the difficulty of checking for everyone's age but stated, "It is our responsibility under the law to be firm." Hirst went on to say young girls were the worst offenders. "This leads to more critical developments in the spread of vice in the city."[44]

The *Wyoming Eagle* in September reported a crime that, according to Hirst, illustrated the need for stiff penalties for selling liquor to minors. Two operators of the Mayflower Café and a waitress were fined $100 each and given six-month suspended jail sentences for serving alcohol to two minors. One was an eighteen-year-old soldier at Fort Warren, and the other was a sixteen-year-old girl. After getting four drinks, the soldier took the girl to Holiday Park and "brutally raped her." He was arrested, court-martialed, and given a dishonorable discharge from the army, and given a life sentence in a federal penitentiary. The girl testified that she and the soldier received drinks from the Mayflower, which led to the fines and a suspended sentence. Hirst said this case "demonstrates the necessity" to enforce the law prohibiting the sale of liquor to minors. "Perhaps if it had not been for the liquor, this attack might never have occurred." He went on to say that the law places responsibility for determining customers' ages on the operators, and that he would charge both the server and the owners for violating the law.[45] However, selling alcohol to minors was not the only violation of state liquor laws.

By November, the Wyoming Liquor Commission, headed by Governor Hunt as the president of the commission, ordered the Wyoming Highway Patrol to begin a statewide campaign to enforce the state's liquor laws. According to Captain William Bradley of the state patrol, the objectives were to prevent the sale of alcohol on Sunday; prevent sale to minors; "require strict adherence to the legally specified closing times" of businesses serving alcohol; to prevent non-taxed alcohol from entering Wyoming; and to "eliminate other illegal operations in liquor sales." One immediate result of the campaign was that charges were brought against the Plamor Club for selling liquor on Sundays. The club was located south of Cheyenne outside of the city limits. The complaint was made by a Cheyenne patrolman and filed in Justice of the Peace F.A. Stennet's court by county attorney Hirst. The liquor commission issued this statement: "The Wyoming Liquor Commission has been aware, as has everybody else, that certain retail liquor establishments have been flagrantly violating the laws governing these establishments. An increasing number of complaints have been coming to the liquor commission from various parts of the state, and it has been necessary for the state to take action in several instances." The commission decided unanimously to inspect every business selling alcohol in the state. Any violations by any outlet that are not corrected immediately will lead to the commission withholding liquor sales from those retailers.[46] Cheyenne Justice of the Peace Stennet jointly fined the two owners of the Plamor nightclub $100 plus costs.[47]

A month before the declaration by the Wyoming Liquor Commission about the statewide campaign to enforce liquor law, the Cheyenne Liquor Dealers Association pledged to support law enforcement agencies and the liquor commission to enforce all liquor rules and regulations. The organization passed a long resolution on October 6 approving the enforcement of the state's laws, acknowledged that the wartime conditions have changed the hours, customs, and methods of selling alcohol, stated their members would assist "in the enforcement thereof in order that unauthorized and illegal sales of liquor thru the sinister practice of bootlegging, illicit distillation and distribution, over-charging sales to minors and all other practices may be brought to an end," and "hereby proffer" to enforce the laws to ensure the welfare of the "service men" in the area, and the association said it would distribute the resolution to Wyoming's Congressional representatives, the Wyoming Liquor Commission, commanding officers of the varied units at Fort Warren, the state's law enforcement agencies, and Wyoming's governor.[48] The sale of alcohol by Cheyenne's businesses was important to the city's revenue; in 1942, liquor license sales brought in $30,480.[49]

The approval of liquor licenses was under the purview of the Cheyenne City Council. Of course, the council, made up of the city's mayor, Ed Warren, and two council members, Kay and Buchanan, dealt with other issues as well, such as complaints about speeding and the running of stop signs in the city,[50] but the determination of which businesses would hold liquor licenses was certainly an important responsibility.

In March 1942, the city council addressed the issue of liquor licenses for several businesses. At that time, retail liquor licenses were granted for one year and were not awarded until a fee of fifteen hundred dollars had been paid. A limited retail liquor license cost $100.[51] When a license was up for approval or renewal, opposition to the license was allowed. At the March 23 meeting, Fort Warren military authorities expressed their opposition through letters regarding the renewal of retail liquor licenses belonging to Samuel Marchick's Tivoli Bar (301 West 16th St.), Anna Shuman (1515 Carey Ave.), R.E. Yeoman, Earl's Bar (309 West 16th St.), and Jack Shuman (422 West 16th St.). The complaints from the Fort personnel stated the businesses run by those four "were being operated in violation of the Wyoming Statutes and to the detrement [sic] of the enlisted military personnel at the Fort." These comments came from Colonel George Blair, the Commanding Officer at Fort Warren. At the Shuman and Marchick places of business, the letters stated, "that alleged houses of prostitution were operated in the same buildings with the liquor stores." The general's statement certainly implied the connection between liquor sales and prostitution. The Yeoman place "was charged with being unsanitary and frequented by men and women of bad repute." In addition to complaints from Fort Warren, the Cheyenne Chamber of Commerce highlighted concerns about those four establishments in a letter to its members. Signed by secretary Robert Hanesworth and president L.A. Miller, the letter stated that there are females employed at the Tivoli bar who "are commonly known as 'B' girls or 'come-on' girls,' and are a direct cause of considerable drunkenness and fighting among the soldiers." It also accused the bar of being an "alleged house of prostitution." Shuman's Bar also employed women, and it was directly under the Trail Rooms, "an alleged house of prostitution." The chamber's letter also said Shuman's Bar was directly under the Gen Rooms, again alleged to be a house of prostitution. Finally, the letter described Earl's Bar, besides being dirty and unsanitary, is visited by undesirables and "women of questionable character."[52] At the meeting, the council denied the renewal for Yeoman, but for the other three, the council determined further investigation was necessary. At the same meeting, many renewals were granted, including those for the Plains Hotel, the Mayflower restaurant, and the Crown Liquor Co. Approval for renewal of Limited Retail Liquor licenses was granted for the B.P.O Elks Club and the Cheyenne Country Club.[53]

At the next council meeting on March 30, the commissioners again addressed the renewals from the week before. This time, the council members heard letters read from the Cheyenne Chamber of Commerce, members of the Women's Club, and several others, all against the renewals of Marchick, Shuman, and Shuman. Also attending the meeting was Captain Tom Hembree, personal representative of Colonel Blair. Hembree told the council members that Blair's comments in his letter from the previous week still stood.[54] Even though the council at the previous meeting had voted to deny Yeoman a renewal, his attorney, Vincent Carter, argued for his client's license to be renewed. He said Yeoman's Earl's Bar, "among other things," did not employ bar maids, which at the time was not legal in Cheyenne. Attorney Walter Phelan, representing Jack Shuman, brought out what he considered a constitutional question: "that no one could deprive a person of his property without the due process of law." Others who spoke against renewing the four licenses were Rev. Ronald Terry of the Cheyenne Ministerial Association and a representative from the Provost Marshal's office at Fort Warren. At that point, Commissioner Kay asked for a vote. Warren moved that the matter be held over for another week in order to give the four applicants the "opportunity to show cause why their applications should not be denied in the face of the protests received from the military and other government authorities and other sources ..." He said he felt "a moral obligation in hearing the arguments of both sides before taking away the means of livelihood of these four applicants." The motion passed with Kay voting no. After the vote, Warren spoke about the importance of following the law if a business is granted a liquor license because if the law is not followed, the license will be denied or not renewed.[55]

At the next city council meeting on April 6, the commissioners heard the requests for renewal of their liquor licenses again. The four attorneys representing the businesses spoke in favor of renewal, and Anne Shuman and Samuel Marchick also spoke on their own behalf and urged "that their applications be approved and that they be given another chance." Speaking against the applications were the president of the Cheyenne Chamber of Commerce, L.A. Miller, Captain Hembree, who spoke for the fort's commander, and the Cheyenne Ministerial Association. After everyone had spoken, for and against, Warren asked for a motion. Kay moved that the four applications be denied, and the motion passed unanimously.[56]

The Cheyenne City Council often addressed issues related to applications and renewals for retail liquor licenses. The meeting on March 29, 1943, for example, was typical of such approvals, with all of the applications and renewals approved, including the one for Ida B. Schwartz, for her business, Schwartz's Bar and Bronco Room at 207 West 16 Street, managed by her husband, Sydney Schwartz.[57] However, the meeting on May 10, 1943, probably brought back memories to the council members of the March and April 1942 meetings.

Jack Shuman again requested a liquor license on May 10, 1943, although this time it came in a different way. A month earlier, a liquor license had been approved for Edmund A. Yarter. At the May meeting, attorney Ed Lazear, representing both Yarter and Shuman, asked the council to approve the transfer of Yarter's license to Shuman. This was the license previously held by Shuman at 422 West 16th Street. The commissioners discussed the request "at length." For the past year the business had been owned by Yarter and Shuman worked as the manager. Since no violations, such as those noted a year earlier, had been brought forward by military authorities or the city police, "no reason could be seen why the request, made in full compliance with the provisions of Chapter 90. S.L. 1941, to approve the sale and transfer of this license from Yarter to Jack Shuman, should not be granted, and that an injustice would be imposed upon both of the interested parties by refusal of the Council to approve the sale and transfer." Commissioner Buchanan moved to approve the sale and transfer of the license, and the council approved the motion unanimously.[58] Approval of liquor licenses could be contentious, and even though a business received a license in 1943, that did not guarantee it would receive one a year later.

CHAPTER 3 ENDNOTES

1   Hirst's biographical information provided by items in Hirst Papers, American Heritage Center, University of Wyoming.

2   Starnes advertisement appeared in the *Wyoming Eagle*, October 29, 1938, 18.

3   Ken Starnes advertisement, October 22, 1942, 2, and October 30, 1942, 3.

4   "Experience Fits Starnes to Be County Attorney," *Wyoming Eagle*, October 30, 1942, 3.

5   "Hirst Well Trained for Public Post," *Wyoming State Tribune*, October 30, 1942, 14; Hirst advertisement, *Wyoming State Tribune*, November 2, 1942, 8.

6   "Gop Sweeps County Offices: Tuck Beats Carroll, Big Gains," *Wyoming State Tribune*, November 4, 1942, 1.

7   "GOP Makes Gains; Tuck Swamps Carroll; GOP Leads Legislature," *Wyoming Eagle*, November 4, 1942, 1.

8   "Winners in County Give Statements," *Wyoming Eagle*, November 5, 1942, 2.

9   "County Returns," *Wyoming Eagle*, November 5, 1942, 2.

10   Letter, Ed Warren, Mayor, to Mr. N.E. Tuck, Chief of Police, June 18, 1940, RG 3001, City of Cheyenne, Cheyenne Mayor Records, Administrative Files, Cheyenne Mayor-Police Department, Dec. 1933-Dec. 1942, box 4.

11   "Tuck May Resist Dismissal, Harvey Jackson Sworn In: Mayor Warren Charges Police Chief With 'Inefficiency,'" *Wyoming State Tribune*, December 19, 1940, 1 and 14; "Cheyenne Has Two Chiefs of Police," *Wyoming Eagle*, December 20, 1940, 1 and 8.

12   Three lists of reasons for dismissal of Tuck as chief of police, all dated December 20, 1940, RG 3001, City of Cheyenne, Cheyenne Mayor Records, Administrative Files, Cheyenne Mayor-Police Department, Dec. 1933-Dec. 1942, box 4.

13   "Captain Tuck Resigns From Police Force," *Wyoming Eagle*, July 4, 1942, 2.

14   See "Helen E. Lewis Asking Divorce," *Wyoming Eagle*, March 23, 1943, 4, and *Wyoming State Tribune*, February 21, 1943, 3.

15   "Perkins Must Stand Trial on Murder Count," *Wyoming Eagle*, January 9, 1943, 1 and 21.

16   "Murder Trial of Negro Man Is Begun Here," *Wyoming Eagle,* 1 and 8; "Perkins Must Stand Trial on Murder Count," *Wyoming Eagle*, January 9, 1943, 1 and 21.

17   "Murder Trial of Negro Man Is Begun Here," *Wyoming Eagle*, March 6, 1943, 1 and 8.

18   "Perkins Claims Self Defense in Fatal Fight," *Wyoming Eagle*, March 13, 1943, 1 and 8.

19   "'Coon Can' Given Life," *Wyoming Eagle*, March 22, 1 and back page.

20   "Carroll Again Freed of Blame in Death of Boy," *Wyoming Eagle*, November 6, 1943, 1 and 21. See also "Charges Against Carroll Dismissed," *Wyoming State Tribune*, October 21, 1943, 1 and 9.

21   "Charges Against Carroll Dismissed," *Wyoming State Tribune*, October 21, 1943, 1 and 9; "Complications Caused Boy's Death, Inquest Jury Decides," *Wyoming Eagle*, October 16, 1943, 1 and 8.

22   "Complications Caused Boy's Death, Inquest Jury Decides," *Wyoming Eagle*, October 16, 1943, 1 and 8.

23   "Charges Against Carroll Dismissed," *Wyoming State Tribune*, October 21, 1943, 1 and 9.

24   "New Hearing to Be Asked for Carroll," *Wyoming State Tribune*, October 25, 1943, 1 and 11.

25   "Carroll Case Argued Here: Justice Asks for More Evidence," *Wyoming State Tribune*, November 5, 1943, 1 and 9; "Carroll Again Freed Of Blame in Death of Boy," *Wyoming Eagle*, November 6, 1943, 1 and 21. Services for Charles Bowersock were held on October 15, 1943, burial was in Beth-El Cemetery. "Bowersock Rites Conducted Here," *Wyoming Eagle*, October 16, 1943, 13.

26   "F.B McVicar Is Named to City Juvenile Post," *Wyoming Eagle,* April 3, 1943, 1.

27   "'Red' Smith to Open Probe of Vice in County Today," *Wyoming Eagle*, August 11, 1943, 1 and 8.

28   "County Takes Action to Clear Up Vice," *Wyoming State Tribune*, August 4, 1943, 1 and 7.

29   "All Must Help," *Wyoming Eagle*, April 11, 1943, 6

30   *Ordinances of the City of Cheyenne, Codified and Compiled 1938*, Codified, Compiled, and Edited by Mildred Pease, Wyoming Labor Journal Publishing Company, 51 and 52.

31   "Gambling Houses In City Closed, Hirst Announces," *Wyoming Eagle*, August 18, 1943, 1 and 8.

32   "How Army Paper Sees City: Yank, Which is Distributed Only to Men In Service, Describes Wartime Boom," *Wyoming State Tribune*, September 13, 1943, 6.

33   "Gamblers Equally Guilty With Operators, Warned," *Wyoming Eagle*, September 15, 1943, 1 and 24.

34   "Slot Machines Seized at Four Places in City," *Wyoming State Tribune*, January 5, 1944, 1 and 11; "County Seizes Slot Machines At Four Establishments Here," *Wyoming Eagle*, January 5, 1944, 1 and 11.

35   "Court Orders Slot Machines Be Destroyed," *Wyoming Eagle*, January 8, 1944, 1.

36   "Slot Machines Seized in Raid Are Destroyed," *Wyoming Eagle*, January 12, 1944, 1 and 16.

37   Cheyenne City Council Minutes, August 17, 1942, p. 98, Wyoming State Archives.

38   "Jackson Warns of Gain in Juvenile Delinquency; Curfew to Be Tried," *Wyoming State Tribune*, February 26,1943, 1.

39   "10 P.M. Curfew and New Juvenile Officer Slated," *Wyoming Eagle*, March 5, 1943, 1 and 8.

40   "Radio Series on Delinquency to Be Continued on Thursday," *Wyoming Eagle*, April 7, 1943, 7.

41   "Court of Juveniles Urged Here," *Wyoming Eagle*, April 3, 1943, 1 and 8.

42   "Jobs Sought for Youths of 16 and 17," *Wyoming Eagle*, March 6, 1943, 8; "Report Gain in Fight on Delinquency," *Wyoming State Tribune*, June 7, 1943, 7.

43   "The Eagle's Critic Eye," *Wyoming Eagle*, November 20, 1943, 15.

44   "Serving of Youths in Bars Probed," *Wyoming State Tribune*, August 16, 1943, 1 and 9.

45   "Stiff Penalties Set For Liquor Sale To Minors," *Wyoming Eagle*, September 10, 1943, 1 and 8.

46   "Night Club Faces Charge As State Acts to Crack Down on Liquor Violators," *Wyoming Eagle*, November 2, 1943, 2. See also "Patrol Launches Drive to Enforce State Liquor Law: Plamor Club at Cheyenne Faces Charge," *Wyoming State Tribune*, November 1, 1943, pp. 1 and 9, and "State to Aid Counties in Enforcing Liquor Statute: Hunt Urges Alertness in Drive," *Wyoming State Tribune*, November 4, 1943, 1.

47   "Operators of Plamor Fined on Guilty Plea," *Wyoming Eagle*, November 3, 1943, 9.

48   "Liquor Dealers Pledge Full Cooperation in Enforcement of Law," *Wyoming State Tribune*, October 6, 1943, 12, and "Liquor Dealers Pledge Strong Cooperation in Enforcing Law," *Wyoming Eagle*, October 7, 1943, 22. In 1941, apparently Warren did not see great cooperation from the liquor dealers regarding following the law. In March 1941, the mayor sent a memorandum "To All Liquor Dealers in Cheyenne" about their repeated promises to live up to the provisions by the State Liquor Law and Cheyenne city ordinances. He had received complaints about closing hours not being complied with and that juveniles were being served. Memorandum To All Liquor Dealers in Cheyenne, from Mayor Ed Warren, March 24, 1941, RG 3001, City of Cheyene, Cheyenne Mayor Records, Administrative Files, Cheyenne Mayor Liquor Licenses, Feb. 1940-May 1942, box 4. Also during that month Warren sent a memorandum to the operators of taxis in the city. He had received complaints that the illegal sale of alcohol was going on "by cab people." He warned the operators they could lose their license for their cab company if this behavior continued. Memorandum To All Operators of Cheyenne Taxi Cab Companies, from Mayor Ed Warren, March 24, 1941, RG 3001, City of Cheyenne, Cheyenne Mayor Records, Administrative Files, Cheyenne Mayor Liquor Licenses, Feb. 1940-May 1942, box 4.

49   "Liquor License Fees Lead City Income in 1942," *Wyoming Eagle*, February 13, 1942, 9.

50   The Cheyenne City Council addressed the issue on August 17, 1942. The council called upon the police department "to make every effort to apprehend such violators and bring them into Police Court." See Cheyenne City Council minutes, August 17, 1942, 98, Wyoming State Archives. The *Wyoming State Tribune* ran an editorial about the issue, stating some motorists were traveling at 40, 48, and 50 miles an hour. The council responded to such complaints. "Penalty for Speeding," *Wyoming State Tribune*, August 13, 1942, 4

51   The 1938 City of Cheyenne Ordinances set the fee, to be paid in advance, at $1,500. *Ordinances of the City of Cheyenne, Codified and Compiled 1938*, 141.

52   Letter, Cheyenne Chamber of Commerce, News Letter, To all members, RG 3001, City of Cheyenne, Cheyenne Mayor Records, Administrative Files, Cheyenne Mayor-Liquor Licenses, Feb. 1940-May 1942, box 4. The letter is not dated, but clearly refers to the cases brought to the Cheyenne City Council in March 1942.

53   Cheyenne City Council minutes, March 23, 1942, 75, Wyoming State Archives.

54   Letter, Colonel George Blair to Honorable Edward Warren, mayor of Cheyenne, March 16, 1942, RG 3001, City of Cheyenne, Cheyenne Mayor Records, Administrative Files, Cheyenne Mayor Liquor Licenses, Feb. 1940-May 1942, box 4.

55   Cheyenne City Council minutes, March 30, 1942, 77-78, Wyoming State Archives.

56   Cheyenne City Council minutes, April 6, 1942, 80, Wyoming State Archives.

57   Cheyenne City Council minutes, March 29, 1943, 123, Wyoming State Archives.

58   Cheyenne City Council minutes, May 10, 1943, 134, Wyoming State Archives.

Prostitution and Disorderly Houses

It will not surprise anyone that the city of Cheyenne has had a long history of prostitution. This dates to the summer of 1867, when the newly founded city, then known as the end-of-track town, was established to serve the needs of the Union Pacific Railroad as it laid track westward. That early period of time, the so-called hell on wheels period, did not last long, relatively speaking, but prostitution had for many years a presence in the territorial and state capitol of Wyoming, and that certainly included the World War II years.

Only a few months after the railroad passed Cheyenne in November 1867 and headed toward the new end-of-track-town of Laramie, the local residents who did not follow the railroad and stayed in the soon-to-be territorial capital, hoped the presence of "bagnios" (brothels) could at least be less visible. The *Cheyenne Leader*, in its March 2, 1868, issue, noted the city council had prohibited dance houses from the main thoroughfare and then wanted the council to do the same for "dens of ill repute."[1] Nearly two weeks later, the Cheyenne newspaper, in reporting on a fire in downtown Cheyenne, called for the city to remove "these dens of crime" from the downtown business area. The article ended: "Close up those haunts of bad men and worse women, and property owners will feel some sense of security."[2]

More than a year later, Cheyenne residents were still aware of the presence of prostitution, but perhaps were more resigned to the fact of its recurring presence. In September 1869, the *Leader* included an article titled "immorality in Cheyenne," speaking about "harlotry." The newspaper saw this and other crimes driving people away from settling in Cheyenne and asked every "good citizen" to do what could be done to banish "the evils of prostitution and gambling" from the city. The *Leader* realized these crimes could not be eradicated entirely, but hoped those evils would not be as apparent so respectable people "may at least not be ashamed to appear on a street or in a public place, for fear of insult by the low and vicious that have hitherto had full run in this city."[3]

At that time, one can see how Cheyenne dealt with the issue of prostitution. In October, the newspaper reported numerous instances of individuals being fined for the offense. Sam Anderson was charged with "keeping a disorderly house" (a euphemism for a house of prostitution, which endured even to the World War II years). He was fined $300 and court costs. Kate Bennett ran a "bawdy house," pleaded guilty, and was fined $30. Another disorderly housekeeper had to pay $100. Ida Hamilton and Emma Cleveland kept bawdy houses and were fined $50. Charles Stanley and Big Anna also maintained a bawdy house and pled guilty, although their fine was $30.[4] The use of fining both the businesses and the prostitutes was commonly used in Cheyenne.

The idea of removing those "dens of ill repute" to other parts of the city arose again in 1911. At that time, the city had an area called the "Red Light District," a common name for areas of prostitution, located on the west side of Cheyenne. In March 1911, a group called the West Cheyenne Improvement Association met. The members were concerned about property on the west side being rented for "immoral purposes." The area of most concern was near the intersection of Eighteenth and Bent streets. The city had laws against renting property for such purposes, and the association wanted the violators arrested and convicted.[5] A few days after that meeting, the *Cheyenne State Leader* published a column titled "Two Affronts to Decency." The topic raised was the proximity of houses of ill repute to the post office, only two blocks away. The paper suggested relocating the houses to the west side of Cheyenne, a more remote location, preferably around Crow Creek, and perhaps west of the stream.[6] Just a week later, "A Suggestion To Mayor Bresnahen," appeared in another Cheyenne newspaper with the same concern about the "West End problem." The column implored the mayor to deal with the houses of prostitution located on a number of city streets. The author's idea was to build a high stockade around two or three city blocks, enclosing all such houses. The area would have only one entrance and two policemen to watch over it. The surrounded area could be easily controlled. Going further, the author even suggested "a similar but separate place could be arranged for the colored people."[7] Stockades were not constructed for the Red Light District or for the African American population of the city, but some "houses" in the Red Light

District were closed only two months later.[8]

During early May, Prosecuting Attorney Charles Rigdon issued an order that proprietors of "houses of ill repute" in the Red Light District close. According to the *Cheyenne State Leader*, those businesses closed their doors the night of the order. The attorney for the West Side Improvement Association also wanted the order obeyed.[9] It is unclear the houses stayed closed, but it is unlikely, since the West Side Improvement Association's executive committee met with Cheyenne Mayor L.R. Bresnahen in late May. The association told the mayor that their organization would no longer object to the district, provided it was located in a certain section on the west side. They suggested the northern boundary should be between Eighteenth and Nineteenth streets; the southern boundary would be the alley between Sixteenth and Seventeenth streets; the east boundary would be the Colorado and Southern tracks; and the western boundary would be Crow Creek. This location was recommended because the area would be on a hillside and "is hidden from view by the crest of the hill, from any part of the city except that within a block of the district."[10]

Even with the proposal to hide the Red Light District where it would not be seen by other city residents, there were still complaints. Some of these concerns were discussed at a meeting in the city at the end of November. It started as a debate between Reverend L.C. Hills and J.H. Walton. The title of the newspaper article reporting on the debate was "Hottest Meeting Of Year." Apparently, both participants were good debaters, but the majority of the attendees supported the reverend against the Red Light District and the sale of liquor in such houses, and they were vocal about it. When the debate ended, others had the chance to speak on the issue. One who spoke "eloquently" was local attorney William B. Ross,[11] speaking about the liquor traffic. According to the newspaper, another speaker made the case that the West End improvement movement "had ended in failure insofar as any regulation of the sporting element was concerned for the reason that the district since peacefully moving across the tracks was more bold and lawless than ever and it is relying on the mayor for support." Another raised the issue that half of the soldiers hospitalized at Fort D.A. Russell were there for venereal disease "contracted in all probability in the Red Light District" as well as many instances of robbery of soldiers and arrests of soldiers for disorderly conduct in the district. Only a few days later, a soldier from the fort wrote a letter to the *Tribune* and made the same case about the mistreatment of soldiers in the saloons and houses of ill repute. Perhaps it may be doubtful that all soldiers at the fort shared these concerns, but prostitution continued in Cheyenne, although during the World War I years, the charge of dealing with this issue passed from the city to the federal government.[12]

With the beginning of World War I, Congress deemed it important to protect the country's soldiers from what were determined to be the three principal vices affecting the army: prostitution, drinking, and gambling. With the passage and signing of the Selective Draft Act of May 18, 1917, Congress attempted to address those issues. Section 12 of the act restricted the sale of alcohol near military installations. Section 13 authorized the Secretary of War to take whatever action was necessary to "suppress and prevent the keeping or setting up of house of ill fame, brothels, or bawdy houses" near a "military camp, station, fort, port" or any training facilities. Any activities related to prostitution could not be within five miles of the military installations. If anyone violated the act by providing or drinking alcohol or being involved in prostitution would be charged with a misdemeanor and "be punished by a fine of not more than $1,000, or imprisonment for not more than twelve months, or both."[13] The goal was to stamp out prostitution and thereby reduce the possible spread of venereal disease, which would reduce the loss of training time for the troops and relieve some of the stress on the army's medical personnel. Certainly, during wartime, most, if not all, military installations in the country dealt with the proliferation of prostitution in neighboring communities. Of course, this applied to Fort D.A. Russell and Cheyenne, not just in World War I, but also in the Second World War.

In the years leading up to the war, prostitution in Cheyenne was addressed in Section 161 of the city charter. The section was broader than just "prostitution and disorderly houses" and included the prohibition and suppression of bowling alleys, billiard tables, and gambling houses, and even "desecration of the Sabbath day." At that time, it was common for the police to have monthly arrests of women engaging in prostitution, which would bring in between thirty and 112 prostitutes at a time. The usual fine was $10, although a fine of up to $100 was possible. With the passage of the Selective Service Act of 1917, enforcement of the law fell to the military police, with assistance from local officials. The result was an increase in the monetary amount of fines and the possibility of jail sentences. However, after the war, federal government involvement in these matters ceased in March 1919. Once again, the enforcement of city ordinances regarding prostitution and the running of disorderly and bawdy houses fell to the city. [14] The 1926 city ordinances provided direction in dealing with this problem, and Chapter 8, Articles 8-100 to 8-104 of the "Ordinances of the City of Cheyenne, Codified and Compiled 1938" dealt with the issue of a "Disorderly House" forbidding the visit or keeping of such a house "for the purpose of fornication, adultery, prostitution, or any other lewd or immoral practices." Any violation of this ordinance was a misdemeanor. The 1938 ordinances were in place during World War II and although it clearly was a city issue, that did not mean the federal government might not attempt to influence the enforcement of the laws in some ways.

As the war years approached, Cheyenne kept a record of the city's immorality in what may have been seen as an efficient form of documentation. For example, attached to the city's Police Justice Docket was a typed list of two law violations, "Immorality" and "Traffic." Usually, those charged with sexual vice were listed first, and those fined for traffic violations were listed below the immorality charges. Of course, the lists of traffic violations were just about always longer. No specific charge was included for either offense; only the fine was specified. For traffic violations, such as speeding or parking violations, the usual charge was $1.00, although some were higher, perhaps up to $5.00. In 1942 and 1943, the justice docket recorded fines of $50 or $100 for driving under the influence. As one might expect, the fines for immorality were higher, starting at $10.00, although they went as high as $60.00. A fine for a prostitute was generally $10.00, as was seen in earlier times, but if the fine was higher, it may have been for operating a "disorderly house." [15]

During the first week of January 1941, all those charged for immorality were fined at least $20.00. Some charges were individual women, but there were also what might be described as disorderly houses. They were: Modern Rooms ($40.00), 1505 ½ Carey Avenue, Dixie Rooms ($20.00), 210 ½ E. 15th Street, Federal Rooms ($40.00), 1519 Carey Avenue, Elite Rooms, (50.00), 219 ½ West Lincoln Way, Trail Rooms ($40.00), 1517 1/2 Carey Avenue, and Tivoli Rooms ($50.00), 1520 Carey Avenue. Some of these "rooms" were located very near the Union Pacific Depot, where trains passed through the city at all hours of the day and night, often carrying troops. [16]

For example, the violations listed in the police docket between May 1 and May 12, 1941, shows those fined for immorality were Gem Rooms ($40.00),

Paris Rooms ($30.00), the other "rooms" mentioned earlier, and Lola West ($60.00), who ran the Black and Tan Club, and Susie Baker ($20.00). These neatly typed lists document the difficulty Cheyenneites had in following traffic rules, and the constant presence of vice in the city, continuing through 1941 and into 1942. During the first two weeks of December 1941, seven women and five houses were fined for immorality. These were the Federal Rooms ($50.00), Jean Mack ($50.00), Dixie Rooms ($40.00), Susie Baker ($30.00), Lola West ($20.00), Tivoli Rooms ($60.00), Ramona Brooks ($50.00), Georgia Brown ($50.00), Trail Rooms ($30.00), Jo Eva ($30.00), and Ramona Brooks ($20.00).[17]

The year 1942 brought an interesting discussion in Cheyenne about whether the city had rid itself of all prostitution or if it still existed. In February, Mayor Ed Warren sent a letter in response to a complaint from Fort Warren's post commander, Colonel George Blair, regarding how the city was dealing with the issue of prostitution. "I know of no other appropriate action for the City other than to continue to make arrests and assess fines when this condition is found to exist."[18] The discussion continued a few months later when the *Wyoming State Tribune* on April 21 reported Warren's response to Blair's most recent query about the issue of prostitution, saying that the city would cooperate "to the fullest extent" to abolish the houses of prostitution in the city. However, unnamed city officials responding to Blair's request to end all prostitution in the city commented that in some communities where some of the houses have been closed down, the practice had moved to residential and outlying areas. Another said, "While I am against such a practice on moral grounds, I've been around enough to know that such a condition cannot be curbed." The article concluded by stating that no action had been taken to fulfill the mayor's promise. Just so everyone would know, the newspaper concluded the article with the obvious statement that prostitution was illegal in Cheyenne.[19] However, the following day, the newspaper reported what must have seemed to be a contradiction of the earlier report.

Harvey Jackson, the city's police chief, said there had not been any houses of prostitution in the city for the past three months. The chief clarified his statement by saying there may still be some prostitution in Cheyenne, but there is no organized prostitution, as apparently Blair had charged. He acknowledged that some women had been arrested in some of the "so-called high-class hotels," but it was "ridiculous" to expect to completely stop all

POLICE JUSTICE DOCKET

THE STATE OF WYOMING,
County of Laramie, } ss.   Before _______________________
City of Cheyenne,

CITY OF CHEYENNE
vs.

Immorality and Traffic Violations Aug.1st to 17th Incl.1941.

Immorality

Gem Rooms	40.00	Billy Powell	50.00
Paris Rooms	50.00	Margaret Jones	50.00
Mary Julian	40.00	Marie Dayton	40.00
Georgia Brown	40.00	Black and Tan	30.00
Susie Baker	30.00	Trail Rooms	30.00
Joeva Rooms	40.00	Paris Rooms	10.00

Traffic

Aaron Bergman	1.00	N.Buffington	1.00
F.H.Porter	1.00	Frank Tremaine	1.00
Mrs.Cliff Petrie	1.00	Geo.Davis	1.00
Phil Vissenberg	1.00	Ben Vissenberg	1.00
R.E.Wilson	1.00	Mrs.D.C.Martin	1.00
W.L.Sellers	1.00	Arthur Black	10.00
Robt.Altizer	5.00	P.M.Cunningham	1.00
Bert Crist	1.00	Walter Miller	5.00
Clifford Patton	1.00	Ray Desmond	1.00
J.S.Fudie	1.00	Wm.Aylward	1.00
Henry Mitchell	1.00	Louis Higardea	1.00

List of "Immorality and Traffic Violations, Aug. 1st to 17th Incl. 1941," Police Justice Docket, State of Wyoming, County of Laramie, City of Cheyenne, Wyoming State Archives.

prostitution with the present police force. He indicated it would take a tripling of the force to accomplish that goal. Jackson said police records indicate seventy-one women had been arrested in March "on suspicion of being prostitutes." In April, 57 women had been arrested on similar charges, according to the police chief. And, he said, every one of those had been fined, jailed, or ordered out of town. Jackson noted that many of the prostitutes are part of the usual influx of prostitutes into a city adjacent to an army post. The mayor did not respond, but Blair did. He told the newspaper he raised the issue because a confidential federal investigation of prostitution in Cheyenne indicated there were eight to twelve houses of prostitution active in the city.[20] Probably surprising to many readers of the *Wyoming Eagle*, as an article titled "Prostitution Is Ended in City, Official Says" appeared on page one of the May 2nd issue. The official mentioned was Blair, who said the mayor had informed him that the city was following the military request to end the practice in the area. However, the article did not provide any specific information about how this was accomplished.[21] Blair's interest in the topic of prostitution in Cheyenne at that time may have resulted from a directive he received in early April from the Provost Marshal Office of the Army, which stated that post commanders would be held "strictly accountable" if official army policies were not followed regarding the suppression of prostitution.[22]

A few weeks before these articles were published, the city stopped including the typed list of those charged with immorality. The docket still included a list under the heading of Traffic, but that was all, so it is difficult to verify Jackson's numbers. However, in the docket of April 20, 1942, a woman named Hattie May was arrested for operating a disorderly house and selling liquor on Sunday. She forfeited a $200 bond.[23] Throughout the rest of 1942, a number of docket entries listed women charged with prostitution or running a disorderly house. These arrests and fines certainly made it clear that Cheyenne had not ended the scourge of prostitution in its city limits by May 1942.

Two months after the announcement of the end of prostitution in the city, the FBI held a conference for law enforcement personnel from southeastern Wyoming and northern Colorado. The conference was held in the Elks Lodge on July 17. One of the speakers was Dr. M.C. Keith, the director of the state health department, who spoke about the incidence of venereal disease in the military. He stated that of the Wyoming military selectees examined, about two and one-half percent were infected with syphilis. He also stated that about two percent of the state's adult population had syphilis. The doctor also reported that the incidence of the disease at Fort Warren was lower than at other military installations in the region.[24]

Another speaker at the conference was FBI Special Agent G.A. Nicholson. He discussed the May Act, which Congress passed during the summer of 1941. The goal of the act was similar to the World War I Selective Service Act of 1917, which prohibited prostitution near military areas. The agent spoke about the need for local and military authorities to work together in the effort to suppress prostitution. The act, which allowed federal intervention if deemed necessary, was never invoked in Cheyenne during the war, although the federal government found other ways to pressure the city to fight the incidence of prostitution.[25] Cheyenne's mayor had already been notified about the May Act in February 1942. He received a letter from Heber R. Harper, the coordinator for the Health, Welfare, and Related Defense Activities of the Federal Security Agency. The letter enclosed a copy of the May Act, which was intended "To prohibit prostitution within such reasonable distance of military and/or naval establishments as the Secretaries of War and/or Navy shall determine to be needful to the efficiency, health, and welfare of the army and/or Navy." Of course, one of the main concerns regarding the military's health was the prevalence of venereal disease.[26]

Like many cities across the country, Cheyenne faced the challenge of determining how to address the increasing number of cases of venereal disease. The Laramie County Health Unit, responsible for the community's health, provided monthly reports on its activities. The health officer's report for March 1942 stated that the Venereal Health Clinic saw 234 individuals for diagnosis or treatment. Of those, 76 were admitted to medical services, and 71 to nursing services.[27] The numbers for those admitted stayed fairly constant, with 77 admitted for services in September 1942 and 88 in October.[28] The state legislature also passed legislation regarding venereal disease during the 1943 session. The bill titled "Marriages—Parties Must Be Free From Venereal Disease" was approved on February 1, 1943. This amended a previous bill, which only ruled that male persons be tested and free of venereal disease before marriage. This bill included women, and both parties had to be tested by a duly licensed physician thirty days before the marriage.[29] After passing by large majorities in both houses, Governor Hunt signed the bill immediately, and it became effective on May 21. The Wyoming Health Department saw it as "a victory for the people of Wyoming." Dr. M.C. Keith, the state health officer, said, "Much of the credit for this accomplishment is also due to the medical profession, women's clubs, and other groups which have urged its enactment."[30] The Woman's Christian Temperance Union of Laramie, Wyoming, sent a letter and petition to Cheyenne's mayor in June 1942 asking the mayor to "secure legislation against the sale of alcoholic beverages to men in uniform and the removal of houses of prostitution in the vicinity of our training camps."[31]

As noted, several groups, such as women's clubs, provided advice on handling venereal disease in the city, and others wrote to Mayor Warren with their suggestions. A Cheyenne resident living on Warren Avenue sent the mayor a condensed version of an article in *Collier's The National Weekly*. The article, titled "Leesville Against Syphilis," discussed efforts in Leesville, Louisiana, near Camp Polk. Providing some context, the story stated that, dating back to the Civil War, venereal diseases have hampered war efforts. During the Civil War, one out of every five soldiers had a venereal disease; in World War I, it was one out of every ten. The numbers declined during World War II, but the problem remained. In Leesville in April 1942, the army, local law enforcement, health officers, and state police began a roundup and testing of those who might be considered to be at risk for venereal disease, such as food handlers and unescorted girls, some just arriving in the town on buses. Those found to be positive were taken to the hospital and treated at what were termed treatment centers. More similiar centers were established across the country.[32] Another letter to the mayor on the topic of venereal disease was written by a former Cheyenne resident living in Salt Lake City, Utah. His letter of July 25, 1943, suggested something quite different from what was done in Leedsville. The writer had published an article on controlling venereal disease in an Ogden, Utah, newspaper, and his idea drew on the past. He wrote that he had been talking to officers around the country and "they think the same as I do. They would rather have the old red-light districts than what they have to contend with now." He did not understand how anyone could keep men away from women, which is clearly shown in his concluding sentence: "In closing, I'd just like to say that if all women would go to China, the men would swim over after them."[33]

To put all of this in proper context, it should be noted that the Laramie County Health Unit and the Wyoming Health Department had much more to address than just venereal disease. The medical profession dealt with other communicable diseases, such as scarlet fever, measles, smallpox, and diphtheria, as well as maternity services. To assist with managing these medical issues, the Laramie County Health Unit hired a Sanitarian. In March 1942, County Sanitarian Edward Mann inspected the city's milk plants and producers to make sure sanitary procedures were followed. In a February 1942 report, he stated he had inspected dairies, eating and drinking establishments, private premises, and schools. He also initiated a survey of private sewage disposal methods to identify where "private privies" can be replaced with sewer connections. His report concluded the conditions in a great number of eating establishments were "deplorable." Cheyenne's medical community had major challenges regarding the health of the city and its citizens.[34]

Cheyenne's city ordinances specified how the community was to address communicable diseases. Article 7-200 dealt with contagious diseases requiring physicians to report any communicable disease to the city health officer. If quarantine was necessary, it was permissible to isolate an individual at home. If such actions were necessary, the health officer would "post in a conspicuous place, at both front and rear doors of every abode wherein communicable disease exists, a white cardboard sign, authorized and approved by the Mayor or City Council, as a warning that such abode is under quarantine ...” A "STRICT QUARANTINE" was ordered if the disease was scarlet fever, smallpox, or diphtheria. However, whenever the mayor and city health officer decided isolation was necessary, someone could be placed in what was called a pest house (short for pestilence). As one would expect, those who suffered from venereal disease were included as patients who could be sent to the pest house.[35]

The state had a statute specifically for the examination and treatment of persons with venereal disease. It provided that state, county, and municipal health officers could examine those suspected of the disease, detain them when necessary, and if found to be infected, require their treatment "until cured." If, in the health officer's judgment, it is necessary to protect public health, those infected may be isolated or quarantined. The end of the statute related to prostitution: "It shall be the duty of all local and state health officers to investigate sources of infection of venereal disease, to cooperate with the proper officials whose duty it is to enforce laws directed against prostitution and otherwise to use every proper means for the suppression of prostitution."[36]

Many communities around the country had pest houses. During the war, the one in Cheyenne was located at what is today Southwest Drive and West Lincolnway. However, the 1945 *Cheyenne City Directory* listed it as an Isolation Hospital with its location one-half mile west of Cheyenne. An early case of a Cheyenne citizen taken to a pest house occurred in December 1900. A person employed as a waiter in the city discovered he was suffering from smallpox, and he was taken to the pest house, although it is unclear where it was located at that time.[37] It was not until early 1943 that the city decided to use the pest house to isolate individuals with venereal disease, as well as other communicable diseases.[38]

During the early part of 1943, the Cheyenne newspapers kept their readers somewhat informed about the issue of venereal disease in the city. The *Tribune* reported in March that 59% of such cases in 1942 occurred in Laramie County. The total number of cases in the state for that year was 883.[39] Two months later, the *Eagle* ran a story that probably intrigued many readers. It was titled "Health Department Would Segregate 'Victory Girls.'" It reported on a study by the Wyoming Health Department, which stated, "the internment of the so-called 'victory girls' and other infectious cases is necessary to curb the spread of venereal disease." The story discussed the findings of a social hygiene conference recently held in Denver, where it was discussed "that nearly all soldiers who contracted venereal diseases were infected through contact with the so-called 'victory girls' who were ones who frequented taverns and other 'hot spots', apparently seeking amusement.[40] However, only days after this announcement, the *Tribune* reported that the Federal Security Agency had begun an investigation into the problem of venereal disease in the capital city.

On June 3, Harold M. Slutes, regional representative for the Office of War Services, Social Protection Division (SPD) in the Federal Security Agency, met with Fort Warren officials, Cheyenne's mayor and chief of police, and several army officers about the conditions that contributed to the spread of venereal disease. The SPD was organized in 1941, and one of its main functions was to check the spread of venereal disease through the containment of prostitution. At the meeting, Slutes told everyone local conditions regarding this topic must be improved, although he did admit that "the percentage of infection in Cheyenne was comparatively low." Even with that admission, he said it is necessary for the city to begin cleanup measures. If such action was not done, Slutes said, "Much preventable venereal disease will be acquired by both soldiers and civilians if action is not taken." He went on to say, "The soldier is the most important individual in the world today," and that it was up to Cheyenne, the federal government, and parents to ensure that nothing disastrous happened to them. He acknowledged that the city had already taken some action, but Slutes recommended a four-step cleanup program. 1. Cheyenne should take steps to close all houses of prostitution. Actions taken at this step have already reduced the number of venereal cases by 30 to 76 percent. 2. Adequate policing of places where prostitutes and victory girls meet soldiers, such as restaurants, taverns, theaters, or any other place where the public gathers. 3. Adequate policing of places of exposure, such as hotels, tourist camps, and rooming houses. 4. Health services which provide free exams and treatment for venereal disease, along with adequate places of detention where someone could be quarantined and given medical treatment.[41]

Mayor Warren responded to Slutes the day after the conference, June 4. In his letter, the mayor wrote that he and the city would cooperate in any way to "prevent the practice of prostitution" in Cheyenne. He acknowledged that stopping prostitution in parks, alleys, and tourist camps was a "big order," but he promised the police department would be "vigilant" to stop the practice, and regarding hotels and rooming houses, the laws would be enforced "to the limit of their ability." Warren had made a similar commitment at the meeting with Slutes, and the letter concluded with the statement: Every effort will be made by the City to cooperate with you in your program for the prevention of prostitution.[42] It is likely that, among those commitments, an effort led by Chief of Police Harvey Jackson emerged.

Jackson and Police Captain Fred Sinclair investigated a number of establishments that had been reported as possible houses of prostitution. Their report, dated June 9, listed seven houses and the results of their investigation. In addition to the report noted on the next page, the file contained a short notice dated June 7 from Warren instructing the chief of police to take action to prevent prostitution in Cheyenne.[43] The last four listed here were located on the city's West Side:

1. Federal Rooms, 1519 Carey Avenue. Billy Powell ran the boarding house and she apparently told Jackson and Sinclair there are six rooms to rent and all were rented by Union Pacific Railroad workers. One woman stayed with Powell who was her daughter-in-law and whose husband was in the army. The report also mentioned the "place has a very complete register."

2. Modern Rooms, 1505 ½ Carey Avenue. Georgia Mason operated the house and she had seven rooms to rent. It has been closed for about a week since she was painting and doing other remodeling work. The renters were transients, she said, some were women with husbands. She had one "colored maid" who had worked there for two years and she kept "a very good register."

3. Dixie Rooms, 210 ½ E. 15th Street. Mary Julien ran the place and had five rooms to rent, mainly to transients. For two people the rent was two dollars and three dollars for two renters. Julien paid rent in the amount of forty-three dollars per month. "She was questioned closely about permitting prostitution in her place and she denied it."

4. Black and Tan Café, 901 W. 18th Street. Lola West owned the café and had ten rooms to rent. At that time two were rented to Union Pacific workers, one to a man who works at the airport, one to West's

sister who does domestic work, one room to a soldier and his wife, one to a soldier's wife who receives his allotment, one vacant room at that time, one room to an Indian girl who works at the lunch counter and receives a government check, one room to her daughter-in-law, and finally one room to a maid. Since it is a café she has ten tables, a lunch counter, dance hall, and "jute box."

5. Jo-Eva Rooms and Sandwich Shop, 1709 Bent Avenue. Joe Eva Davis operated the business. Her rooms were rented, two to soldiers' wives who received their husbands' allotments and the other two rooms were rented to her employees, one a waitress and the other the cook. The restaurant served meals, soft drinks, and sandwiches, and the business had two jute boxes.

6. Susie Stowers, 616 West 18th Street. She had the largest boarding house with thirteen rooms to rent. Two were empty at the time of the investigation and ten were rented to workers at the Union Pacific and war industries. The last room was rented to a soldier and his wife. She mentioned two rooms are rented to women who work for her, one the maid and a cook. She had one jute box.

Lola West in the Black and Tan Café, ca. 1941. Courtesy Alonzo Reed Family.

Children in front of the Black and Tan at 901 W. 18th St. Three are children of the Alonzo Reed Family, Rena, Joyce, and Lester, ca. 1941.
Courtesy Alonzo Reed Family

7. The Red White and Blue Café, 610 West 18th Street. George Howard operated the restaurant and had two rooms to rent. One to a soldier and his wife and the second was vacant. Howard served meals and soft drinks and had two jute boxes.

The report's conclusion stated: "We have questioned all the above, and they deny that they have permitted the practice of prostitution at any time. We found no evidence of prostitutes or prostitution in any of these places." Signed by Harvey T. Jackson, Chief of Police, and Fred Sinclair, Captain of Detectives.

Attached to the report is a page containing the mayor's comments. He clearly said prostitution in Cheyenne was a thing of the past, and he made it clear his assurances given to Slutes both verbally and in writing that the city will continue to stamp out prostitution are sincere, and he will continue to follow through to keep prostitution from the city.[44]

Describing what Jackson and Sinclair did as an investigation would be difficult. Certainly, they were aware of the times the establishments and some of the operators had been fined for "immorality" in the recent past, as recorded in the police justice docket, so their acceptance of statements that prostitution had never occurred at any time seems unbelievable. Anyway, the report noted above may have come a day too late, since on June 8, Slutes sent a short telegram to Eliot Ness, director of the Social Protection Section of the Federal Security Agency, which stated: "Local Officials refuse to close houses. Concur with Washington officials on immediate off-limits action for entire city. Report follows."[45]

The headlines on the front page of the June 9, 1943, edition of the *Wyoming Eagle* must have shocked many Cheyenneites. It read: "VICE PROBER SAYS CITY TO BE CLOSED TO ALL SOLDIERS: Authorities Deny They 'Failed to Cooperate' With Federal Officials." The article quoted Slutes stating that "no soldiers would be permitted in Cheyenne's city limits." The city would have been deemed "out of bounds" for soldiers. The ban needed approval by what was described as "official Washington channels," so it did not take effect immediately. However, the threat of keeping thousands of soldiers at Fort Warren from entering the city and visiting its businesses could have significantly harmed many businesses and Cheyenne as a whole. This was not something city officials were willing to accept without a fight. The city attorney, Carleton A. Lathrop, responding to Slutes' demands to close and padlock various houses of prostitution, said the demands put upon the city by Slutes and the government were a "clearly unconstitutional action" and were not things the city was able to grant. At a meeting with Slutes the day before, the attorney went so far as to say he did not have the power to suspend the Constitution. Slutes responded that he "was not concerned with the means or methods used, and walked out of the meeting."[46]

Slutes continued to claim, as reported in the newspaper, that his investigation revealed the city had active houses of prostitution, although he refused to name them or specify how many. He said that if "the city would go all the way in carrying out the government program of venereal disease control," this action would not be needed. Lathrop retorted that Slutes "would not produce any evidence of law violations on property which he had demanded be padlocked, except the hearsay statements of unknown parties, which statement and names of persons he has refused to give me or Chief of Police Harvey Jackson." Even officials from the fort stated that they had not received any reports of violations of the law from the locations identified by Slutes. Lathrop went on to describe the federal representative and his actions: "In the case of Mr. Slutes, it is just another incident of an arrogant and egotistical official from Washington attempting to dictate and take away property of this sovereign state by illegal and unconstitutional means." The article in the *Wyoming Eagle,* in its conclusion, attempted to end on a positive note, stating that because of the amicable relations that had existed between the city and the fort, even if the city was placed "out of bounds" for military personnel, it would only be a temporary measure.[47]

Two days later, the mayor responded. Warren acknowledged the anxiety in the city about the need to meet Slutes' demands to avert the city's closure to personnel from the fort, and he reiterated the city's complete cooperation in assisting the fort in cleaning up prostitution and addressing the spread of venereal disease. He mentioned that some of the houses Slutes wanted closed were badly needed to help offset the city's housing shortage. "It is against the demand that these aforementioned houses be definitely closed and padlocked, rather than cleaned up morally, that the city takes exception." In support of the mayor and city officials, the Cheyenne Kiwanis club gave full approval to those officials and the stand they took on Slutes' demands.[48]

On the same day as Warren's response, the *Eagle's* editorial page included a column titled "We Can't Work Miracles," relating to the difficulty of meeting all the demands from the federal government.

"Since the days of Sodom and Gomorrah, prostitution and venereal diseases have plagued every era, every generation and every nation. For hundreds if not thousands of years, the most brilliant minds of the medical, legal and sociological professions have combatted these twin evils. Governments have spent millions and tried every known device to elevate the morals of their peoples. Progress has been made but much remains to be done. It cannot be done in a week or a month or a year as the 'community war services investigator' seems to think."

The editorial continued that the city has, for many years, cooperated with officials at Fort Warren to protect the soldiers stationed there, and that the state of Wyoming and its boards of health have attempted to control venereal disease; even Slutes had commented that the rate of disease is better now than it has been. The column said the Federal Security Agency "is to be praised for its zeal to eradicate social diseases and to purify the human race." That effort is certainly supported by everyone in Wyoming. However, the editorial ended with a strong statement. "Having done everything asked by army officials, the threat by a civilian agency to declare Cheyenne out of bounds for soldiers at great cost to merchants and great inconvenience to military personnel is an autocratic move that should be resisted to the limit."[49]

In the end, neither the Social Protection Agency (with approval from Washington) nor Fort Warren put Cheyenne "out of bounds." The capital city was not the only community during the war to be threatened with such action. In Texas, which hosted many military bases, some base commanders used the same threat, and some cities acquiesced to the military's demands.[50] Slutes must have gone back to Washington, D.C., and continued his and Ness' campaign to fight prostitution across the country to protect soldiers from getting venereal disease.

At the end of June, however, the *Wyoming Eagle* published an article that may have pleased some of the Cheyenneites who had dealt with Slutes and his threats a few weeks earlier. Perhaps including the story in its June 29th edition continued the resistance against what some considered overreach by the federal government. The article's title was "Vice, Disease and Delinquency Are Found Rampant in Nation's Capital." The story described Washington, D.C. as vice-ridden and dirty and in danger of "disastrous epidemics." The incidences of syphilis and gonorrhea among soldiers "had increased 147 percent in the last six months of 1942, and there was no improvement in the first three months of 1943." Cases of Meningitis and tuberculosis also increased.[51] Cheyenne was doing much better than where Ness and Slutes had their offices.

Even after Slutes left, Cheyenne continued its fight against venereal disease. By mid-June, state public health service funds were made available for rapid treatment centers in cities and counties where necessary for those infected with syphilis. The funds were provided to cover free laboratory services and medications for the four free venereal disease clinics in Casper, Rock Springs, Laramie, and Cheyenne.[52] In early July the state health department planned a "Venereal Disease Drive," a title that perhaps could have been misinterpreted, but which was an attempt to conduct a "statewide contact tracing program to find the infectious cases and keep them under treatment until cured …"[53] Shortly after the start of that drive and perhaps somewhat surprisingly, Cheyenne's mayor received a letter from Eliot Ness, still the director of the Social Protection Division. In his letter, Ness included a booklet titled "Techniques of Law Enforcement Against Prostitution." Ness was mailing copies to all law enforcement personnel in the country in the hope that some of the procedures listed could help in the fight against prostitution and the spread of venereal disease. According to Ness: "In past wars, these diseases increased to several times their peacetime rates. In this war, the rates in the armed forces are now the lowest in history." The low numbers were due to "vigorous law enforcement programs." The booklet's contents provided information on how to deal with prostitution in taverns and bars, hotels, tourist and trailer camps, and taxicabs, as well as other information.[54]

Despite the federal booklet's advice and Wyoming's actions to combat venereal disease, the problem persisted. An early September article in the *Wyoming Eagle* reported that 424 Wyoming selective service registrants were rejected at induction because of syphilis, as reported by the state health department. Broken down by county, 48 were from Laramie County, 58 in Fremont County, and 50 in Natrona County. The lowest county was Teton, with one; Crook had only two.[55] The state health department reported an increase in the disease in the previous September and again in late October, although the numbers were reduced: 25 in September and only 11 in October. The total for 1943 was 662, compared with 398 the previous year.[56] The fight against venereal disease continued into 1944, but with the election of the mayor and city council in the fall of 1943 and the new mayoral administration taking office in January 1944, the city of Cheyenne turned its attention to other pressing matters.

CHAPTER 4 ENDNOTES

1. "Centra bons Moves," *Cheyenne Leader*, March 2, 1868, 1. The article included the term bagnios.

2. "Incendiaries About," *Cheyenne Leader*, March 14, 1868, 1.

3. "Immorality in Cheyenne," *Cheyenne Leader*, September 21, 1869, 1.

4. *Wyoming Weekly Leader*, October 9, 1869, 7; *Wyoming Weekly Leader*, October 16, 1869, 5.

5. "Start War Against Red Light District," *Cheyenne State Leader*, March 5, 1911, 1.

6. "Two Affronts to Decency," *Cheyenne State Leader*, March 10, 1911, 4.

7. "A Suggestion To Mayor Bresnahen," *Wyoming Semi-Weekly Tribune*, March 17, 1911, 8.

8. "Red Light District Resorts Are Closed," *Cheyenne State Leader*, May 5, 1911, 1.

9. "Red Light District Resorts Are Closed," *Cheyenne State Leader*, May 5, 1911, 1.

10. "Agree on Location Red Light District," *Cheyenne State Leader*, May 28, 1911, 7.

11. William B. Ross became the governor of Wyoming in 1923 although he died in office late in 1924. His wife, Nellie Tayloe Ross, ran to replace him and won the election, becoming Wyoming's first woman governor in January 1925. She ran for reelection in 1926, but lost.

12. "Hottest Meeting Of Year: Utter Disregard For Law and Order by the Saloons and Bawdy Houses—Lax Enforcement of Ordinances," *Tribune Stockman Farmer*, November 28, 1911, 1 and 2; "Soldier Criticises City For Red Light Conditions," *Wyoming Tribune,* November 30, 1911, 4.

13. Buchanan, John G., "War Legislation Against Alcoholic Liquor and Prostitution," *Journal of the American Institute of Criminal Law and Criminology*, February 1919, 520-529; Selective Draft Act of 1917, ch. 15, S201 40 Stat. 76.

14. Druery, Tawnya, K. "Disorderly Dollars: Penalty, Prosperity and Prostitution, Cheyenne, Wyoming, 1915-1922," (M.A. Thesis), Department of History, University of Wyoming, 2002, 20-28, 37-38, 55-56.

15. See "Immorality and Traffic," lists, July 22nd to July 30th, 1940, and August 1st to 5th, 1940, Cheyenne Police Register, Wyoming State Archives.

16. "IMMORALITY AND TRAFFIC, JAN 1st to JAN. 6th Incl. 1941," Cheyenne Police Justice Docket, Wyoming State Archives.

17. "IMMORALITY AND TRAFFICE VIOLATIONS," December 1st to 14th, 1941, Cheyenne Police Justice Docket, Wyoming State Archives.

18. Letter from Ed Warren, Mayor, to George Blair, Colonel, Fort Francis E. Warren, February 20, 1942, RG3001, City of Cheyenne, Cheyenne Mayor Records, Administrative Files, Police-War, box 4, Wyoming State Archives. On January 31, 1942, Fort Warren's Medical Corps Surgeon, Colonel D.W. McEnery, sent a brief message to Blair on the subject of Houses of Prostitution. He stated there have been rumors that certain Cheyenne houses are used for prostitution. "While I have been informed not to have anything to do with such a situation, it is the policy of the War Department to suppress such houses as a danger to the post personnel." From D.W. McEnery to Commanding Officer of Fort Francis E. Warren, January 31, 1942, RG3001, City of Cheyenne, Cheyenne Mayor Records, Administrative Files, Police-War, box 4, Wyoming State Archives.

19. "City to Aid In Curbing Prostitution," *Wyoming State Tribune*, April 21, 1942, 1; "Officials Silent On Request For Ending Of Prostitution," *Wyoming Eagle,* April 18, 1942, 8.

20. "Reports on Houses of Prostitution Conflict: Police Chief's Statement Conflicts With Claim Made by U.S. Agency," *Wyoming State Tribune*, April 22, 1942, 10; "Jackson Says No Houses of Prostitution Operate Here," *Wyoming Eagle*, April 22, 1942, 1 and 8.

21. "Prostitution Is Ended In City, Official Says," *Wyoming Eagle*, May 2, 1942, 1 and 21.

22. "Prohibition of prostitution," from Francis S. Drath, Provost Marshal, to Commanding Officers, Fort Francis E. Warren, Wyoming, April 7, 1942, RG3001, City of Cheyenne, Cheyenne Mayor Records, Administrative Files, Police-War, box 4, Wyoming State Archives.

23   Cheyenne Police Justice Docket, April 20, 1942, Wyoming State Archives.

24   "Danger of Prostitution to War Effort Stressed at FBI Session," *Wyoming Eagle*, July 18, 1942, 1 and 21.

25   "Police Conference On May Act Enforcement Opens Here Today," *Wyoming Eagle*, July 17, 1942, 1; "Danger of that of the first million enlistees and draftees in the armed forces at the beginning of the war sixty thousand were rejected because of venereal diseases."

26   Letter from Heber R. Harper, Federal Security Agency to Hon. Edward Warren, Mayor of Cheyenne, February 21, 1942, RG3001, City of Cheyenne, Cheyenne Mayor Records, Administrative Files, Police-War, box, 4, Wyoming State Archives.

27   Laramie County Health Unit, Cheyenne, Wyoming, "Nurses" Report for March, 1942, Cheyenne City Records, Cheyenne Mayor-Health Unit, Feb. 1943-May 1945, box 4.

28   Laramie County Health Unit, "Nurses' Report for September 1942 and "Nurses" Report for October 1942," RG3001, City of Cheyenne, Cheyenne Mayor Records, Administrative Files, Cheyenne Mayor-Health Unit, Feb. 1943-May 1945, box 4, Wyoming State Archives.

29   Session Laws of Wyoming, 1943, Chapter 7 (Original Senate File No. 2), "Marriages—Parties Must Be Free From Venereal Disease," 6.

30   "Pre-Marital Law Covering Women Seen as Victory in People's Fight for Health," *Wyoming Eagle*, February 9, 1943, 13. Governor Hunt signed the bill in early February 1943. Upon signing the bill he commented: "I think this provision is something that will lead to better health of children, fewer divorces, and generally improved social and health conditions in the state. It is a splendid bill, one that has long been overdue in Wyoming." "Hunt Signs Bill For Premarital Test of Women," *Wyoming Eagle*, February 2, 1943, 1 and 8.

31   Letter, Laramie, Wyoming, Woman's Christian Temperance Union, to Mayor Ed Warren, June 17, 1942, RG3001, City of Cheyenne, Cheyenne Mayor Records, Administrative Files, Cheyenne Mayor-Petitions from Citizens, Oct. 1940-Aug. 1942, box 4, Wyoming State Archives.

32   Letter to Mayor Warren, from Mr. Peacock, June 11, 1943; "Leesville Against Syphilis," condensed from *Collier's*, by J. D. Ratcliff, April 10, 1943, RG3001, City of Cheyenne, Cheyenne Mayor Records, Cheyenne Mayor Records, Administrative Files, Police Department Jan. 1943-Nov. 1945, box 4, Wyoming State Archives.

33   Letter Nathan Bregman, Salt Lake City, Utah, to Cheyenne Mayor Ed Warren, July 25, 1943, and article "Moral Reform Moves Are Blamed for Sex Crimes," RG3001, City of Cheyenne, Cheyenne Mayor Records, Administrative Files, Cheyenne Mayor, Police Department Jan. 1943-Nov. 1945, box 4, Wyoming State Archives.

34   Laramie County Health Unit, "Health Officer's Report for March, 1942, and "Sanitarian's Narrative Report for Month of February, 1942," RG3001, City of Cheyenne, Cheyenne Mayor Records, Administrative Files, Cheyenne Mayor-Health Unit, Feb. 1943-May 1945, box 4, Wyoming State Archives. Laramie County's health officer at the time was Dr. Walter S. Kotas. In March 1943, the county health unit recorded 15 cases of scarlet fever, 56 of measles, 146 cases of smallpox, and 198 cases of diphtheria, 5 years and over. Laramie County Health Unit, "Nurses" Report for March, 1942, RG3001, City of Cheyenne, Cheyenne Mayor Records, Administrative Files, Cheyenne Mayor-Health Unit, Feb. 1943-May 1945, box 4, Wyoming State Archives.

35   *Ordinances of the City of Cheyenne, Codified and Compiled 1938*, Codified, Compiled, and Edited by Mildred Pease, Wyoming Labor Journal Publishing Co., 1938, Article 7-200, 43-44.

36   Wyoming Statute Title 35, Chapter 4, Public Health and Safety, Article 1, 103-235. "Examination and Treatment of Persons Suspected of Being Diseased." This also applied to those imprisoned in the state. If upon their discharge prisoners were still infected they could be isolated or quarantined. Wyoming Statute Title 35, Chapter 4, Public Health and Safety, Article 1, 103-236, "Prisoners Infected With Venereal Disease."

37   "Taken to the Pest House," *Cheyenne Daily Leader*, December 31, 1900, 4. That same month the *Leader* included a story about Laramie's pest house. "Suit Over Pest House," "A dispute has occurred at Laramie between the county and city authorities over the title to the pest house at that place and the question may be adjudicated in the courts. Cheyenne people fight—over young ladies, but draw the line at pest houses," *Cheyenne Daily Leader*, December 20, 1900, 4.

38   "Pest House to Be Used by County To Confine Cases," *Wyoming State Tribune*, February 12, 1943, 3; "City May Use Pest House In Vice War: Detention Home is Needed Here, Mayor Reports," *Wyoming State Tribune*, June 10, 1943, 1 and 7.

39   "Venereal Disease Is Centered Here," *Wyoming State Tribune*, March 3, 1943, 9.

40   "Health Department Would Segregate 'Victory Girls,'" *Wyoming Eagle*, May 27, 1943, 1.

41   "Social Disease Cleanup Said Needed in City," *Wyoming State Tribune*, June 4, 1943; "Improvement in Vice Conditions Here is Sought," *Wyoming Eagle*, June 4, 1943, 4; "Venereal Disease Study Under Way," *Wyoming State Tribune*, June 3, 1943, 7.

42   Letter, Mayor Ed Warren to Howard M. Slutes, June 4, 1943, RG3001, City of Cheyenne, Cheyenne Mayor Records, Administrative Files, Cheyenne Mayor-Police Department, Jan. 1943-Nov. 1945, box 4, Wyoming State Archives.

43   Note from Ed Warren, Mayor, June 7, 1943, RG3001, City of Cheyenne, Cheyenne Mayor Records, Administrative Files, Cheyenne Mayor-Police Department, Jan. 1943-Nov. 1945, box 4, Wyoming State Archives.

44   Report, Harvey T. Jackson, Chief of Police, and Fred Sinclair, Captain of Detectives, June 9, 1943, RG3001, City of Cheyenne, Cheyenne Mayor Records, Administrative Files, Cheyenne Mayor-Police Department, Jan.1943-Nov. 1945, box 4, Wyoming State Archives.

45   Telegram, Howard M. Slutes to Eliot Ness, Director Social Protection Section, Federal Security Agency, Washington, D.C., June 8, 1943, RG3001, City of Cheyenne, Cheyenne Mayor Records, Administrative Files, Cheyenne Mayor-Police Department, Jan. 1943-Nov. 1945, box 4, Wyoming State Archives.

46   "VICE PROBER SAYS CITY TO BE CLOSED TO ALL SOLDIERS: Authorities Deny They 'Failed to Cooperate' With Federal Official," *Wyoming Eagle*, June 9, 1943, 1 and 8.

47   "VICE PROBER SAYS CITY TO BE CLOSED TO ALL SOLDIERS: Authorities Deny They 'Failed to Cooperate' With Federal Official," *Wyoming Eagle*, June 9, 1943, 1 and 8.

48   "City Repeats Desire to Aid Vice Cleanup," *Wyoming Eagle*, June 11, 1943, 1 and 4.

49   "We Can't Work Miracles," *Wyoming Eagle*, June 11, 1943, 9.

50   David C. Humphrey, "Prostitution in Texas From the 1830s to the 1960s," *East Texas Historical Journal*, vol. 33, iss. 1, 34.

51   "Vice, Disease and Delinquency Are Found Rampant in Nation's Capital," *Wyoming Eagle*, June 29, 1943, 3.

52   "Health Funds Available For Syphilis Cases," *Wyoming Eagle*, June 18, 1943, 2.

53   "Venereal Disease Drive Is Planned By Health Office," *Wyoming Eagle*, July 8, 1943, 3.

54   Letter, Eliot Ness, Director of the Division of Social Protection in the Federal Security Agency, to Cheyenne Mayor Ed Warren, July 26, 1943, RG3001, City of Cheyenne, Cheyenne Mayor Records, Administrative Files, Cheyenne Mayor-Police Department, Jan. 1943-Nov. 1945, box 4, Wyoming State Archives.

55   "424 Wyoming Men Rejected For Syphilis," *Wyoming Eagle*, September 9, 1943, 14.

56   "14 New Cases of Syphilis Listed," *Wyoming Eagle*, September 30, 1943, 2; "Increase of Syphilis in State Shown," *Wyoming Eagle*, October 28, 1943, 2. During the fall of 1943 there was discussion about building a new "Health Unit" in Cheyenne. In 1942 an agreement on the building was reached between the federal government and city and county governments. In September 1943, the construction contract had already been awarded to a Worland company. The building was to be built for $22,000 and to be located on Carey between 19th and 20th streets. However, city and county officials believed the building was unnecessary and opposed it in October 1943. The reasons were that it would mean additional expense and it only provided some office space, but not wards or treatment facilities. Patients still would have been treated at the already operating health facility and the pest house. See "New Building Is Okayed for City," *Wyoming State Tribune*, December 24, 1942, 2; "Health Unit Will Be Built," *Wyoming State Tribune*, September 30, 1943, 1; "Health Unit Plans Opposed," *Wyoming State Tribune*, October 6, 1943, 1 and 11; "Health Unit Proposal Is Turned Down," *Wyoming State Tribune*, October 8, 1943, 2.

Good Clean Government

During the 1940s, Cheyenne's mayor and council had two-year terms, with elections held in odd years. Four candidates entered the 1943 mayoral primary election. They were Ed Warren, the incumbent mayor; Ira Hanna, the county assessor; businessman John J. McInerny; and John W. Howard, also a businessman. Nine men ran for a seat on the city council, including two incumbents, J.A. "Buck" Buchanan and Al Kay. The others were Gus Fleishli, Bruce Jones, Daniel Wolcut, Everett "Ed" Shaw, Fred L. Thompson, Archer Lapham, and G.E. "Red" Porter. The primary election was held on October 19, reducing the number of candidates running for mayor to two and for council to four. The general election was held on November 2, just two weeks after the primary.

Warren was the first to announce his candidacy for mayor. He had already served two terms in Cheyenne's highest office, and in running for his third term, noted there were still many problems "which in most instances are vitally connected with the war effort." Warren believed his experience over the previous four years made him the most qualified person to manage the issues still facing the city.[1] This may have been the case, but his ads in Cheyenne's newspapers focused more on what he had accomplished during his years as mayor.

Warren's campaign consisted of running advertisements in the *State Tribune* and *Eagle* with the slogan, "Cheyenne Should Have A Business Man For Mayor." His ads mostly discussed the "five promises" he made and kept during his time in office. He had promised to solve the traffic problem, and after much study, the city council "endorsed parking meters," freeing up parking spaces downtown, as well as bringing in revenues of about $55,000. One ad mentioned another positive outcome of adding parking meters. "Figures show that gas and rubber saved by drivers heretofore driving around the block looking for a parking space is more than equal to the money spent in the meters."[2] Another promise he had made was to remove the city dumps. Apparently, this had been promised by politicians for thirty years, and completing that promise "improved sanitary conditions in South Cheyenne and enhanced the value of its property."[3] The development of the airport was another promise fulfilled. Warren was always sure to give credit to others who were instrumental in completing these goals, and in this instance, he listed the contributions of the officials at the Cheyenne airport and the Municipal Airport Board, whose members understood the value of a "great airport." He said that their combined efforts led to "the greatest airport expansion since the airport's inception." Federal money funded a five-million-dollar improvement in the airport's runways and modification hangars. The ad also claimed Cheyenne had "one of the greatest airports in the country."[4]

The other promises Warren had made were "Increased Water Production" and "Reduction in City Taxes." According to his October 15 ad, during his tenure as mayor, the city had increased its water supply by seven million gallons. Reducing taxes was accomplished by revising fifty-year old water agreements with two of the largest water users. One user paid nothing for their water, and the other paid a "a very small rate." The extra income from these new water payments allowed the city to retire some of its indebtedness. Warren called this "one of the greatest business accomplishments in Cheyenne's history and was the result of untiring work on the part of the Water Board and the City, together with fine cooperation from the two big water users in question." The mayor also cited some positive accomplishments he did not promise, but that happened anyway. These included a new fire station in South Cheyenne, another one in North Cheyenne, and one that would probably be built in East Cheyenne. His ad stated: "These unquestionably will mean reduced fire insurance rates."[5]

Warren's last ad was what he called "A Non-Political Plea from Ed Warren, Mayor of Cheyenne." In this ad, he said that if you had read his previous ads, you knew what he accomplished during the past four years, and included a plea for everyone to vote, "regardless of who your choice might be. It is not only a privilege ... one of which is being fought for ... but is one of your duties. VOTE!!"[6]

The second candidate to announce his run for Cheyenne's mayor was Ira Hanna. He was the only candidate who did not come from the business world. Hanna had served as the deputy county treasurer, county treasurer, and at the time of the election, he was the county assessor. Hanna believed the taxation experience he gained in those various offices "should be of advantage to the people of Cheyenne in administration of their municipal government." He had lived in Cheyenne for about twenty-five years and had been active in the city's civic affairs. Hanna told the newspaper that announced his candidacy that "I will serve the interests of the people of Cheyenne, all the people, to the best of my ability."[7]

Hanna's ads were strikingly different from those of the other three candidates. His were more visual with larger font sizes and short statements about how he would manage. His first ad in the *Wyoming State Tribune,* dated October 11, 1943, was headlined "Elect Ira Hanna for Mayor." The ad went on to state he had proven his "administrative and executive ability," certainly highlighting his twenty years in county government. The ad also stated that he would be a "Full-Time — Around-the-Clock Mayor," and that he had shown "Honesty and Fairness as a Public Officer." Where other candidates listed the problems facing the city, he just included "He Promises to Devote All of His Ability to Their Solution," meaning Cheyenne's problems. The same ad was published in the *Wyoming Eagle* the following day.[8] Another ad, the following week, also did not address any of Cheyenne's main issues in 1943, although he pledged to be a "Round-the-Clock Mayor if Elected." He apparently was willing to be a "Twenty-Four Hour Man."[9] In his third ad, he pledged cooperation with the people of Cheyenne and the two city council members. It stated: "Give Me Your Support — I'll Give You My Best, Vote for Ira Hanna for Mayor, 'The No. 1 Man.'"[10] He also had ads in the two papers the day before the election and one on election day. These were the same ads previously published on October 12.[11]

The third candidate to join the race for mayor was John W. Howard. He announced his candidacy for the office in early September. Howard had lived in Cheyenne for thirty-five years and had been the contractor for a number of local buildings, several of which are landmarks. Unlike Hanna, he believed that his business experience "would be of value to the taxpayer, particularly in view of the great increase in municipal business due to the recent growth of the city."[12]

Howard ran three ads: one on October 8 in the *Eagle,* a second on October 18 in the *State Tribune,* and a third on October 19 in the *Eagle,* the day of the election, which was the same ad from the day before. His slogan

Ira Hanna's campaign advertisement used in his 1943 campaign for Cheyenne mayor against John McInerney. Hanna promoted "Good, Clean City Government," and he also insisted on a "Clean Campaign," as shown in this advertisement in the *Wyoming State Tribune*, October 25, 1943.

was "Elect a Builder for Mayor." Howard did not see himself as a politician, but he ran because of the support he received "from many sources, including both men and women, working people, business heads and big and little taxpayers, all of whom promised support …." To support his claim as a builder, the ad contained photographs of three buildings in Cheyenne, all well known in the city and around the state. The first was the Supreme Court Building, with the caption "Built by John W. Howard." The second was the Capitol Building, with the caption "Doubled in size by John W. Howard." The third was of the City and County Building, with the caption "Built by John W. Howard." This ad contained Howard's "Platform." In the ad, he stated he had been "fairly successful during the many years I have been a resident and a contractor and builder in Wyoming." He recognized that water was an important issue for the city and promoted the construction of "another large purification basin" on top of Round Top, which had plenty of room for expansion. Howard supported more street construction and maintenance, and he believed there would be a need for more housing for "people of moderate income" in Cheyenne once the war ended. He supported a beautification program for the capital.[13] Howard's second ad, published in both newspapers, had the headline "South Side's Growing And Offers Opportunity For Further Development." He noted growing traffic congestion on the South Side between the Frontier Refining Company and Orchard Valley, and on the Riner Viaduct between the South Side and downtown Cheyenne. The ad ended with this statement: "There are many other opportunities in Cheyenne requiring careful thought and attention, which I hope to discuss later."[14]

Prominent businessman John J. McInerney was the fourth person to announce a candidacy for the office of Cheyenne mayor. In the article about his intention to run, he said, if elected, "I will seek to give the city a progressive, business administration. My policy will be to cooperate with the other commissioners in all matters for the best interest of Cheyenne." McInerney had lived in the city all his life, born in 1886, and had served as a city council member in the early 1920s and, ten years later, as a county commissioner. He had run for mayor in 1939 and 1941, losing the latest election by approximately 400 votes.[15]

Having run twice for the mayor's office in the past two elections certainly provided McInerney with campaign experience and familiarity with the issues facing Cheyenne during the war. His campaign strategy, as illustrated by his published ads, was quite different from that of his three opponents. McInerney's ads started with a question that he then answered, making direct statements that addressed many of Cheyenne's issues. His first ad asked, "What Is Cheyenne's Number-One Question Today?" His answer was "WATER." "Without an adequate water supply, Cheyenne cannot grow. With adequate water, Cheyenne's growth can be unlimited. So water is the key to our future here in Cheyenne." This applied both to an "equitable water rate" and an adequate supply. The ad ended: "So, when you vote for me at the Primary Election, on October 19, vote for more water and, hence, Cheyenne's entire future."[16]

The next issue may have caught the attention of the County Attorney, Hirst, and Sheriff Tuck. The question was "What Shall We Do About Gambling in Cheyenne?" He acknowledged that "gambling is pretty well closed in Cheyenne, after a period of wide-open violations." His concern was that the same pattern would repeat: lax enforcement would create a need to clamp down on gambling. His policy as mayor would be to ban public gambling. He also made an interesting statement: "Certainly an administration which condones this illegal practice invites suspicion of its integrity and destroys the confidence of the people in their elected representatives." McInerney also said those who would be involved in gambling during wartime would be most useful if employed in the war effort.[17]

Another topic McInerney addressed was "Cheyenne's Mayor Must Lead – or Be Led." He noted that the mayor and the council members "are alike in their voting power." There is no boss. But to McInerney, it was "conceivable that a strong Commissioner, or even an outsider, could lead the Mayor, and be the Mayor in fact, if not in name." He said the mayor must lead, or risk being led.[18]

Other topics McInerney addressed in his primary election ads included his belief that Cheyenne must be run by a businessman, since city government is, in fact, the city's largest business enterprise. Regarding the issue of appropriate taxation, he said he would have the lowest taxes, which allows for "good government." Like the other candidates, McInerney said he would foster good relations with Fort Warren. He was also aware that the city was losing good employees due to the government's salary structure, and he wanted Cheyenne to provide its employees "benefits consistent with good government." The last ad before the primary election was titled "Will You Vote For

Me Tomorrow?" He summarized the issues he had brought up previously and ended with this: "I shall appreciate your support and shall strive to give you, who elected me, the most efficient and understanding city administration Cheyenne has ever had. Will you vote for me?"[19]

The city council race was also underway, with 9 candidates vying for 2 seats. The two incumbents ran several ads. Buchanan had the most detailed ad, explaining that while on the city council, he served as Commissioner of Public Improvements, and that, through his work with Senator Joseph O'Mahoney, thousands of Cheyenne taxpayer dollars were saved by having federal funds appropriated to repair the airport runways. He also mentioned that new curbs and gutters had been installed in the city, that fire stations were planned for different areas of Cheyenne, and that the city-installed parking meters provided a new source of revenue.[20] Al Kay, the other incumbent, ran a number of ads, but none nearly as detailed as Buchanan's. Kay always included that he was the Commissioner of Finance, Parks, and Public Improvement, and in one, added "Honest-Independent-Progressive."[21]

The other seven candidates also published ads in the newspapers, but not nearly as many as the mayoral candidates. Archer Lapham indicated that he would "express the people's wishes in City Administration." He had resided in Cheyenne for eighteen years and was a homeowner.[22] Ed Shaw was an "insurance man," serving as manager for two large Cheyenne insurance agencies. He promised to "make Cheyenne a bigger and better city in which to live," and he would get the job done.[23] Daniel J. Wolcut, the city building inspector, was well aware of Cheyenne's problems at the time and would give attention to law enforcement.[24] Fred L. Thompson, originally from Fremont County, although he had lived in Cheyenne for twenty-eight years, served as a Laramie County Representative in the state legislature. His ad stated he was experienced in city affairs and was conscientious and reliable.[25] G.E. "Red" Porter was a long-time resident of Cheyenne and had "worked on the streets and alleys" in the city, and with that experience, he believed he could manage efficiently and economically.[26] Gus Fleischli had worked in the automobile business for 25 years. His ads stated he was responsible for the "retention and enlargement" of Cheyenne's zoo and, during the Depression, had served as chairman of the Boy Scouts Council and helped save scouting in the city during the economic downturn. Fleischli was also active with the Chamber of Commerce.[27] The last city council candidate was Bruce S. Jones. He was an insurance man and, at the time, a state representative in the state legislature. He also had served as the county chair of the Red Cross, and his ad stated that it would be his "policy to work for the best interests of Cheyenne at all times."[28]

Cheyenne citizens voted in the primary election on October 19. The turnout was light, according to both the *Eagle* and the *State Tribune*. In the mayoral race, McInerney came in first with 1,593 votes and Hanna second with 1,310 votes. Howard placed third, and Warren, the incumbent, was fourth, with fewer than 1,000 votes cast. Surprisingly, Cheyenne's voters did not want Warren for another two years, even with all he had accomplished. As for the city council race, the four who would run in the general election were Kay, who came in first with 1,808 votes; Fleischli, second with 1,468; Jones, third with 1,399; and Buchanan, fourth with 1,329. The *State Tribune* noted that even with the increase in Cheyenne's population since the 1941 election, the total vote was 769 fewer votes than that year.[29]

Hanna and McInerney both thanked Wyoming voters and then continued their campaigns. In Hanna's thank-you letter, he wrote that he made no promise he could not keep and that he would fulfill every one if elected on November 2. Hanna signed the letter, "Ira L. Hanna, The Round-the-Clock Candidate."[30] McInerney wrote that the acceptance of his candidacy showed that many agreed with his ideas and principles, and that, if elected, he would put them into practice. He appealed for votes on November 2 and said if he was elected, Cheyenne would be "where we can do business without interference and at a profit, a city where we can rear our families in safety... a city of sound American principles."[31]

During the general election campaign, Hanna continued using the same type of ad he had used in the primary. On October 25, his ad, in a large font, announced: "Ira Hanna Offers Good, Clean City Government." The ad mentioned some of the issues facing Cheyenne, such as the need for increased water supply, adequate street repairs, higher pay for city employees, and a lower tax rate. However, one element of the ad is rather puzzling. The ad read: "But I insist on a Clean Campaign," which is followed by this statement: "To combat Dirty Rumors, Mean Insinuations, Consider my Reputation and Twenty Years Public Service. For A 'Round-the-Clock Mayor Elect Ira Hanna." This ad was placed in the *State Tribune* on October 25, and the same ad appeared in the *Eagle* the following day.[32] It is unclear what rumors or insinuations

Ira Hanna campaigned in his run for Cheyenne mayor in 1943 for the necessity of law enforcement and that he would enforce the law. This advertisement appeared in the *Wyoming State Tribune*, October 26, 1943.

the ad referenced. No other mention was made of those rumors. Hanna's ads used football images and references. "Let's Go Over the Goal for Clean City Government with Ira Hanna" featured an image of football goalposts. The ad included the lines, "Good Sportsmanship Is My Keynote," and "Law Enforcement Is Necessary For A Good, Clean City Administration." Hanna promised that the law "will be enforced," perhaps referring to those rumors and insinuations.[33] Hanna's final ad featured an image of a soldier and boldly stated, "Let's Win The War First," alluding to his belief that unnecessary construction can wait until after the war. The issues Hanna considered necessary were cooperating with the Water Board, enforcing all laws, cooperating with all civil and military authorities, granting pay raises to city employees, encouraging new industry, and even encouraging more musical activities in the city.[34]

As Hanna continued his campaign strategy, McInerney again used ads with his questions and explanations. His first ad, published on October 27, asked whether Cheyenne should go forward or backward. McInerney saw the city at a crossroads and wanted it to grow, prosper, and become a "metropolitan city." According to the ad, Cheyenne needed a mayor with vision who would lead a "constructive city administration." He put it upon the electorate to choose the right man, and he was the right man.[35] McInerney was a World War I veteran, and his second ad warned that Cheyenne must be prepared to receive the many veterans returning home at the end of the war. He wanted to make sure there would be jobs "which will enable these men to re-establish themselves and add to the happiness and prosperity of our city." Who would be better to ensure this than someone who had gone through it himself?[36]

McInerney also asked, "What Does Cheyenne Really Need in a Mayor?" His response included someone with a broad business background, vision and imagination, courage to fight for what is right, someone who has the confidence of the city's citizens, one who is a leader, and "one who has Cheyenne's interests at heart all day, every day."[37] McInerney's final ad listed what he stood for: everything constructive, law enforcement, low taxes, increased pay for city employees, a modern city plan, and "everything Cheyenne needs." He asked the Cheyenne voters to "Vote For The Right Man."[38]

The front-page headline of the *Wyoming Eagle* on November 3, 1943, the day after the election, read: "Ira Hanna Defeats McInerney." The winners in the race for the two city council seats were Bruce Jones and Gus Fleischli, who defeated the two incumbents. Apparently, the city's citizens wanted a fresh start, first defeating the incumbent mayor, Ed Warren, and then Buchanan and Kay, the two sitting city council members. Hanna received 3,079 votes, and McInerney received 2,765. Jones led the city council race with 3,472, followed by Fleischli with 3,244. Kay had 2,632 votes, and Buchanan came in last with only 1,763. The *Eagle* described the vote as light, with only 5,877 voting in the general election, and compared it to two years earlier, when 6,817 voted.[39] McInerney published a thank you in the *State Tribune* the day after the election. He said, of course, he was disappointed, but he would support everything Hanna did for the good of Cheyenne. "All of us together should now proceed to build a greater, more prosperous Cheyenne."[40]

In an editorial titled "Three Competent Leaders," published on November 4, two days after the election, the *Wyoming State Tribune* wrote: "Cheyenne may look forward with confidence to the administration of municipal government" because of the elections of Hanna, Jones, and Fleischli.

"Here are three admirable gentlemen selected for important, arduous public service by the majority of their fellow citizens." The *State Tribune* believed the "city validly may expect to continue to go forward under their leadership."[41]

The other Cheyenne newspaper, the *Wyoming Eagle*, on January 1, 1944, just a few days before Hanna took office, published an editorial titled "A Good Ending." The paper wrote about Warren's service to the city, including his six years as a county commissioner and four years as mayor. The editorial also spoke to the issues Cheyenne had faced over the past two years. "It is no overstatement to say that the past two years have been the most difficult in Cheyenne's history in more than one way. The city's population increased by approximately 8,000. Personnel at the military post were upped more than six times over the number stationed there in pre-war years. The demands on every service rendered by the city were multiplied. Unprecedented financial burdens were placed on the city treasury. The problems imposed on the police department were staggering." It did mention some positives from the past two years, such as a new fire station on the south side and new downtown parking meters, which markedly solved some of the traffic problems while contributing to city revenues. The editorial concluded that the coming two years also would be difficult, but "We believe the new officials will measure up to the heavy responsibilities that will rest upon them. We bespeak for them the cooperation of every citizen of Cheyenne."[42] Apparently, many in Cheyenne believed that Hanna would be the "Round-the-Clock Mayor" and would enforce all laws in the city.

CHAPTER 5 ENDNOTES

1   "Ed Warren Is First To Enter Mayor's Race," *Wyoming Eagle*, August 13, 1943, 1.

2   Ed Warren Advertisement, *Wyoming Eagle*, October 9, 1943, 17.

3   Ed Warren Advertisement, *Wyoming State Tribune*, October 8, 1943, 2.

4   Ed Warren Advertisement, *Wyoming State Tribune*, October 13, 1943, 2.

5   Ed Warren Advertisements, *Wyoming Eagle*, October 15, 1943, 20, and *Wyoming State Tribune*, October 14, 1943, 5.

6   Ed Warren Advertisement, *Wyoming State Tribune*, October 19, 1943, 8.

7   "Hanna Will Be Candidate for Mayor's Post," *Wyoming State Tribune*, August 18, 1943, 1.

8   Ira Hanna Advertisement, *Wyoming Eagle*, October 12, 1943, 14.

9   Ira Hanna Advertisement, *Wyoming Eagle*, October 16, 1943, 19.

10   Ira Hanna Advertisement, *Wyoming State Tribune*, October 18, 1943, 7.

11   Ira Hanna Advertisements, *Wyoming State Tribune*, October 18, 1943, 7, and *Wyoming Eagle*, October 19,1943, 7.

12   "John Howard to Run for Mayor," *Wyoming Eagle*, September 4, 1943, 22.

13   John W. Howard Advertisement, *Wyoming Eagle*, October 8, 1943, 14.

14   John W. Howard Advertisements, *Wyoming State Tribune*, October 18, 1943, 11, and *Wyoming Eagle*, October 19, 1943, 14.

15   "McInerney Is Candidate for Mayor's Post," *Wyoming State Tribune*, September 8, 1943, 1 and 9.

16   "What is Cheyenne's Number-One Question Today?" *Wyoming State Tribune*, October 1, 1943, 2.

17   "What Shall We Do About Gambling in Cheyenne?" *Wyoming State Tribune*, October 4, 1943, 6.

18   "Cheyenne's Mayor Must Lead—or Be Led," *Wyoming State Tribune*, October 6, 1943, 7.

19   "Put Cheyenne on a Business Basis," *Wyoming State Tribune*, October 8, 1943, 5; "No More 'On-Again-Off-Again' Policy for Cheyenne Taxpayers," *Wyoming State Tribune*, October 13, 1943, 8; "A Frank Statement About Cheyenne and The Military," *Wyoming State Tribune*, October 14, 1943, 8; "Our City Employees And Their Pay Envelopes," *Wyoming State Tribune*, October 15, 1943, 11; "Will You Vote For Me Tomorrow?" *Wyoming State Tribune*, October 18, 1943, 8.

20   J.A. "Buck" Buchanan Advertisement, *Wyoming State Tribune*, October 18, 1943, 8; J.A. "Buck" Buchanan Advertisement, *Wyoming Eagle*, October 16, 1943, 8.

21   Al Kay Advertisements, *Wyoming Eagle*, October 15, 1943, 13; *Wyoming State Tribune*, October 15, 1943, 7; *Wyoming Eagle*, 16, 1943, 4.

22   Archer Lapham Advertisement, *Wyoming State Tribune*, October 18, 1943, 7.

23   "'Ed' Shaw is Candidate in City Election," *Wyoming State Tribune*, September 9, 1943, 1; Ed Shaw Advertisement, *Wyoming State Tribune*, October 4, 1943, 3.

24   "Wolcut and Fleischli Are Commisisoner Candidates," *Wyoming Eagle*, August 14, 1943, 1; Daniel J. Wolcut Advertisement, *Wyoming State Tribune*, September 24, 1943, 3.

25   "Thompson to Seek Seat on City Council," *Wyoming State Tribune*, October 1, 1943, 1 and 9; Fred L. Thompson Advertisement, *Wyoming State Tribune*, October 15, 1943, 2.

26   G.E. "Red" Porter Advertisement, *Wyoming State Tribune*, October 12, 1943, 8.

27   "Wolcut and Fleischli Are Commissioner Candidates," *Wyoming Eagle*, August 14, 1943, 1; Gus Fleischli Advertisements, October 13, 1943, 3, and October 18, 1943, 5.

28   "Bruce S. Jones Candidate for Commissioner," *Wyoming Eagle*, September 17, 1943, 1 and 4; Bruce S. Jones Advertisement, *Wyoming State Tribune*, October 18, 1943, 6.

29   "Warren Beaten in Primary," *Wyoming State Tribune*, October 20, 1943, l; "McInerney and Hanna Win in Mayor Race; Warren Fourth," *Wyoming Eagle*, October 20, 1943, 1. In the commissioner's race, Wolcut was fifth, Shaw sixth, Thompson seventh, Lapham eighth, and Porter ninth.

30   Hanna Thank You Letter, *Wyoming Eagle*, October 21, 1943, 12.

31   "Thank You, Cheyenne," *Wyoming State Tribune*, October 20, 1943, 7.

32   Ira Hanna Advertisement, *Wyoming State Tribune*, October 25, 1943, 3; *Wyoming Eagle*, October 26, 1943, 14.

33   Ira Hanna Advertisement, *Wyoming State Tribune*, October 26, 1943, 2.

34   Ira Hanna Advertisement, *Wyoming State Tribune*, November 1, 1943, 2; *Wyoming Eagle*, November 2, 1943, 5.

35   "Cheyenne Is at The Crossroads," *Wyoming State Tribune*, October 27, 1943, 3.

36   "Suppose YOU Were a Soldier Returning to Cheyenne When the War Is Over," *Wyoming State Tribune*, October 28, 1943, 10.

37   "What Does Cheyenne Really Need in a Mayor?" *Wyoming State Tribune*, October 29, 1943, 10.

38   "Be Sure You Vote On Tuesday And Vote For The Right Man," *Wyoming State Tribune*, November 1, 1943, 10.

39   "Ira Hanna Defeats McInerney," *Wyoming Eagle*, November 3, 1943, 1; "Hanna Elected Mayor," *Wyoming State Tribune*, November 3, 1943, 1 and 9.

40   "Thank You For Your Confidence," *Wyoming State Tribune*, November 3, 1943, 2.

41   "Three Competent Leaders, *Wyoming State Tribune*, November 4, 1943, 4.

42   Editorial, "A Good Ending," *Wyoming Eagle*, January 1, 1944, 5.

Round-the-Clock Mayor

Cheyenne's new administration, Mayor Ira Hanna and city council members Bruce Jones and Gus Fleischli, took office on January 3, 1944. The swearing-in ceremony took place in the council chambers during the morning and was broadcast on KFBC.[1] Other changes also occurred as a result of the election.[2] Since Hanna was the county's assessor, having been elected to the four-year position in 1941, he submitted his resignation in early December, with it taking effect on January 3.[3] Chief of Police Harvey Jackson, who had served in the position since 1940, resigned at the end of November because Hanna planned on appointing someone else as the new leader of the Cheyenne Police Department. Before serving as police chief, Jackson was the Chief of Detectives, and he returned to that position when his resignation took effect on December 1, though he served as acting chief until January 3.[4] Rumors about who would be the next chief spread, including the names of Fred Sinclair and Jesse Miller, both members of the Wyoming Highway Patrol. In fact, Miller told County Attorney Byron Hirst that he was offered the job, but he would not accept it at the current salary of $185 per month. According to Miller, Hanna told him the salary could be worked out after he began working in the position.[5] However, Hanna already seemed to have someone else in mind.

The first city council meeting took place the afternoon of January 3, and Jess Ekdall was sworn in as the next Cheyenne Chief of Police. Ekdall was born in Cheyenne and, at the time of his appointment, worked as the state manager of the Hamilton Depositors Corporation. He had graduated from Cheyenne's high school and had quite a career in sports, winning all-state honors in football and track. He graduated from the University of Wyoming Law School in 1933, and during his college years, he won the Rocky Mountain Conference boxing championship. At Lusk High School, he coached boxing for three years before accepting the position at the Hamilton

Depositors Corporation. Upon accepting the position of Chief of Police, he said, "I intend to see law enforced in Cheyenne during my term in office."[6] Ekdall had a law degree but apparently had no law enforcement experience. When the city council took up his appointment at their meeting on January 3, there must have been some surprise when it came to Ekdall's nomination. The council voted 2-1 to appoint him as Chief of Police. Hanna and Fleischli voted yes, but Jones voted no. Unfortunately, there is nothing in the city council minutes as to why he voted against Ekdall's appointment.[7]

Ekdall's lack of experience as a law enforcement professional became apparent fairly quickly in the Cheyenne Police Department. Only a few weeks into his term as chief of police, officers in the department contacted Hirst, concerned about how Ekdall was enforcing gambling laws. In response, the county attorney wrote a letter to the new chief of police: "I have received several requests from officers in your department about the proper procedure in enforcing the gambling laws and ordinances, and in conducting gambling raids. Therefore, this brief summary of the law is furnished to you for your department." In the letter, he explained how to secure evidence and the need for a search warrant as well as the importance of "voluntary statements of participants in the game." Hirst also discussed when taking a case to court that evidence should be "clear and conclusive." He ended the letter: "I shall appreciate continuance of your cooperation by bringing prosecution in Police Court and in preparing cases for prosecution in the District Court."[8]

Once beginning his tenure as Chief of Police, Ekdall quickly made some changes. He dismissed T. Joe Cahill from the police department. Cahill had been a former chief of police and, at the time of his dismissal, was the manager of the radio communications department.[9] About a week later, Ekdall announced a reorganization of the police department. Gerald J. Morris (nickname Jet), who had been the desk sergeant, was promoted to acting captain, a newly created position, and E.K. Violette (called Eckie or Ekky), who had been a detective, was assigned as the acting desk sergeant. He also said the department wanted to hire more patrolmen. Applicants had to be residents of Cheyenne, between 25 and 40 years old, at least 5 feet 9 inches tall, and weigh at least 165 pounds.[10]

On Wednesday, January 12, Mayor Hanna did what Cheyenne mayors do. He spoke before the Rotary Club, planning to explain the objectives of his administration and ask for suggestions regarding city government.

Hanna Says He Is Not In Favor of 'Open Gambling'

Brands Report as 'Damn Lie' in Talk to Rotary Club; Cites Condition of City

"It's a damn lie!"

So forcifully and unequivocally, Mayor Ira L. Hanna responded Wednesday to a question whether report was, or was not, true that the new Cheyenne administration was in favor of "open gambling" here.

The question was put by James H. Walton at a meeting of the Rotary club at which the mayor outlined objectives of the administration and invited suggestions concerning civic government.

Walton said that both before and after the city election, there had been widely circulated reports that the administration might be influenced and dominated by "an individual or group" interested in gambling.

Responding, Mayor Hanna said that he, too, had heard such reports, and said:

"I am not in favor of open gambling—there's nothing to it."

Further discussion, in which the recent seizure and destruction of slot machines by county authorities was mentioned, evoked from the municipal chief executive statement that the administration was not in favor of slot machine gambling or any other "open gambling," and the emphatic, and denunciation of any report that the administration favored gambling as "a damn lie!"

Views of News . . .

Comment and conjecture concerning the significance of happenings reported in today's edition of this newspaper.

By DEWITT MACKENZIE

While expectation of imminent wholesale Nazi collapse on the Russian front is unwarranted at this time, it is a fact that they are laboring under such terrific Red pressure that both German and Allied high commands are

Wyoming State Tribune, January 12, 1944

However, one question he was asked must have taken him aback. James Walton asked whether his administration favored open gambling in the city. Hanna responded: "It's a damn lie!" According to the article in the *Wyoming State Tribune*, Walton said there have been rumors about someone, "an individual or group," who could dominate Hanna's administration and was interested in gambling. The discussion turned to slot machines, and the mayor noted that his administration was opposed to slot machine gambling and any other form of gambling. That law enforcement continued to confiscate and publicly destroy slot machines was still true, as illustrated by the photo of Hirst and Tuck demolishing machines in a vacant lot the same day Hanna spoke to the Rotarians.[11] After that discussion, Hanna mentioned some of his plans for the city. He referenced marking streets with signs elevated above the street, replacing the curb markings, which would get covered by snow. Speaking of the fire and police departments, Hanna hoped to provide greater allowances for employees to purchase and maintain their uniforms, and he also favored wage increases for them, a point raised by several mayoral candidates. According to the article, "The mayor's statements evoked hearty applause."[12]

Another duty of the mayor was to promote the city. On February 21, Hanna responded to a query about Cheyenne from Miss Rose A. Luetmer of Cincinnati. It is unclear why she wrote, but the mayor provided a mostly positive picture of the capital city. He reported that the population was 25,000 and that Fort Warren had 15,000 soldiers. He mentioned it was difficult to find "suitable living quarters" at that time, but one could stay at one of the two large hotels, the Plains or the Frontier. To get around the city, there was a good bus system, while Cheyenne had four "attractive and modern theaters for entertainment" and many parks. Hanna, of course, also mentioned the "Daddy of 'Em All," the well-known Cheyenne Frontier Days celebration held every summer in the city. One negative Hanna mentioned was that "food prices are rather high."[13]

After the eventful Rotarian meeting, city business continued. The city council approved an appropriation of $345,000 to fund the government for the coming year. This was an increase over the previous budget, and a portion of the extra money budgeted was allocated for city employee salary raises. However, administrative employees and elected officials were not included in the salary increase. An allowance for police and fire department personnel was also granted, authorizing $30 to purchase a uniform and an extra $10 per month for uniform maintenance.[14]

The city also looked for ways to increase its revenues. During February, the mayor and city council members discussed raising funds by imposing fees on juke boxes and pinball machines. Hanna proposed an ordinance that would have imposed a $1,000 license fee on operators of pinball machines and juke boxes. The committee voted this down, but did pass an ordinance imposing a $25 license fee on each jukebox and a $10 fee on each pinball machine in Cheyenne.[15] Of course, during wartime, more organizations than the city needed funds. On March 1, Hanna issued a proclamation naming March the Red Cross Month and encouraged Cheyenne's citizens to "make their Red Cross gifts larger than ever this year."[16] Just a few days after the Red Cross appeal, Cheyenne's newspapers covered two topics in detail: one, the sad news about the passing of a young woman, and the other, positive news about a thriving business in downtown Cheyenne.

The thriving business was the Schwartz Bar and Bronco Room, managed by Sydney (Syd) Schwartz, located at 207 West 16th Street. Both Cheyenne newspapers printed a two-page ad of the newly renovated bar in the March 10 editions. The *Wyoming Eagle* also included a short article about Schwartz. According to the article, Schwartz was beginning his third year in Cheyenne, and before leaving California, he was "a former operator of the Hollywood 'Trocadero' and the fashionable San Francisco 'Montgomery' club." Syd's renovation of the business included "some 200 exhibits creating an atmosphere reminiscent of the old west and Cheyenne Frontier Days." The ad claimed that since 1943, the bar had served 347,892 patrons and included "Our Thanks and Gratitude" to those who frequented it. In large font, the ad also shouted that the Schwartz Bar and Bronco Room had "The Longest Bar in the United States." Also, not forgetting this was a time of war, adding "Drink Less Liquor, Buy More War Bonds." Schwartz and his wife became parents for the first time in January, when their son was born at Memorial Hospital.[17]

The young woman who had passed away was Helen Ann Phelan. Twenty-one years old, she attended the University of Wyoming in her junior year, and on February 11, she became ill and returned to the Phelan home, and then entered Memorial Hospital on the fifteenth, and she died on the evening of March 9. Both Cheyenne newspapers covered her untimely death on their front pages on March 10. She was well-liked, and her father, Walter Phelan, was a Cheyenne attorney and, at the time, chairman of the Wyoming Democratic Party. The presumed cause of her death was a fall from a horse on September 8, 1943, while riding with her friends. The fall resulted in head injuries and three weeks in the hospital. She was born in Cheyenne and attended St. Mary's Academy, and while attending Cheyenne Junior High School, she served a year as the student body president.[18] Certainly, her family and many friends mourned her untimely death, and those who knew her questioned why someone so young had to die. Many more questions would be raised by Cheyenne citizens in less than two weeks about events most did not see coming.

Two-page ad for the Schwartz Bar and Bronco Room in the March 10, 1944, issue of the *Wyoming Eagle*. The bar was located at 207 West 16th Street and claimed it was famous coast to coast.

CHAPTER 6 ENDNOTES

1   "Cheyenne's New Administration To Start Jan. 3," *Wyoming Eagle*, January 1, 1944, 1 and 6; "New City Administration Takes Office at Cheyenne," *Wyoming State Tribune*, January 3, 1944, 1 and back page.

2   Sound scriber recording of conversation between Byron Hirst and Jesse Miller, Byron Hirst Papers, Old West Museum. Transcript in author's collection.

3   "Hanna Resigns as Assessor: Two Seek Job," *Wyoming State Tribune*, December 7, 1943, 1 and 11.

4   "Police Chief Here Resigns: Harvey Jackson to Return to Post as Detective," *Wyoming State Tribune*, November 29, 1943, 1 and 2. The Cheyenne City Council accepted his resignation at their meeting on November 29, 1943. Cheyenne City Council Minutes, November 29, 1943, 165, Wyoming State Archives.

5   Sound scriber recording of conversation between Byron Hirst and Jesse Miller, Byron Hirst Papers, Old West Museum. Transcript in author's collection.

6   "Jesse Ekdall Will Be Police Chief January 1," *Wyoming Eagle*, November 30, 1943, 1 and 8.

7   Cheyenne City Council Minutes, January 3, 1944, 172, Wyoming State Archives.

8   Letter, Edward Byron Hirst, County and Prosecuting Attorney, to Jess B. Ekdall, Chief of Police, Cheyenne, Wyoming, February 2, 1944, Byron Hirst Papers, Old West Museum, Cheyenne.

9   "'T.Joe' Is Out As New Regine Steps In Here," *Wyoming Eagle*, January 4, 1944, 16.

10   "Local Police Department Reorganized," *Wyoming Eagle*, January 12, 1944, 1 and 11.

11   *Wyoming Eagle*, January 12, 1944, 1.

12   "Hanna Says He Is Not In Favor of 'Open Gambling,'" *Wyoming State Tribune*, January 12, 1944, 1 and 9.

13   Letter, Ira L. Hanna, Mayor, to Rose A. Luetmer, February 21, 1944, RG3001, Cheyenne City Records, Cheyenne Mayor Records, Administrative Files, Cheyenne Mayor-Misc. Correspondence, Jan. 1944-June 1944, box 4.

14   "City Budget Up Slightly This Year," *Wyoming Eagle*, January 22, 1944, 1 and 8.

15   $25 Fee on Jukeboxes Is Proposed," *Wyoming State Tribune*, February 22, 1944,.3; Cheyenne City Council Minutes, February 14, 1944 and February 21, 1944, 184 and 187, Wyoming State Archives.

16   "Mayor Hanna Asks Support Of Red Cross," *Wyoming Eagle*, March 2, 1944, 15.

17   Advertisement, "Syd Schwartz Proudly Presents To a Famous City 'Cheyenne,'" *Wyoming Eagle*, March 10, 1944, 8 and 9, *Wyoming State Tribune*, March 10, 1944, 6 and 7, and "Schwartz Bar Bronco Room Redecorated," *Wyoming Eagle*, March 10, 1944, 3. The notice about the birth of Schwartz' son was in the *Wyoming State Tribune*, January 17, 1944, 6.

18   "Helen A. Phelan, Popular Local Girl, Succumbs," *Wyoming Eagle*, March 10, 1944, 1 and 5; "Ann Phelan Dies Here," *Wyoming State Tribune*, March 10, 1944, 1.

CHAPTER 7

We Are Running The Show

If you were at home in Cheyenne on March 20, 1944, waiting for the Monday afternoon *Wyoming State Tribune*, you may have been shocked by what you saw on the front page, perhaps mystified at how this could happen in Wyoming's capital city. The leading headline remained in readers' memories for many years. It read, in bold letters all capitalized: "BRIBERY CHARGE FILED AGAINST MAYOR, CHIEF OF POLICE AND TWO PATROLMEN." The story was accompanied by photographs of Mayor Ira Hanna, Chief of Police Jess Ekdall, Captain G. J. Morris, and Sgt. E. K. Violette. The story stated that all pleaded not guilty.[1]

The other headlines were also surprising, and certainly somewhat puzzling. One read: "Schwartz Denied License Renewal." Another one read: "Syd Schwartz Faces Charges." In the lower right-hand corner of the page was "Ekdall Is Removed As Chief of Police" and "41 Negroes Arrested in Raids Here."[2] Those "arrested" were on the city's West Side. Readers must have asked, "What is going on around here?" and perhaps wondered if these stories could be connected in some way, and what headlines would be in the next morning's edition of the *Wyoming Eagle*.

The morning *Eagle* of March 21 did not disappoint, with page one leading with the headline "HIRST SAYS MAYOR HAD THREE MARKED $5 BILLS." Following the headline was "Shorthand Reporter, Dictograph Used to Get Other Evidence." The newspaper asked the condemning question: "Who's Mayor?" Schwartz was not left off the front page: "City Officials Refuse Renewal of License for Schwartz's Bar." Finally, in the bottom-right corner of the page, there was a "Federal Statement" congratulating the city of Cheyenne for ferreting out the alleged graft in the city administration. Included were photographs of the results of the previous day's raid on Cheyenne's west side.[3] People must have wondered what this all meant, and it would have been natural for those who voted for Hanna (and for those who

BRIBERY CHARGE FILED AGAINST MAYOR, CHIEF OF POLICE AND TWO PATROLMEN

Schwartz Denied License Renewal

Plead Innocent At Hearings in District Court

Ekdall, Morris and Violette Named With Chief Executive; Bonds Set for Group

WYOMING STATE TRIBUNE

Cheyenne, Wyoming, Monday, March 20, 1944 — Price 5 Cents

FORTY-SEVEN ARRESTED IN CHEYENNE VICE RAIDS

ARMY POLICE TAKE PART IN WIDE ROUNDUP

Mayor, Chief and Two Officers Are Set Free on Bond.

Charges of Corruption

20 Given Permits By City

City Council Takes Action Against Bar Operator

Syd Schwartz Faces Charge

Allowed Woman to Work as Barmaid, Warrant Claims

Ekdall Is Removed As Chief of Police

F. B. McVicar Is Named Acting Chief of Police; Other Officials Not Affected

Negro Troops From Ft. Warren Moved To Colorado Camp

41 Negroes Arrested in Raids Here

Cheyenne Police And MPs Carry Out Raid

Yanks Win Battle for Admiralties

21-Day Fight Ends In Victory for M'Arthur's Force

Spring Arrives

Cheyenne Native Will Direct U. S. Grazing Service

11 Flyers Who Parachuted From Bomber Found

The front page of the March 20, 1944, issue of the *Wyoming State Tribune*, with headlines about the arrests of the mayor, chief of police, and two other Cheyenne police officers, as well as two stories about the arrest of Sydney Schwartz and the city council not renewing the Schwartz Bar liquor license, and in the bottom right hand corner, a story about "41 Negroes Arrested in Raid Here." At some point, someone pasted on to the page a headline from the March 21, 1944, issue of the *Denver Post* titled "Forty-Seven Arrested in Cheyenne Vice Raids." This page is mounted on cardboard and is located in the Byron Hirst Papers, American Heritage Center, University of Wyoming.

did not) to remember Hanna's ads from only a few months before promising a "good, clean city government," and that he had an unquestioned reputation for honesty." It must have seemed ironic that when running, Hanna asked for a "clean campaign," apparently not promising the same for his administration.

The following day, an editorial in the *Wyoming Eagle* attempted to explain what had happened.

> Nothing more sensational could have occurred in municipal affairs than what happened here Monday—the arrest of the mayor, the chief of police, and two police officers. To say that the community was astounded puts it mildly—as evidenced by the long lines of people waiting in line to get detailed news as fast as it rolled from the presses. Here was one story that crowded war news off the front page and made Cheyenne people, for a time, more concerned with local affairs. The charges against the mayor and police officers were prepared by County Attorney Edward Byron Hirst and were supported by affidavits signed by citizens of this community. It is unnecessary to state that this is a matter in which county authorities were not able to be governed by their personal inclinations or desires. Sworn evidence was placed in their hands, which required the filing of information and the issuance of warrants. The warrants having been issued, the sheriff had no other choice than to make the arrests. The court, in due process of law and recognizing the legal rights of the accused. Granted bail in a reasonable amount.

The editorial went on to compliment the "citizens who assisted the investigators by giving evidence to which they were willing to sign their names." It added that if there is wrongdoing, "it should be punished," but also stated that everyone deserves a fair trial.[4]

At that time, of course, only a few knew when and how the alleged wrongdoing began, and how Hirst, Tuck, and others had gathered enough evidence to lead to the arrest of the mayor and three law enforcement officers. It is not known when Hanna and others began planning what could be called a shocking betrayal of Cheyenne voters who had trusted Hanna and Ekdall, believing they would follow through on their promises and declaration to enforce the law. Did it start before the election or after Hanna won the vote in November, or would it have waited until Hanna began looking for a chief of police who had similar intentions? We cannot say for sure, but what we do know is that it started in early March.

Not quite two months into Hanna's term as mayor, he, Ekdall, Morris, and Violette began to visit African American businesses on Cheyenne's West Side. On March 1, during the afternoon, the Chief of Police and Acting Captain visited the Black and Tan Café. They spoke with Lola West, the owner of the business. According to West, Morris told her, "We came down to see about a shake-down." She asked how much it would cost her. The two police officers explained they knew she was selling whiskey and beer (she did not have a liquor license) and accused her of having prostitutes in the café. She denied that, and in response, she was told, "You have got women around here, put them to work." West refused. Morris said they would only expect fifty dollars this week, but one hundred dollars per week after that, and if business increased, the weekly payment would increase to one hundred and fifty dollars from then on. The officers said that if this were agreed to, the Black and Tan Café would receive protection from the Cheyenne Police Department and the Military Police from Fort Warren. Ekdall also reiterated to West that she should put the women who live there to work. When she responded, these were soldiers' wives, he said, "Put them out and get women that will hustle." The following evening, Hanna and the other three visited West at the Black and Tan Café, and Hanna reinforced that everything told her yesterday "was all right" and that she should go and talk to "Pop" Grimes at the Porters and Waiters Club — that he would explain everything.[5]

The next African American business four men visited was Susie Stowers' boardinghouse at 616 West 18th Street. In the evening of March 2, the mayor and the three police officers spoke with her about opening her house and having "girls." According to Stowers, Ekdall "told me they were opening up the houses because of the rape cases…. He said that they had to do something to protect the city." (By opening up the town, Ekdall meant allowing prostitution, gambling, the sale of illegal alcohol, and other vices that could be profitable. They reasoned that if Black businesses had enough prostitutes for the African American soldiers, other women would be less at risk.) If a girl agreed to prostitution, she would have to pay twenty-five dollars to Hanna and the others, and Stowers would have to pay one hundred twenty-five dollars a month. The girls also had to go to a doctor at Fort Warren for any treatment. "He, Chief Ekdall, said that everything was already fixed with the doctor to take care of them." Besides paying the money, Ekdall said, "The girls would not be allowed to go on the streets except one day a week."[6]

Shortly after seeing Stowers that evening, Hanna and the others went to the Porters and Waiters Club at 1804 Bent Avenue to see W.C. "Pop" Grimes. In his statement, Grimes said the chief asked: "How would I like to gamble, sell whiskey, and have a few girls around here?" Grimes responded, saying gambling was fine, but he could not get any alcohol, and "I didn't deal in girls." Still, according to Ekdall, "You will have to come in line just the same." When Grimes asked if this was a payoff, he asked how much, and the chief said, "$100 a week." Grimes said that for as long as he had been in Cheyenne, he had never made a "pay-off." Ekdall corrected him, saying he knew otherwise. "I know Harvey Jackson had a pay-off man down here, and we were all paying him and Fred Sinclair." Grimes fired back that Tuck and Jackson had never taken any money, and he went on to clarify that he had always "lived up to the rules as laid down by the Chief of Police and the Ft. Warren authorities." On March 3, Violette (known as Eckie or Ekky) visited Grimes and made it clear that Harvey Jackson was not to know anything about what was going on at all and he said that Lola West and Mildred Brooks, who ran the Cottage Restaurant at 1720 Bent Avenue, should give their money to Grimes and that he would return at 4:00 on Saturday, March 11, to pick up the payoffs. That day would turn out to be an important one in the prosecution of Hanna and the others.[7]

Contrary to Violette's order, West, Grimes, and Stowers went to Chief of Detectives Jackson. The statements they made in the presence of Jackson and Glenn Peterson, another member of the Cheyenne Police Department, are dated March 4, immediately after being offered protection by Hanna and his cohorts. It is not known where the statements were made, perhaps in the Cheyenne Police Department, but apparently, other members of the department were not aware of what Jackson was doing with the West Side business owners. Shortly after the fourth, they all spoke to County Attorney Hirst, making him aware of the offers of protection. From there, planning began for an effort to gather more information about Hanna's illegal activities and the involvement of the police officers, which would lead to their arrests on March 20.

The day before Violette was to return to the Porters and Waiters Club on March 10, various law enforcement officials and others met at the county building to discuss steps to obtain evidence against the mayor and the three police officers. That day, Jackson called L.D. Parker, who was an investigator for the Alcohol Tax Unit, a federal office under the Treasury Department, asked him to join him for a meeting with Hirst, City Council Member Bruce Jones, Glen Peterson, George Smith, and Court Reporter Clarence Feguson.[8]

Hirst led the meeting and told Parker they had information that might interest him. The county attorney produced the statements made by West and Grimes a week earlier. In a statement about the meeting dated April 22, 1944, Parker described the two business owners as "operators of houses of ill repute." After hearing about what the mayor and the three police officers were doing with the West Side businesses, Parker agreed to cooperate with their investigation. He then called Special Investigator John Schooley in Denver, Colorado, and asked him to join the investigation and to come to Cheyenne the next day (March 11) with the unit's recording equipment.[9]

About mid-afternoon on the eleventh, Parker, along with Schooley and Court Reporter Ferguson, who would transcribe the meeting in shorthand,[10] and Fred M. Taylor, another investigator from the Alcohol Tax Unit, went to the Porters and Waiters Club to set up the equipment to record the meeting between West, Grimes, Hanna, Ekdall, Morris, and Violette. Grimes had agreed to allow the taping of the meeting in his business. To prepare for the meeting, Schooley bored a hole in the wall between Grimes' office and the stairway, ran a wire into the office, and placed a microphone under the desk. The wire then ran up the stairway, where it was attached to a radio and the recording equipment in a room on the second level.[11] Schooley ran both machines while Parker and Taylor stationed themselves in the hallway next to a door leading into the office. "This door had a glass panel in the top part, which was covered with a common type of window shade. In this curtain, there were two or more holes large enough to allow observation of the occupants of the office room."[12] Everything was set to record the meeting. The recording began at 4:35 when newly promoted Desk Sergeant Violette entered the office.

POP GRIMES: Come on in.[13]

After Violette entered the office, Grimes went out the west office door and "returned with a pint of whiskey and a Coca-Cola which he placed on the desk in front of Violette, who poured himself about half a water glass of whiskey and finished filling the glass with Coca-Cola. Pop took a drink from the bottle.[14]

POP GRIMES: Well, that is what I want to talk to you about ….

Here is what we want to know: what protection will we get from the police?"

SGT. VIOLETTE: I know what protection you will get if you don't pay off.

POP GRIMES: There is twenty-five. (Handing paper money to Sergeant Violette).

Grimes handed Violette several other envelopes. One contained twenty-five dollars from Lola West, although, according to Violette the amount was supposed to be one hundred dollars.

SGT. VIOLETTE: You tell Lola to have that other seventy-five bucks over here … I'll be here at eight. You tell her to have that money here by seven o'clock, or else.

POP GRIMES: All right, I'll tell her to have that hundred dollars here at seven.

SGT. VOLETTE: You tell her that's just the way it is … And you tell her to have that money over here at three o'clock every Saturday afternoon … If she don't have it over here, I'll padlock her God damn door … All of you claim making no money. We know better.

(Sgt. Violette left the room at 4:50 p.m.)

(The following proceedings commenced at 7:50 o'clock p.m., March 11, 1944, at the same place.)

(Lola West and Pop Grimes in room. Captain Jet Morris and Sgt. E.K. Violette entered room at 7:50 o'clock.)

Millie Brooks was also in the room, although Violette asked her to leave. Brooks ran the Cottage Restaurant at 1720 Bent Avenue. Lola asked Violette and Morris if all the rest had paid, and Violette answered yes. Lola asked why didn't the police just load up the entire west side and put it in jail. The sergeant responded that he doesn't want to do that. He just wanted to padlock it.

CAPT. MORRIS: Listen, these people, they are all paid. That's none of your business. We are going to tell you one thing, that's for sure, and if you don't pay you won't be in business by Thursday. You got away with murder for about fifteen years, so if you want to … There is no use denying it … You just go on down there and lock your door and you run everybody out.

LOLA WEST: No, I will let you do that.

CAPT. MORRIS: All right, we are going to do it. We are going to put you out of business.

LOLA WEST: All right, let me talk to the Chief and let me find out what I'm supposed to pay and who I'm supposed to pay.

SGT. VIOLETTE: That's right.

LOLA WEST: And the Chief told me that he would get the girls and the whiskey.

SGT. VIOLETTE: You got the girls.

LOLA WEST: I ain't got no girls ….

CAPT. MORRIS: You have been running gambling games.

LOLA WEST: Christ O Mighty!

Discussion continued between Lola, Morris, and Violette about whether she had girls working for her right now. Parker described it as "just a general argument and cuss fight"[15] between the three. Violette also accused Lola of "making more money than anybody in the God damn town." She responded get me some girls and "I will make some." The threats to close the Black and Tan Café continued.

CAPT. MORRIS: Get hold of Eddie and tell them to close it up, tell them to put a lock on the door and lock her up. Call Eddie and see if you can get hold of the Chief … Yes, but the phone is disconnected … We will go out and get him. If she wants to see the Chief, we will go out and get him. We will get them right together.

It is unclear who Eddie is. It may have been a misspelling in the transcript for Ekky, or perhaps it was another member of the police department.

LOLA WEST: Everybody is going to padlock me. Go ahead and padlock me. You want to let me talk to the Chief.

SGT. VIOLETTE: I am going to get the chief. We will get the Mayor, too. Do you want the Mayor, too.

LOLA WEST: Yes.

SGT. VIOLETTE: All right, we will bring them both.

LOLA WEST: Get them both … I want to talk to both of them.

CAPT. MORRIS: We are going to get them pretty quick. We are the small guys.

LOLA WEST: That's all right, you are just as big as the next one to me. We will have to know something, too. I want to know something. I want to know, where is my protection coming from. You bring me a written statement from the Post where I can run and keep girls, but, by God, I am not going to stick my neck out there in the loop, without. I ain't going to do it.

The arguing continued. Violette and Morris brought up one of the women working for Lola and said she has been hustling. Lola disagreed and said that if she has been hustling, it has not been in the Black and Tan Café. The two officers leave Lola and Grimes alone for a short time.

(Officers have left Lola and Pop alone for a few minutes. Lola and Pop repeat numbers on some bills, apparently writing numbers down.)

They were writing down serial numbers from some of the five-dollar bills, which would be turned over to the mayor and the officers. When Violette returned, he asked Lola how much she paid Harvey Jackson. She said not "one dime." He then accused her of running a crap game in her café, which she denied. He also said Lola had been selling whiskey, which she also denied.

According to Parker's account, "In a long argument about who was designated at a prior meeting to do the collecting, Violette contended that he had been assigned, and Lola said Jet (Morris) was named as the one to do the collecting. Violette said, "The Mayor and the Chief and I were all right there, and it was agreed that I would be the one who would see you — I would handle it."[16]

During a discussion about whether Lola had girls hustling in the Black and Tan Club, she commented, "You can go by the Plains Hotel and find the biggest whore house of any place —"

Morris and Violette left for a while, and at 9:50 p.m., those two and Hanna and Ekdall entered the office. Lola sat in a chair while Grimes and the others stood. Violette told Lola, "Go ahead and talk," and she responded, "Just hold your horses, I am going to talk." There was discussion about what Lola had to pay. At this point, Morris and Violette left the room.[17]

LOLA WEST: You said you would settle for fifty.

CHIEF EKDALL: The first two weeks — You see, we passed up a whole week. We told you it would be a hundred a month — a hundred a week.

LOLA WEST: You first told me a hundred and fifty.

CHIEF EKDALL: That is all right, that's out. Well, Pappy's paying himself.

LOLA WEST: A hundred and fifty?

CHIEF EKDALL: Yes, and that's what … We consider you and Pappy and one other, you are doing the volume of business. We have had an opportunity to check and find out. We haven't bothered you for two months. We didn't touch you because we had to find out what was going on.

LOLA WEST: Well, I don't —

CHIEF EKDALL: We are not making any —We are not making any mistakes.

LOLA WEST: I don't have no girls in the house, and I don't want none. That is a fact. And I don't mind, you know, as I said, if it takes them from that Fort —You know how that is —

CHIEF EKDALL: You are getting the protection from the Fort as well as from — (pause) — our office.

LOLA WEST: I am?

CHIEF EKDALL: Now listen: You are paying a license, nothing else, your license to us for your protection.

LOLA WEST: A license to run? I want to know just what it is all about.

CHIEF EKDALL: I will tell you what it is all about —

LOLA WEST: My understanding is the best in the world, don't you think so? I want to know what I am paying for.

CHIEF EKDALL: We are running the show —

LOLA WEST: That is what you told me.

CHIEF EKDALL: Anything that happened in the past, any rules or regulations, or enforcements, are out. Now, if they get their nose in it, they'll be out, too, because we are sitting on the seat. They might think we are dumb down there. We don't say very much; keep our mouth shut; and half the time some of the big guys that think they are big think we are pretty damn dumb. But we know what the score is. We know that — We know what we are doing. And when we say that you are being protected, not just from us, but you are being protected from our (one unintelligible word here) too. We don't have to involve ourselves. That's all we have to do, go to one person out at that Post, to put you out of bounds. And we are going to protect ourselves; the city isn't going to be involved.

Now, that's the connection we have, and we can assure you of that. And I think that letting these places be operated there before, that that amounts to two or three hundred dollars a week, just for gambling alone. But after all, everybody wants to make a little living, and that's a damn cheap license. Now, if you have girls, or don't have girls, that's your business. Yes, sir, that's your business ….

Ekdall continued.

CHIEF EKDALL: You don't know, Lola; I think you are fair and I think you are honest. You don't know that your girls—You don't know that your girls—They are married girls, and you know and I know that a married woman, her boyfriend is some place else, they have had it all their lives, and they want to make a little on the side theirselves. And they don't let you know that, no; no, they don't let you know that. But mark my words, if you don't want to play ball, if your place isn't shut up by Wednesday, I'll kiss your left foot.

LOLA WEST: Well, I—I—I'm going to play ball, but I do want to know where I am at.

CHIEF EKDALL: You know who you are talking to now. (Few unintelligible words). We want Pappy, he is willing to just go ahead, just keep you folks in order — not a go-between, or anything like that — he is going ahead, he is paying his license just like the rest of you. He didn't ask for a thing. Now, that's the truth, and it's damn nice of him to take and … (Unintelligible words). We have asked Ekky because he did some work for us down there, to help us see that things are getting along, because four people can do a job a lot better than two. Now, we hated to ask Ekky … (Several unintelligible words). The Mayor is fair… but it doesn't involve anything like that. You can get Ekky on the 'phone all day long, and our other man on the 'phone there; anything that goes to our office, regardless of whoever person it goes to, the man on the 'phone knows it.

MAYOR HANNA: (Few unintelligible words) … and I know what I am talking about, too. No matter who has been telling you before this, from now on we are doing the telling. You determine tomorrow what you want to do … and just forget what has been said here tonight … (Several voices here).

MAYOR HANNA: I know who was doing the knocking down before, I know who has been collecting, and I know all about it, but we are running the show.

LOLA WEST: For the next two years you are running the show, I guess, you are running the show.

MAYOR HANNA: No, it is not only going to be just for two years. If we all stick together, it will be for eight years, and we are all going to get along.

LOLA WEST: A hundred dollars a week, though, is a hell of a lot of money. I don't care, that's a *hell* of a lot of money. That is more money than I am making. I haven't made a hundred dollars this damn week.

(inaudible)

CHIEF EKDALL: You can make more now. We are going to tell you some things now.

LOLA WEST: I don't want no girls, and I wouldn't have none. I wouldn't have one of the sons-of-a-bitches in my house. I have suffered from that grief, and I don't want no more girls; but I guess — I guess either you or — (inaudible) — just cutting our throat …

CHIEF EKDALL: Cutting your throat (inaudible)

CHIEF EKDALL: Everything is all right now.

(Pause)

Morris and Violette reentered the room.

LOLA WEST: that's a hundred.

MAYOR HANNA: I will count it later on.

(Pause)

SGT. VIOLETTE: You thought I was lying to you, didn't you?

LOLA WEST: You can never tell anything about it.

The conversation ended when Pop Grimes said "All right, your captains. Everything is fixed now." Lola said, "That's right."

Over the next week, Hirst must have reviewed everything and spoken with Parker and Taylor. During the evening of March 19, Parker, Taylor, and Hirst's secretary went to the Black and Tan Café. There, Lola gave Parker a list of the serial numbers she recorded from the five-dollar bills she had given Hanna as part of her "fee" for that week. He asked her to write her name on the list for identification. "I then marked the list with my initials for identification and delivered the list to Byron Hirst." With this and everything else gathered during the past weeks, Hirst was ready to make the arrests the following morning.[18]

CHAPTER 7 ENDNOTES

1   *Wyoming State Tribune*, March 20, 1944, 1.

2   *Wyoming State Tribune*, March 20, 1944, 1.

3   *Wyoming Eagle*, March 21, 1944, 1.

4   Editorial, "Let The Probe Be Thorough," *Wyoming Eagle*, March 22, 1944, 2.

5   "Statement by Lola West, March 4, 1944," Byron Hirst Papers, Old West Museum, Cheyenne, Wyoming.

6   "Statement by Susie Stowers, March 4, 1944," Byron Hirst Papers, Old West Museum, Cheyenne, Wyoming.

7   "Statement by W.G. Grimes, March 4, 1944," Byron Hirst Papers, Old West Museum, Cheyenne, Wyoming.

8   "Statement of L.D. Parker, Investigator—Alcohol Tax Unit, Cheyenne, Wyoming," April 22, 1944, Byron Hirst Papers, Old West Museum, Cheyenne, Wyoming.

9   "Statement of L.D. Parker, Investigator—Alcohol Tax Unit, Cheyenne, Wyoming," April 22, 1944, Byron Hirst Papers, Old West Museum, Cheyenne, Wyoming. L.D. Parker also testified at the trial of Hanna and the others. See "Federal Man Tells Court of Hearing 'Payoff Discussions,'" *Wyoming Eagle*, May 4, 1944, 1 and 24, and "State To Rest Case Today In City Trial," *Wyoming Eagle*, May 5, 1944, 1 and back page.

10   Clarence Ferguson was the court stenographer for the First Judicial District Court. However, only days after the March 11 meeting he was taken to the hospital for an appendectomy. It was reported he was progressing satisfactorily, but on March 19 he died. "Dolezal to Work in Local Court," *Wyoming State Tribune*, March 19, 1944, 3, "Reporter of Court Dies: Ferguson Succumbs Unexpectedly at Hospital Here," *Wyoming State Tribune*, March 20, 1944, 6.

11   "Statement of L.D. Parker, Investigator—Alcohol Tax Unit, Cheyenne, Wyoming," April 22, 1944, Byron Hirst Papers, Old West Museum, Cheyenne, Wyoming. See also "Evidence of F.M. Taylor," Byron Hirst Papers, Old West Museum, Cheyenne, Wyoming.

12   "Evidence of F.M. Taylor.

13   The selected quotes from the recorded meeting come from the "Transcript of Recordings made at Porters and Waiters Club, 1804 Bent Avenue, Cheyenne, Laramie County, Wyoming, on March 11, 1944," Byron Hirst Papers, Old West Museum, Cheyenne, Wyoming. The quotations will be exactly as written in the transcript.

14   "Statement of L.D. Parker," 2.

15   "Statement of L.D. Parker," 5.

16   "Statement of L.D. Parker," 7.

17   "Statement of L.D. Parker," 8.

18   "Statement of L.D. Parker," 11.

An Invitation for Graft

Monday, March 20, 1944, must have started like any other beginning of the usual work week. The city council was meeting, led by Mayor Ira Hanna, and city council members Bruce Jones and Gus Fleischli were in attendance. At the same time, courts were hearing cases. And, early that morning, the Laramie County Prosecuting Attorney presented charges against Mayor Ira Hanna, Chief of Police Jess Ekdall, Captain Jet Morris, and Sergeant Ekky Violette. Supporting the charges were affidavits by Lola West and Pop Grimes. According to the *Wyoming State Tribune*, West's statement said, "the officials solicited and received $100 from her March 11 as 'pay-off' for 'protection.' Grimes' affidavit made the same allegation, but the amount was $25." Judge Thompson quickly issued bench warrants that morning for the four, and within the hour, County Attorney Hirst and Deputy Sheriff Ward entered the city council chambers.[1]

Certainly disrupting the council meeting, Hirst and Ward arrested Hanna and took him to the Laramie County Sheriff's Office. Ward also arrested Ekdall, while Sheriff Tuck, William Bradley, head of the Wyoming Highway Patrol, and Jess Miller of the Highway Patrol soon arrested Morris and Violette. These three were also taken to the sheriff's office. Investigator L.D. Parker was in the office when all four were searched. He related: "I saw the money taken from each of them and put in an envelope. Byron Hirst handed me a list and asked me to check each man's money against the numbers on the list. I asked Deputy Sheriff Joe Filer to assist me. I then opened the envelopes in the presence of Filer and Ekdall. I opened Hanna's envelope first, and from the bills in it, I found three five-dollar bills with serial numbers corresponding to numbers on the list which had been handed me by Mr. Hirst." Parker then asked Investigator F.M. Taylor to verify the numbers, which he did, and after this, Parker placed them in a safety deposit box at American National Bank.[2]

At the hearing before Judge Sam M. Thompson, all four pled not guilty. The judge specified the bonds would be $4,000 for both Hanna and Ekdall ($2,000 for each charge) and $3,000 for Morris and Violette ($1,500 for each charge). The specific charges were soliciting and accepting money "to influence them with respect to their official duties."[3] The four posted bond, so they did not go to the county jail, but they were listed on the Laramie County Sheriff's Prison Calendar. The entry for Hanna stated, "chg'd with taking bribe." The column titled "Committed" listed the time he was booked into the jail at 9:50, and included under the arresting officers were the names of Hirst and Ward. As for Ekdall, who was listed immediately below Hanna, the entry stated "same as above," and booked in the jail at 9:55 with the same arresting officers noted. Of course, Hirst did not have arresting authority, but he must have wanted to be present for the arrests. Morris and Violette were also included on the prison calendar; both had the same reason for arrest, "bribe," and both were booked in the jail at 10:30. The arresting officers were Tuck, Miller, and Bradley. However, on the register between Ekdall and Morris was the name of someone who also had been named on the front page of the *Tribune* that day. That was Sydney Schwartz. He was arrested for "employ(ing) female waitress in liquor bar." He was booked in the jail at 9:45, and the arresting officers were Tuck and Ward.[4]

The amount of money for the bonds was considerable at the time. The four who were charged did not pay their bonds. According to the *Tribune*, "Mrs. Ekdall became bondsman for her husband, and jointly with Mrs. Ida Schwartz, for Morris. Mary Kalman and Lilly Stone became bondsmen for Hanna. Mrs. Schwartz became bondsman for Violette." The women did not need to pay at that time, but their signatures meant they would pay the amount if the defendants failed to appear when the court summoned them.[5] Mrs. Ida Schwartz, owner of the Schwartz Bar, was the wife of Sidney Schwartz, who also owned and managed the Schwartz Bar.

After Hanna left the city council meeting, the two remaining council members took immediate action in response to the four arrests. Fleischli moved that Ekdall be removed from the office of Chief of Police. Jones seconded the motion, which passed. They said Ekdall had violated his oath of office and was not performing the duties as Chief of Police. A second motion by Fleischli, again seconded by Jones, was to appoint F.B. McVicar, the current juvenile officer, as Acting Chief of Police. Since McVicar was present at the meeting, he was sworn in to that position immediately. Jones went on to say that, with the mayor's arrest, he became the acting mayor under state statutes and Cheyenne's city ordinances. This would hold as long as the present circumstances kept Hanna from performing the duties of the office.[6]

The following morning, the *Wyoming Eagle* provided more details about the efforts that led to the arrest of Hanna and the three law enforcement officials. The headlines noted that Hanna had three marked five-dollar bills in his possession. Hirst and other official sources told reporters about the bills and the serial numbers, and he also mentioned that law enforcement used a dictograph and that a shorthand reporter recorded the conversations of that meeting at the Porters and Waiters Club on March 11. Unfortunately, the reporter, Ferguson, had passed away just two days before the arrests. The *Eagle* reported that all four of the defendants had been seen going into "certain colored houses and cafes in the West end and explicitly explained to the owners they would have to pay off for protection, and specified the amounts." What was perhaps even more surprising was that Hirst had acquired five affidavits from other business operators on the West Side. These were referenced in the article.[7]

The new affidavits told stories similar to those West and Grimes told in their statements. It is important to note that all the businesses on the West Side approached by the four were run by African Americans. Jordan Davis, who owned a hotel at 1806 Bent Avenue, reported the mayor had come to his place of business one night and mentioned to Davis that he had a "nice clean place." It was Violette who told him that "all places would have to pay something if they were to run." The charge for Davis' business was $100 per week; he paid the sergeant that amount on March 18, and he was expected to repeat it every Saturday. Davis said he could make that money by selling liquor and gambling, but he would not get involved in "hustling." Another affidavit was provided by Alma Marie Banks, who worked at the Cottage Café. She was from Louisiana, was twenty-one years old, and had been in Cheyenne for about ten months. Banks had waited tables, but "when Mildred Brooks, who runs the Cottage cafe, told me that the chief of police in Cheyenne said it was all right for girls to hustle, and I started hustling then at the Cottage café. I charged $7 a trick and out of this I paid Mildred $2 a trick and kept $5 a trick." Brooks expected Banks to pay her ten dollars per week for protection, which helped her pay the chief of police. She told Banks this was the order from the chief of police.[8]

Another affidavit was submitted by Joe Eva Davis, the wife of Jordan Davis. According to her, their business was a rooming house where they rented rooms to soldiers and their wives. In the rooming house was a sandwich shop and a bar, where they served "pop and other soft drinks." She admitted to keeping liquor on hand, but it was just for parties, such as when her son, who was in the army at the time, came to visit. She related that Hanna and Ekdall had visited their business and asked for $100 per week. "For that money, we were supposed to have girls hustling and gambling. I understood they were going to give us protection and we could have gambling and girls and liquor." On Saturday, March 18, she paid Violette $100. "I let my bills go and paid them the $100." She was encouraged to get some girls for their rooming house, but Davis said no, those rooms were for soldiers and their wives. After she paid Violette, Davis asked for a receipt, but none was forthcoming. He just told her, "Go ahead and take care of my business and make my money."[9]

The *Eagle* that morning also included a "Federal Statement" from the Social Protection Division of the Federal Security Agency. Howard F. Feast, the regional social protection representative, acknowledged Jackson, Hirst, Tuck, McVickers, and others for conducting an effective investigation that uncovered many legal violations. He said his agency had "been very much concerned about conditions in Cheyenne for some time." He also noted that if a community tolerates illegal behavior, it "is an invitation for graft, and a community that tolerates such conditions should likewise be under indictment with its officers who might become involved in illegal practices." Feast specifically mentioned prostitution, which, according to him, contributes to an increase in venereal disease and often leads to violations of the law in communities. He ended his statement: "We are wholeheartedly behind all activity which will eliminate entirely the prostitute, the facilitator, and all those profiting from her effort."[10]

That issue of the *Eagle* answered one important question: whether Hanna could legally continue his duties as mayor. The answer was yes. The article stated that legal authorities said Wyoming statutes allowed a public official to be removed by petition, which would need to be signed by 25% of the votes cast in the general election. A petition could be submitted to the county clerk, who would then call for a special election to decide who would serve as mayor. Such a petition was never submitted.[11] Once released on bond, Hanna was able to continue the duties of mayor.

The *Tribune's* edition on the afternoon of March 21 repeated some of the earlier story in the *Eagle*, such as the affidavits collected, but it also provided new information. City Council member Jones spoke with Hanna, who said he would not resign as mayor. Both Jones and Fleischli said they would continue to work with the indicted mayor. Also discussed in the newspaper was that Morris and Violette had been suspended for five days, as required by the police department's civil service commission regulations.[12] Of interest was a short article in the bottom-right corner of the front page titled "Wyoming Bribery Statute Carries Stiff Provisions." According to the article, being prosecuted and found guilty under Wyoming's bribery law can result in a sentence of up to 14 years. Hirst told the newspaper about the law earlier that day.[13]

Hirst also released a statement. He apparently wanted everyone to know that the four defendants were all involved in the bribery scheme and that Hanna had the three five-dollar bills with serial numbers documented by West and Grimes. Hirst's statement made clear that the investigation "was made possible by the alert and intelligent action by Chief of Detectives Harvey Jackson." He also acknowledged Glenn Petersen of the police department, as well as Tuck and the sheriff's office. His statement ended, "Cheyenne in the past has been a clean town. With the cooperation of the good citizens of Cheyenne, the various law enforcement agents will see that Cheyenne is a clean town in the future."[14]

The *Tribune* also included an editorial titled "Courts Place for Judgment," about the events of the past few days, attempting to express what the citizens of Cheyenne were feeling. It did not mention the names of the four arrested and charged, but mentioned the officials' accepting bribes and selling protection, and described it as "illegal and immoral pursuits of the rottenest category. The citizenry of the city, doubtless with very few exceptions, are astounded and profoundly mortified." The editorial also alluded to the unverified connection between the mayor and the three policemen to "the so-called 'underworld,' but these were not sufficient to prepare the public mind for information so devastating as that which has been officially released in explanation of yesterday's events." It continued that many in Cheyenne have already convicted the four defendants, but said they are entitled to the presumption of innocence. The newspaper also congratulated Hirst, Jackson, and McVicar. "They are demonstrating that Cheyenne fundamentally is a law-abiding community which is determined to remain that way."[15] Unfortunately, the editorial did not commend those West Side business owners, West, Grimes, Stowers, and others who stood up for the rule of law and were instrumental in the arrest of Hanna, Ekdall, Morris, and Violette.

Not to be outdone, the following day, the *Eagle* included an editorial titled "Let the Probe Be Thorough." It admitted that the "community was astounded puts it mildly" and the coverage of the arrests and charges was a powerful enough story that "crowded" war news off the front page of the newspaper. The editorial continued that it must have been disagreeable for the officers to arrest other law enforcement officers for their alleged misdeeds, but they held true to their oaths and carried out their duties. Unlike the *Tribune*, the *Eagle* commended those from the West Side who stood up and signed the affidavits, which were essential to bring charges against those who had taken oaths to uphold the law but had failed in their responsibilities. The editorial concluded that now that charges have been filed, everything should be done to ensure justice. "If there has been wrongdoing, it should be punished."[16]

The four charged with bribery appeared in district court on March 27. Judge Sam M. Thompson told them that the court date was only a formality and that they would be summoned again when a trial date had been set. Several days before that hearing, A.D. Walton, the attorney for the four, filed "an affidavit charging him (Judge Thompson) with bias and prejudice in the case." Due to that filing, Thompson was automatically disqualified from serving as a judge on the case, and he stated that he would appoint another judge to take over the case fairly soon.[17] Just a day before that quick hearing, the *Wyoming State Tribune*, in a section titled "Servicemen' News-Letter," which was credited to both Cheyenne newspapers, began the section with this: "IN PROBABLY THE MOST SENSATIONAL case in the city's history Mayor Ira J. Hanna and Chief of Police Jess Ekdall and two police officers were arrested last Monday and charged with soliciting and accepting bribes."[18]

The fact that the Cheyenne newspapers used the word "sensational" to describe the arrests and charges brought against high city officials was certainly appropriate. However, it should not be forgotten that the front pages of the two papers featured two other events during those several days in March. One question that arises is why the arrest of a Cheyenne bar manager appeared on the front page, and why the prison calendar listed him among the four officials arrested. This certainly warrants further investigation.

CHAPTER 8 ENDNOTES

1   "Bribery Charge Filed Against Mayor, Chief of Police, and Two Patrolmen: Plead Innocent At Hearing in District Court," *Wyoming State Tribune*, March 20, 1944, 1.

2   "Statement" of L.D. Parker, April 22, 1944, 11-12, Byron Hirst Papers, Old West Museum, Cheyenne, Wyoming.

3   "Bribery Charge Filed Against Mayor, Chief of Police, and Two Patrolmen: Plead Innocent At Hearing in District Court," *Wyoming State Tribune*, March 20, 1944, 1.

4   Laramie County Wyoming Sheriff's Prison Calendar, March 20, 1944, 166.

5   "Bribery Charge Filed Against Mayor, Chief of Police, and Two Patrolmen: Plead Innocent At Hearing in District Court," *Wyoming State Tribune*, March 20, 1944, 1. In 2024 dollars the $4000 bond would be equal to $71,702 and the $3000 bonds equal to $53,777. These are taken from the CPI Inflation Calculator.

6   "Ekdall Is Removed As Chief of Police," *Wyoming State Tribune*, March 20, 1944, 1. Cheyenne City Council Minutes, March 20, 1944, 192, Wyoming State Archives.

7   "Hirst Says Mayor Had Three Marked $5 Bills; Shorthand Reported, Dictograph Used to Get Other Evidence: County Attorney Has Affidavits From Five West End Operators," *Wyoming Eagle*, March 21, 1944, 1 and 6.

8   Hirst Says Mayor Had Three Marked $5 Bills; Shorthand Reported, Dictograph Used to Get Other Evidence: County Attorney Has Affidavits From Five West End Operators," *Wyoming Eagle*, March 21, 1944, 1 and 6.

9   Hirst Says Mayor Had Three Marked $5 Bills; Shorthand Reported, Dictograph Used to Get Other Evidence: County Attorney Has Affidavits From Five West End Operators," *Wyoming Eagle*, March 21, 1944, 6. All three of the affidavits mentioned in this newspaper article are included in their entirety in the Byron Hirst Papers, Old West Museum, Cheyenne, Wyoming.

10   "Federal Statement," *Wyoming Eagle*, March 21, 1944, 1 and 20.

11   "Who's Mayor?" *Wyoming Eagle*, March 21, 1944, 1.

12   "Civil Service Rules Invoked Against Pair," *Wyoming State Tribune*, March 21, 1941, 1 and 10. "Police Take Affidavits," *Wyoming State Tribune*, March 21, 1944, 1 and 10.

13   "Wyoming Bribery Statute Carries Stiff Provisions," *Wyoming State Tribune*, March 21, 1944, 1.

14   "Dictograph Employed In Preparing Bribery Charge: Statement Released by Hirst," *Wyoming State Tribune*, March 21, 1944, 1 and 10.

15   Editorial, "Courts Place for Judgment," *Wyoming State Tribune*, March 21, 1944, 4.

16   Editorial, "Let The Probe Be Thorough," *Wyoming Eagle*, March 22, 1944, 6.

17   "Judge Thompson Barred From Presiding In Case," *Wyoming Eagle*, March 23, 1944, 1. "Thompson Disqualified In Trial Of Fourt City Officials: Defendants Ask Change in Petition," *Wyoming State Tribune*, March 22, 1944, 1 and 11.

18   Servicemen's News-Letter, *Wyoming State Tribune*, March 26, 1944, 6.

We Are Going to Open This Town Up

Ida Bronstine-Schwartz had lived in Cheyenne for many years, married to Harry Schwartz, a well-known local businessman. Mr. Schwartz was a partner in the Globe Finance Company and owned an interest in the Schwartz-Bobb Liquor Company on Sixteenth Street in Cheyenne. He died in his home on Carey Avenue at the age of forty-six in May 1939 following a two-year illness. After his death, Mrs. Schwartz and her two sons moved to California.[1]

There, Ida met and married Sydney A. Schwartz. They lived for a time in El Passadero, California. In a newspaper article about the wedding, he was listed as S. Allen Schwartz, and it stated that he was the president of the Kenmore Construction Company and engaged in construction work in California. However, an article in the *Wyoming State Tribune* a few years later described his background differently, stating he was a "former operator of the Hollywood 'Trocadaro' and the fashionable San Francisco 'Montgomery' club."[2]

The newly married couple moved to Cheyenne in 1941, and during the summer of 1942, Sydney (generally known as Syd) came up with an idea for the city that would have greatly changed Lions Park. He proposed building an amusement park on the south side of Sloans Lake, with 5% of gross receipts going to the city. Schwartz also wanted to build a dance hall, though his plan called for the city to install the necessary lights, water, and sewer connections. According to the *Wyoming State Tribune*, "Schwartz told the council that as a permanent resident of Cheyenne and a member of the Cheyenne Chamber of Commerce, he is eager to furnish Cheyenneites and men at Ft. Warren with entertainment and amusement 'equal to those furnished in cities many times the size of Cheyenne.'" Schwartz wanted a five-year lease and an exclusive franchise for the sale of food, soft drinks, and cigars. Attorney A.D. Walton represented Schwartz at the presentation to the city council in early August.

Mayor Ed Warren and the two city council members, Buck Buchanan and Al Kay, decided to study the plan further.[3] The council may have expected to take several days or a week to decide, but they quickly heard from quite a few constituents.

What the *Wyoming State Tribune* described as a "wave of vigorous protest" overtook city hall the day after Schwartz presented his proposal. Private homeowners and civic organizations let the mayor and city council members know they strongly opposed the plan. The mayor told the *Wyoming Eagle* they had heard from "hundreds of Cheyenneites, many of them residents of the sector bordering the proposed park site, all requesting denial of the application." The neighborhood near the potential amusement park saw it as a nuisance that would require more law enforcement and fire protection and could even draw business from downtown businesses, including the USO clubs. Also opposed was the Lions Club, stating Lions Park "has been and will be a civic enterprise and the placing of commercial ventures at the location would not be in accord with the Lions' idea of how it should be operated." At the August 10 city council meeting, Warren moved and was seconded by Kay, "that for the best interests of the North Park System of Cheyenne, the application of Sydney A. Schwartz for an amusement concession be denied." All three members voted aye in support of the motion.[4] Despite that setback, Syd and Ida had already begun another profit-making enterprise which would prove quite popular, at least for a while.

Schwartz's Bar and Liquor Store opened at 207 West 16th Street in June 1942. The *Wyoming Eagle* described the bar as a place for "lovers of relaxation and fine liquors" and noted that the new downtown business would be warmly welcomed. The article mentioned Syd would manage the bar, which featured mirrored ceilings, "richly paneled walls and ultra-comfortable seating accommodations" for those who enjoyed the "top-grade liquid refreshments offered." Syd's background was highlighted, noting he had "owned and operated several of California's leading bars and nightclubs." The same issue of the *Eagle* included a full-page ad for the bar which stated: "Visit Schwartz's and See the West at It's Best."[5] Fortunately for the bar, Syd, and Ida—who apparently were co-owners — were granted a liquor license by the city council at their March 23, 1942, meeting. In early March 1944, the bar became the newly renovated "Schwartz Bar and Bronco Room," which made headline news on March 20, 1944, when Syd was arrested.

A front-page headline on the *Wyoming State Tribune* that day read "Syd Schwartz Faces Charge." The warrant claimed he had allowed a woman to work as a barmaid in his bar. If true, it violated city ordinances, which read: "No female shall be employed in a room holding a Retail Liquor License; but this provision does not exclude service from such room by females to connecting rooms where food is served in hotels or restaurants holding the proper license."[6] The woman was Irene Fleming. According to the article, the city, under the Warren administration, had allowed her to be employed by the bar; however, this did not stop Hirst from approaching Justice of the Peace F.A. Stennett to approve two complaints against Schwartz. Apparently, one charge was made by James F. Powers and Willis C. Walker, and the other by Charles F. During and Jacob Weber. The four stated in the complaints that they had been served by Fleming in the Schwartz Bar.[7]

At the same time Schwartz was going through the legal process after his arrest, the city council discussed the requests for liquor license renewals. With Hanna attending to his own criminal charge after his arrest, the two city council members, Bruce Jones and Gus Fleischli, granted twenty liquor licenses, but denied a liquor license renewal for Ida Schwartz and the Schwartz Bar and Bronco Room. During the meeting, a captain from Fort Warren spoke against granting the Schwartz Bar a liquor license. His reason was that "on one occasion (the bar) had sold as many as twelve (12) drinks to one soldier at one time and then gave him one for good measure," which led to him being so intoxicated that military police had to subdue him and take him to the police station. The captain gave one other example, stating a sailor had been given three "double shots" at the bar and passed out before he could return to the fort.[8]

The *Tribune* described other complaints not mentioned in the council minutes, as well as a response from Mrs. Schwartz. In addition to the concern that the bar had hired a female barmaid, there was concern that the license had been granted to Mrs. Schwartz for the previous 2 years, but the bar was run by her husband, implying the person holding the license was not involved in the running of the business. Also, a representative from a number of women's clubs in the community said, "It's not a woman's place to run a bar, and if she (Mrs. Schwartz) has been doing it unlawfully, I certainly believe that the license should be revoked." Mrs. Schwartz attended the meeting and said she was "amazed and astonished" by what had happened, noting she had owned the bar for several years and needed time to comply with any requests from the council. She admitted the bar had a female barmaid, but said she was a "perfect little lady" and added, "She doesn't drink, she serves them." She also stated: "I have thousands upon thousands of dollars invested in that business, I have a family, and I don't think it's fair to take my business without warning." Her attorney asked Jones and Fleischli to give her more time to address the issues raised, but the two members ignored the request. Then, Jones made a statement that may have surprised and astonished some, although others in attendance probably expected to hear what he had to say.

> I don't know how to proceed or what to say. This has proven a very sad occasion for me. The mayor was arrested this morning along with the chief of police and other police officers. The laws have been corrupted. One man had made boasts and brags about what he was going to do, how he was going to have things his way. I think he selected a man whom he was going to use as a tool. He knew he was popular politically and that he could feather his own nest. It is very regrettable and with all respect to Mrs. Schwartz, my heart goes out to her and I don't condemn her, I feel the council should act courageously and clean up the town, therefore I make a motion that the Schwartz license not be granted.

Fleischli seconded the motion, and it passed.[9]

Attending the meeting that morning were many well-known citizens of Cheyenne, including former governor Leslie Miller, Archie Allison, Fred Warren, H.B. Henderson, and L.D. Parker of the alcohol tax unit, "Capt. E.R. Brock, commanding officer of the internal securities district" at Fort Warren, along with members of various church and women's groups.[10] After the council denied the Schwartz Bar license, the two council members granted that license to Art and Ed James, former owners of the Washington Market.[11] With that action, all liquor licenses allowed for Cheyenne had been assigned. None remained. The person Jones referred to as having made boasts was Syd Schwartz. Jones' comments echoed some of the rumors circulating around Cheyenne—that Schwartz chose Hanna to run for mayor and that Schwartz was leading the effort to extort the West Side business owners.

The day after the arrests and the denial of the Schwartz liquor license, the *Wyoming Eagle* reported on several rumors that had apparently been circulating in Cheyenne for several weeks. The newspaper stated, "rumors had been

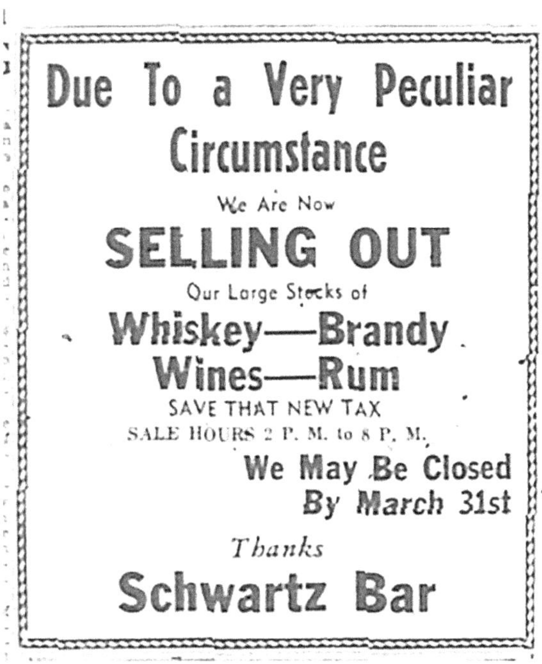

Wyoming Eagle, March 22, 1944

a dime a dozen or less," and most were related to which establishments might lose their liquor licenses. Would the city council's actions by denying a license close a bar, or possibly would the council close two of the "best places" in the city by not renewing their licenses? However, one rumor was fairly accurate, expecting the council not to renew the Schwartz Bar license, with Jones and Fleischli voting not to renew, while Hanna would vote to renew. Of course, the mayor did not have the opportunity to weigh in on the question.[12]

Syd and Ida Schwartz quickly attempted to defend their actions and have their former license returned and renewed. Syd told the *Eagle:* "The charges against me are completely out of line." He said that in his two years in Cheyenne, he had never been charged with any violation, and he added that the mayor's administration had approved the use of a female barmaid because of the "manpower shortage," and that she never mixed drinks or worked behind the bar. She was "merely a waitress and a member of the cooks and waiters union in Cheyenne." When Hanna took office, Syd claimed he had spoken to the new mayor about Fleming, and the still-unindicted mayor said it was all right to employ her in that position. Schwartz also refuted the charge of serving 12 drinks to one soldier, saying the bar had signs posted letting everyone know that only 3 "double shots" or 6 single drinks were allowed per customer. According to Schwartz, "those rules are carried out."[13] Because of Syd's arrest and the denial of the liquor license to Ida, the couple faced several urgent issues.

Without a liquor license, the Schwartz Bar and Bronco Room had to close. Realizing this, the co-owners put an ad in both Cheyenne newspapers. The beginning of the ad said: "Due To a Very Peculiar Circumstance, We Are Now Selling Out." Would the "peculiar" circumstance have been the refusal to renew the license, or could it have been what council member Jones said, certainly implying some possible nefarious activity? The bar owners were looking to sell their supply of whiskey, brandy, wines, and rum. The ad ended with: "We May Be Closed By March 31st, Thanks, Schwartz Bar."[14] Because the city council granted the Schwartz liquor license to another business, there was no question that the Schwartz Bar would have to close, since all available licenses had been distributed. However, that did not stop Ida from pursuing the issue legally.

Before the end of March, Ida Schwartz filed a petition for a "writ of Mandamus" in district court, which would direct the city council to appear and present why the license was not renewed, as well as to renew it. The action stated that Schwartz had a "preferential right" to the license, and that this right was violated when the council voted not to renew. The legal effort submitted by her attorney, Walter Phelan, was presented to Judge Sam M. Thompson, who set March 29 as the date for the arguments to be heard.[15] Schwartz maintained that she had complied with everything necessary for the license to be renewed. Additionally, Ida filed an affidavit "charging District Judge Sam M. Thompson with 'bias and prejudice,' and that she could not obtain a fair trial of the issues" in Thompson's court and requested that another judge be given the case. Once attorney Phelan submitted the affidavit, Thompson had no choice but to select another judge, who turned out to be V.J. Tidball,[16] although the change in judges did not help Schwartz in her effort to reverse the council's decision.

City Attorney C.A. Lathrop quickly filed a demurrer with the court. What the petition stated was that even if Schwartz's filing was true, that was not enough to "constitute a cause for action at law." Tidball granted the city attorney's demurrer, and in response, Phelan said he or his new co-counsel, Tom McKinney, can either file another petition or appeal to the Wyoming Supreme

Court.[17] Tidball ruled that state law says "no person shall have an action against the governing body or its members by reason of denial of a retail liquor license."[18] It was McKinney who filed an amended petition that included more information about the city council hearing at which the renewal was denied. The petition said the decision was unlawful and unfair.[19] Shortly thereafter, Lathrop filed a demurrer to the amended petition, and Tidball scheduled a hearing on the demurrer for May 26.[20] The judge ruled in July, upholding the council's decision not to renew the license. Ida had one last move to make: appeal to the state supreme court, which she did in late September. McKinney and A.D. Walton filed the appeal, and the court dismissed the case on April 16, 1945. The court ruled that the question was moot, as the license would have expired on March 31, 1945.[21] The question about the liquor license was finally settled, but during the early legal work on the non-renewal, Syd faced Hirst's charge against him for hiring a female barmaid.

Schwartz's case was held in H.A. Brookhart's Justice of the Peace Court. It had begun in F.A. Stennett's court, but after an affidavit of prejudice was filed, the case was moved to Brookhart's court. Schwartz's attorney, Phelan, requested a jury trial for his client on April 3. At the hearing, Schwartz pled not guilty and furnished a $400 bond, $200 for each count.[22] Since there were two charges against Schwartz, they would be tried separately. That same day, the sheriff submitted the names of twelve male potential jurors, and the trial began two days later.

The second charge was tried first, and Hirst prosecuted the case. He, Schwartz, and Phelan appeared before the judge on April 5. Six summoned jurors also were in the courtroom, but two of the potential jurors apparently made it clear that Schwartz would get a "fairer trial" if they were not on the jury.[23] They were dismissed. Both attorneys agreed to proceed with a four-man jury. The *Wyoming State Tribune*, covering the trial, wrote that the courtroom "was jammed by a crowd of curious persons, but they were provided little excitement" because of how slowly the trial proceeded with "much discussion by the participants."[24] Sitting next to defense attorney Phelan and Schwartz was Irene Fleming, the barmaid.

Hirst began the prosecution by calling the city clerk and the former city clerk to testify that Ida Schwartz had received a liquor license for the Schwartz Bar in March 1943, and it expired the following year on March 31. Next, he called the Cheyenne Newspapers, Inc. employee charged with advertising to show a photograph of Fleming at the bar, which illustrated that the business was a bar, not a restaurant, and that, according to the city ordinance, she should not have been serving drinks. Next, an accountant who had worked on the bar's books testified that Fleming was an employee of the business. Also called as a witness by Hirst was Willis Walker, co-owner of Plains Airways, and one of the men who signed a complaint against Schwartz. He testified that he and James Powers entered the Schwartz Bar the evening of March 16 and were served drinks by Fleming. Phelan cross-examined the witness, and Walker testified that he then went to Hirst's office to make the complaint against Schwartz. Phelan asked if he found it offensive to see "girls carrying drinks" in the Oak Room of the Plains Hotel. He responded that they handled food as well as drinks. Schwartz's attorney asked: "You don't feel very kindly toward Mr. Schwartz, do you, Mr. Walker?" He replied, "No, I do not." Phelan was ready to cross-examine the other person who filed the complaint. After Powers identified himself on the stand, something unthinkable happened in the courtroom — everyone must have been shocked by what they saw. Phelan collapsed on the courtroom floor with a heart attack.[25]

The court quickly summoned a doctor to examine Phelan, but he was pronounced dead. After that, "on motion of the prosecuting attorney, the Court declared a mistrial and adjourned the trial and dismissed the jurors."[26] Phelan was Catholic, so a priest was called to give him the last rites before he was removed from the courtroom. According to the *Wyoming Eagle*, Phelan had recently spoken to friends about his heart condition. A longtime friend of his, Charlie Wunnicke, told the newspaper that Phelan was "physically crushed by the sudden death of his little girl," Helen Ann, only a month before. The newspaper reported that one of the pieces of evidence Phelan had on his desk during the trial was a newspaper which "carried the death notice and picture of his daughter, and according to witnesses, it is probable that he viewed these many times during the course of the trial."[27]

After what must have been an unsettling day in court, Schwartz needed to decide what he wanted to do. On April 19, in Brookhart's courtroom, he pled guilty to each of the two complaints of hiring a female barmaid in the Schwartz Bar. The Justice of the Peace fined him fifty dollars and sixty days in jail on each count. Brookhart suspended both jail sentences. Surprisingly, Hirst was not in the courtroom when Schwartz was sentenced. He told the *Eagle* "I did not know Schwartz had changed his plea. Passing of sentence is a function of the judge, and in this case, I was not asked for and did not make any recommendation."[28] The suspension of the jail sentences was "on condition that Deft. [Defendant] have no further trouble."[29] Syd and Ida had weathered losing the liquor license, the legal battle to retain it, his arrest, a day in court, and, finally, pleading guilty. However, there was still one more item for the couple to deal with, though it would certainly seem minor compared to the others.

The same day Schwartz pled guilty to hiring a female barmaid (April 19), William T. Harwood, a Cheyenne painter and decorator, filed suit against both Syd and Ida, asking for $266 and court costs for work he had completed at the Schwartz Bar and Bronco Room and for which he was not paid. The petition filed in the district court stated, "That on the 4th day of January 1944, the plaintiff (Harwood) was engaged by the said Sydney A. Schwartz to decorate and paint the interior of the business premises known and operated as 'Schwartz's Bar'...." The two parties came to a verbal agreement to decorate the bar based on Schwartz's wishes. Harwood said he had worked 208 hours on the project, and the agreed rate was $1.80 per hour. The total was $374.40, and an additional $48.60 for materials to complete the work. Also, Harwood valued his murals at $50, so the compensation amount was $473. Only $207 had been paid by the time of the filing, so Harwood asked for the remaining $266. The petition also stated that Harwood had been offered $100 for "full payment of balance," but he rejected it because it was not the full payment.[30]

Ida and Syd responded to the April filing with their own petition filed on May 20. It stated they had contracted with Harwood, but the agreed-upon amount to complete the work was not to exceed $300. They claimed he "should have completed said work for less than said $300; and that at the said time of employment, plaintiff told defendants said plaintiff said work should undoubtedly be less than said sum of $300." They also claimed Harwood did not work "diligently and with reasonable speed." The attorney for Harwood, Ruth Edelman, replied on June 8, denying everything included in the Schwartz's petition. That response was followed by months without any legal filings, and then nearly a year later, the *Wyoming State Tribune* included a very short article in its May 25, 1945, edition, stating that the suit "has been settled out of court."[31] However, the story of Syd and Ida is not yet complete.

Prosecuting Attorney Hirst knew Syd, had conversations with him, and wanted to arrest him with Hanna, Ekdall, Morris, and Violette, and not just for hiring a female barmaid. Before the trial of the quartet, Hirst spoke to a number of people, apparently preparing for the court battle. He had a recording device in his office, and these conversations were stored on sound scriber disks. Hirst spoke to Pop Grimes, Lola West, and her daughter, Bernice Favors. Another person he spoke to was Vaile Ward, a member of the Laramie County Sheriff's Department. During his conversation with the deputy sheriff, Hirst said: "He (Schwartz) told me he was going to open up the town, 'Mayor and I are going to do it. Come on in with us.' That was the way he talked to me." Revealing his desire to arrest Schwartz, he also told the deputy sheriff: "Well, of course I have to go on what evidence I have, but I have got very nearly enough to charge him something or other."[32] He may have been close, but the only charge against Schwartz was the hiring of the female barmaid.

Surprisingly, one of the recorded conversations was with Syd (Hirst called him Syd). Schwartz just seemed to show up in Hirst's office. It is unclear if he knew the discussion was being recorded. Hirst made it clear he would follow the law. He told Syd, "You told me about what you're going to do around here. Yeah, you and Ira. Remember you said, 'We're going to open this town up, we're going to have gambling, we're going to have this, we're going to make money.'" He also told Syd, "I got to get this crap cleaned up around here. We're not going to have all this stuff." Besides that, the two discussed Schwartz's trial for hiring Irene Fleming to work as a barmaid at the Schwartz Bar. Hirst said, "Of course, here's what you're up against, Syd: you're going to be convicted sooner or later anyway on that charge." Schwartz replied, "That's right, that's right." Hirst offered, "You want my advice, you take a plea and let it go at that. But you do what you want to. I don't know what you'll get from Brookhart." Of course, Schwartz did take the plea.[33] Schwartz also mentioned his possible future plans. "I don't expect to stay in Cheyenne. I don't want any business with Cheyenne or with any Cheyenne individuals." Hirst responded, "Yeah," and Syd explained, "Because they're out to frame me, and you know that already." The discussion also briefly mentioned the loss of the liquor license. Hirst did not see that he and Ida had any hope of getting it back, "I don't think so. I don't think you got a good case any way you look at it. I mean the—the law permits that city council will do any damn thing they want to. They did it."[34]

Besides having these discussions with Schwartz, Ward, and others, Hirst also sought to learn more about what was happening in Cheyenne's law enforcement community in another way. He asked a former member of the Laramie County Sheriff's Department about the "general attitude" in the office.[35] The former employee commented that the "efficiency of the office was very low," and some matters that deserved attention were "sadly neglected." He did not know Hanna well and did not know Schwartz at all, but said he (Schwartz) was often at the police department. He said Schwartz's car was frequently parked out in front. "He used to go down to the Police Station quite often. At least, that is the reason given me for the presence of his car. Possible he was in Hanna's office. I knew Schwartz's car, because with the siren and red light prominently displayed, it was one that attracted attention. I understood that Schwartz was very friendly with Ekdall." He was also told by Vaile Ward that Schwartz "put up the money to elect the mayor and named the Chief of Police." Regarding the red light, apparently, it was policy that only law enforcement, ambulances, and fire department vehicles could have a siren and red light. The former employee also asked a law enforcement official, Vaile Ward, if it was illegal for other vehicles to be so equipped. He responded, "that it was, but that Schwartz had 'put up the money' — etc, 'was the big Boss,' and therefore enjoyed these special privileges."

CHAPTER 9 ENDNOTES

1   "Local Business Man Succumbs At Home Here," *Wyoming Eagle*, May 25, 1939, 3; "Schwartz Rites Today in Denver," *Wyoming Eagle*, May 26, 1939, 16.

2   "Ida Schwartz Is Married in California," *Wyoming State Tribune*, September 15, 1941, 6; "Schwartz Bar Bronco Room Redecorated," *Wyoming Eagle*, March 10, 1944, 3.

3   "City Council Will Study Amusement Park Proposal Would Involve Sloans Lake, Lions Grounds," *Wyoming State Tribune*, August 3, 1942, 2; "Amusement Park Plan Is Studied By Council Here," *Wyoming Eagle*, August 4, 1942, 18; Cheyenne City Council Minutes, August 3, 1942, 96, Wyoming State Archives.

4   "Wave of Protests Greets Amusement Park Plan: Lions Club Voices Strong Disapproval," *Wyoming State Tribune*, August 4, 1942, 2; "Amusement Park To Be Denied Here," *Wyoming Eagle*, August 7, 1942, 1 and 3; Cheyenne City Council Rejects Amusement Park Proposal: Schwartz' Appeal Is Turned Down," *Wyoming State* Tribune, August 10, 1942, 2; Cheyenne City Council Minutes, August 10, 1942, 97, Wyoming State Archives.

5   "New Schwartz Bar Is Tops In Liquor Stores," *Wyoming Eagle*, June 17, 1942, 2; full page ad, *Wyoming Eagle*, June 27, 1942, 12.

6   *Ordinances of the City of Cheyenne, Codified and Compiled,* 1938, Wyoming Labor Journal Publishing Company, 141. This is included under chapter 23 which discusses Business Licenses for Alcoholic and Malt Liquors.

7   "Syd Schartz Faces Charge: Allowed Woman as Barmaid, Warrant Claims," *Wyoming State Tribune*. March 20, 1944, 1.

8   Cheyenne City Council Minutes, March 20, 1944, 193.

9   "Schwartz Denied License Renewal: 20 Given Permits by City," *Wyoming State Tribune*, March 20, 1944, 1 and 9; "Soldiers Sold 12 Drinks at Bar Is Charge," *Wyoming Eagle*, March 21, 1944, 1. The man Commissioner Bruce Jones referred to was Sydney Schwartz and he used Hanna as a tool to feather his own nest.

10   "Schwartz Denied License Renewal: 20 Given Permits by City," *Wyoming State Tribune*, March 20, 1944, 1 and 9.

11   "City Officials Refuse Renewal of License for Schwartz's Bar: Action Puts Stop to Rumors on Taverns," *Wyoming Eagle*, March 21, 1944, 1 and 6.

12   "City Officials Refuse Renewal of License for Schwartz's Bar: Action Puts Stop to Rumors on Taverns," *Wyoming Eagle*, March 21, 1944, 1 and 6.

13   "Schwartz Says He Got Permit to Employ Girl," *Wyoming Eagle*, March 22, 1944, 1 and 3.

14   Schwartz Bar advertisement, *Wyoming Eagle*, March 22, 1944, 5, and March 23, 1944, 11; Schwartz Bar advertisement, *Wyoming State Tribune*, March 23, 1944, 12.

15   "Seek to Compel Commissioners To Issue Schwartz Bar License: District Court Petitioned to Issue Writ of Mandamus Ordering Action," *Wyoming State Tribune*, March 20, 1944, 1.

16   "Tidball to Hear Case," *Wyoming State Tribune*, March 28, 1944, 2; "Judge Tidball to Preside in Case," *Wyoming Eagle*, March 28, 1944, 1 and 8. The case's title was "State of Wyoming on the relation of Ida H. Schwartz, plaintiff, vs. Ira L. Hanna as mayor of the City of Cheyenne, Bruce Jones and Gus Fleischli, as commissioners of the City of Cheyenne, constituting the city council of the City of Cheyenne, a municipal corporation, and S.D. Markley, city clerk of the City of Cheyenne, a municipality."

17   "Move to Force Issuance Of Liquor License to Mrs. Ida Schwartz Fails: Tidball Sustains Lathrop's Demurrer; 'Tom' McKinney Enters the Case as Co-Counsel," *Wyoming State Tribune*, April 3 1944, 1; "Attempt to Force Liquor Permit to Be Renewed Fails," *Wyoming Eagle*, April 4, 1944, back page.

18   "Servicemen's News-Letter," *Wyoming Eagle*, April 8, 1944, 17.

19   "Ida Schwartz Files New Petition in Liquor Case," *Wyoming State Tribune*, April 20, 1944, 1 and 9.

20   "Demurrer Is Filed In Schwartz Case," *Wyoming State Tribune*, April 23, 1944, 1; "Hearing Set In Cheyenne Liquor Case," *Wyoming State Tribune*, May 18, 1944, 1.

21   "Ida Schwartz Appeals Case to High Court," *Wyoming Eagle*, September 29, 1944, 1; "Court Dismisses Schwartz Action," *Wyoming State Tribune*, April 17, 1945, 11.

22   Justice Docket, State of Wyoming, County of Laramie, "State of Wyoming vs. Sidney (Sid) Schwartz," Wyoming State Archives; "Schwartz To Ask For Jury At Hearing On Wednesday," *Wyoming State Tribune*, March 30, 1944, 1; "Lawyer Seeks Jury Trial In Schwartz Case," *Wyoming Eagle*, March 31, 1944, 1 and 9.

23   "Schwartz Case Is Postponed Thru Mistrial," *Wyoming State Tribune*, April 6, 1944, 2.

24   Justice Docket, State of Wyoming, County of Laramie, "State of Wyoming vs. Sidney (Sid) Schwartz," Wyoming State Archives; "Schwartz Case Opens With Four-Man Jury: Two Disqualify Themselves: Faces Charge of Employing Barmaid in Cheyenne Bar," *Wyoming State Tribune*, April 5, 1944, 1.

25   "Schwartz Case Is Postponed Thru Mistrial," *Wyoming State Tribune*. April 6, 1944, 2; "Walter Phelan Dies While Defending Case in Court," *Wyoming Eagle*, April 6, 1944, 1 and 8; "Walter Q. Phelan Dies In Cheyenne Courtroom: State Democratic Chairman Stricken by Heart Attack; Daughter Died Early in March of Injuries from Fall," *Casper Star Tribune*, April 6, 1944, 1; "Phelan Rites Are Pending: Heart Attack Is Fatal to Demo Leader, *Wyoming State Tribune*, April 6, 1944, 1 and back page.

26   Justice Docket, State of Wyoming, County of Laramie, "State of Wyoming vs. Sidney (Sid) Schwartz," Wyoming State Archives.

27   "Walter Phelan Dies While Defending Case in Court," *Wyoming Eagle*, April 6, 1944, 1 and 8. Phelan was born in Wisconsin but moved to Cheyenne in 1909. He became one of Cheyenne's most successful and prominent attorneys.

28   "Schwartz Pleads Guilty And Is Fined $100 For Hiring Barmaid," *Wyoming Eagle*, April 20, 1944, 2.

29   Justice Docket, State of Wyoming, County of Laramie, "State of Wyoming vs. Sidney (Sid) Schwartz," Wyoming State Archives.

30   Filing in the State of Wyoming, County of Laramie, in the District Court, First Judicial District, "William T. Harwood v. Sydney A. Schwartz, also known as S. Allen Schwartz, and Ida B. Schwartz," April 19, 1944, Wyoming State Archives. "Action for $266 Judgment Against Schwartz on File," *Wyoming Eagle*, April 2, 1944, 1 and 8.

31   Filing in the State of Wyoming, County of Laramie, in the District Court, First Judicial District, "William T. Harwood vs. Sydney A. Schwartz also known as S. Allen Schwartz and Ida B. Schwartz, May 20, 1944"; Filing in the State of Wyoming, County of Laramie, in the District Court, First Judicial District, "William T. Harwood vs. Sydney A. Schwartz also known as S. Allen Schwartz and Ida B. Schwartz, June 8, 1944"; "Suit Is Settled Out of Court," *Wyoming State Tribune*, May 25, 1945, 11.

32   Hirst interview with Vaile Ward, member of the Laramie County Sheriff's Department. Interview is on sound scriber disk in Byron Hirst Papers, Old West Museum, Cheyenne. The transcript of the interview is in author's collection.

33   Recorded discussion between Byron Hirst and Sydney Schwartz. Discussion is on sound scriber disk in Byron Hirst Papers, Old West Museum, Cheyenne. Transcript is in author's collection.

34   Recorded discussion between Byron Hirst and Sydney Schwartz. Discussion is on sound scriber disk in Byron Hirst Papers, Old West Museum, Cheyenne. Transcript is in author's collection.

35   The name of the former employee of the sheriff's department is not listed in the four-page, single-spaced response. However, the document is in the Byron Hirst Papers at the Old West Museum. The date 5/4/44 is handwritten on the document's first page.

The Raid

Another article appeared on the front pages of the Cheyenne newspapers on March 20. The reporting about this event did not quite make headlines, but it must have caught the attention of interested readers in the Capital City. The *Wyoming State Tribune* began the coverage with the article in the March 20 issue titled "41 Negroes Arrested in Raids Here." "Cheyenne police, with the cooperation of 25 military policemen, arrested 41 Negroes this morning in the west end of Cheyenne."[1] The raid took place from midmorning to early afternoon.[2] "Their arrest was witnessed by hundreds of residents of the West end, inhabited mostly by colored people, who stood outside their houses, or peered thru windows."[3] Several questions arise about this extraordinary event. Why did law enforcement think such a raid was necessary, and why did it occur at the same time as the arrests of Hanna, Ekdall, Morris, Violette, and Schwartz?

The contingent of law enforcement personnel needed to raid the African American community is remarkable. Besides members of the Cheyenne Police Department and the Wyoming Highway Patrol, there were from twenty-five to thirty military police from Fort Warren, along with Brigadier General Horace L. Whittakes, commander of the quartermaster training center, and Colonel Graves B. McGary, commander of Fort Warren. Federal employees joined the force, as did members of the special protection division of the Federal Security Agency, and L.D. Parker, head of the federal alcohol tax unit. The fort's personnel joined in because County Attorney Hirst asked for their assistance, and once the raid was completed, he said they had "cooperated splendidly."[4] From the perspective of those in the West Side neighborhood, they must have been curious and perhaps panicked at seeing their friends and neighbors taken out of their homes and businesses, put into military trucks and police cars, and carted off to the county jail.

Apparently, two reasons triggered the surprise raid on Cheyenne's West

Side and the African American community. According to Parker, his department wanted "to determine what liquor violations were occurring." Confiscated during the raid were ten cases of assorted whiskeys and eleven cases of beer. The federal stamps on the bottles of alcohol indicated that they were purchased from establishments in Colorado and Nebraska. Parker did not plan to press charges against any of the business owners, but he wanted to find the suppliers. The retail value of the whiskey and beer was reported to be $875, which was three to four times higher than the government price. Parker had been working with Hirst on the liquor investigation, so he joined in the raid.[5] Hirst, however, had other reasons for the action taken that day on the West Side.

On March 21, Hirst told the press, "Raids conducted by city, county, military and federal authorities in west Cheyenne yesterday were 'occasioned by' the filing of the charges against the city officials," and stated that "47 Negro men and women" were arrested during the operation. That number contradicted the *Tribune's* story the day before, which stated the authorities "herded 26 women, eight soldiers, and seven civilians, all colored into army trucks and police cars and brought them to the city jail."[6]

The headline of a front-page story in the *Denver Post* read: "Forty-Seven Arrested In Cheyenne Vice Raids: Army Police Take Part In Wide Roundup." The second part of the story on page three exclaimed, "Forty-Seven More Arrested in Cheyenne Raids: Military Police Play Leading Role in Citywide Roundup: Vice and Liquor, Black Market Operations Charged: Mayor, Police Chief and Two Officers Are Released on Bond." This story was certainly sensational, claiming the raid was city-wide, when clearly it was only directed at the city's West Side. The first paragraph of the article dramatically exaggerated a "citywide cleanup of vice, liquor black markets and gambling," but the rest of the article did provide good information.[7]

According to the *Post*, Hirst said his investigation had been ongoing since January, and he was aware of six or eight establishments involved in the bribery scheme by the mayor and others. However, they decided to concentrate on two West Side businesses, "upon which to base the information." These were Lola West's Black and Tan Club and Pop Grimes' Porters and Waiters Club. The newspaper also provided information from the Fort Warren Public Relations office, including that Cheyenne's law enforcement officials asked about and mentioned that forty-one "Negro men and women" had been arrested in the west end of Cheyenne. It added: "From evidence presented to

Fort Warren authorities by local officials and other available information, it appeared the situation existing called for such action." The rest of the article reported on the denial of the Schwartz liquor license and on the use of a dictograph in the investigation. It included a photo of some of the women taken during the raid, showing them being booked into the Cheyenne jail.[8]

The *Wyoming Eagle* on March 21 also featured some interesting photos. The top one was of the city council meeting the day before and showed the two members, Jones and Fleischli. The middle photo displayed "Confiscated evidence" from the raid being labeled by a detective and an aide. Lastly, the bottom image showed two women being "Booked In at the city jail following yesterday morning's raid these Negro girls are shown giving up their jewelry and other possessions as Policeman Tom Morissey Jr. fills out their arrest card."[9]

The newspapers reporting on the West Side raid gave conflicting numbers, either 41 or 47 people arrested. However, the Cheyenne Police Department Jail Register listed 46. This number did not include Lola West, Pop Grimes, and Susie Stowers, who apparently were not targeted by the invading force. One would assume those who were rounded up and booked into the county jail would be charged with some crime, but that was not the case. In the police register, under the column titled Cause of Arrest, beside each person booked was "Inv." This clearly means investigation. One might assume this applied to the question of where the 21 cases of alcohol came from, but it is more likely that it refers to Hirst's investigation of Hanna and the others. The soldiers taken to jail were released to the military authorities. The rest were released on March 20, 21, or 22. The only exception was Pearl Roubideaux. For some reason, she was released to the sheriff's office, seemingly to testify in the upcoming bribery trial. However, she was quickly released. So what did Hirst gain by authorizing such a brazen attack on the Capital City's West Side?

Chapter 8 reported that the day after the arrests, Hirst received additional affidavits from business owners detailing what Hanna, Ekdall, Morris, and Violette were doing to the Black businesses. These business owners were Jordan Davis, Jo Eva Davis, and Alma Marie Banks. Their statements are all dated March 20 and were certainly taken after their "arrests" earlier that day. Eleven more statements were completed by some of those who were taken in military trucks or police cars to the county jail. If Hirst's goal was to get more

Volume XIX. CHEYENNE, WYOMING, TUESDAY, MARCH 21, 1944 Number 211

Hirst Says Mayor Had Three Marked $5 Bills

Shorthand Reporter, Dictograph Used to Get Other Evidence

A Stormy Session was held at the city council meeting here yesterday morning, which dealt with the applications for liquor licenses in the city, as evidenced by the activity shown in this picture. Left to right is shown Commissioner Gus Fleischli, Commissioner Bruce Jones, City Clerk S. D. Markley and a citizen at the hearing. Photo by Francis Brammar.

Confiscated evidence. Detective Henry Dillman and an aid are shown labeling whiskey confiscated in police raids here yesterday morning. Photo by Francis Brammar.

Booked In at the city jail following yesterday morning's raid these Negro girls are shown giving up their jewelry and other possessions as Policeman Tom Morissey Jr. fills out their arrest card. Photo by Francis Brammar.

WHO'S MAYOR?

What is the future official status of Mayor Ira L. Hanna? That was a question that county and state officials had not determined an answer to last night. They would make no statement to the legal proceedings involved in removing Hanna from office.

Legal authorities said Wyoming statutes provide that a public official can be recalled by petition. This petition must bear the names of at least 25 per cent of the number of voters at the preceding general election and in the case of a municipality, the petition must be presented to the city clerk. The clerk then would call a special election to act on the petition and to elect a mayor.

Cheyenne is operated under a special charter, and has adopted a three-man council form of government, which differs from the usual form of city council, and thus has provided a legal problem in the method to be pursued in removing Hanna from office if he is convicted.

COUNTY ATTORNEY HAS AFFIDAVITS FROM FIVE WEST END OPERATORS

That Mayor Ira Hanna when searched upon his arrest by Sheriff Tuck yesterday had three $5 bills in possession, the serial numbers of which corresponded exactly with three of the $5 bills paid as payoff money to police by one of the colored establishments in the West end, that Hanna, Chief Ekdall, Police Captain Morris and Sgt. Violette personally and together visited certain colored houses and cafes in the West end and explicitly explained to the owners they would have to pay off for protection—and specified the amounts—are among the charges that will have to be answered by these four defendants when they come to trial soon in connection with the sensational bribery charges filed against them yesterday.

The statement that Hanna had the three marked $5 bills on his person when arrested is categorically made by County Attorney Byron Hirst.

Evidence against the mayor and police chief, captain and sergeant, according to reliable information given the press last night by of-

(Continued on Page Six) (Column Four)

CITY OFFICIALS REFUSE RENEWAL OF LICENSE FOR SCHWARTZ'S BAR

☆ ☆ ☆

SOLDIER SOLD 12 DRINKS AT BAR IS CHARGE

Capt. Edwin R. Brock, cavalry commanding officer of the Wyoming division and in charge of MP's on train at Cheyenne testified before the city council that the Schwartz bar had, on one occasion sold as many as 12 drinks to one soldier at one time and then gave him one for good measure and that when the soldier arrived at the station to board a train he was so intoxicated military police had a difficult time overpowering and taking him to the police station.

He also testified that a sailor had been sold three "double shots" at the Schwartz bar at one time and passed out before arriving at the station.

This testimony, combined with the filing of a complaint by Hirst charging Schwartz with having a barmaid employed at his place of business against state law was re-

Action Puts Stop to Rumors on Taverns

With a temporarily mayorless city commission yesterday refusing to renew the license of the Schwartz bar, 207 W. 16th, there was quickly ended several weeks of speculation as to which of Cheyenne's bars would and which would not, receive license renewals.

It was chiefly on the grounds that the establishment employs one or more women waitresses, which is forbidden by state law,

(Continued on Page Six) (Column Two)

Federal Statement

The following statement was made Monday afternoon by Howard F. Feast, regional social protection representative of the federal security agency, Mr. Feast maintains his headquarters in Denver.

"The action taken by the citizens of Cheyenne to clean

Front page of the March 21, 1944, *Wyoming Eagle* with headlines about Ira Hanna having three marked five dollar bills, which was important in the case against the mayor for bribery. The newspaper also divulged that a dictograph had been used to gather evidence against Hanna, Ekdall, Morris, and Violette. The photograph in the lower left shows two African American women being "Booked In" the Laramie County Jail after "the raid."

evidence from those approached by Hanna, Ekdall, Morris, and Violette, possibly to strengthen his case against the four, he certainly succeeded.[10]

The statements provided some interesting facts about Hanna's activities and those of his law enforcement associates. Pearl Roubideaux, 1710 Snyder Avenue, gave her statement to L.D. Parker of the Alcohol and Tax Unit on March 20. Roubideaux, listed as a "full-blooded Indian," had only been in Cheyenne for about a week before she was caught up in the West Side raid. She had been in Cheyenne before and then used the name Vivian Russell. Sergeant Bailey helped her find a place to "hustle." She went to Eloise Robinson's house and also worked for Kid Rabbi. The going rate was seven dollars, with Pearl able to keep five dollars. Both places told her that if she got arrested, they would cover the fine, so not to worry, since they were paying for protection. While working for Kid Rabbi, she earned twenty-eight dollars, but she said, "he has not given me any of it."[11]

Golden Hall, 814 West 19th Street, provided his statement to Zac Taylor of the sheriff's department on March 22. Hall had been in Cheyenne for about a year and a half and worked for the railroad for a while, although recently, "I haven't been doing anything and sometimes stay with Alberta Echoles at her house at 1710 Snyder in Cheyenne, Wyoming. A little over two weeks ago I heard some talk about a pay off in Cheyenne and made it my business to find out so I came down here to the office of the Chief of Police in Cheyenne." While in Ekdall's office at the police department, Hall stated that he did not have any girls, but he had two rooms. He had been picked up before and did not want to be picked up again. Hall "offered him $20.00 a week" and Ekdall told him "To go ahead and do whatever I wanted to do and he would make sure I wasnt [sic] picked up for it and wasnt throwed in jail." He was told to pay Grimes, and he made two $20 payments.[12]

Alberta Echoles, 1710 Snyder Avenue, also spoke to Zac Taylor on March 22 regarding her statement. Like Hall, Echoles heard about the town opening up. She had not been "running a sporting house, but a few weeks ago I heard a rumor from some soldiers that the town was to be opened up and there had to be a payoff." Golden Hall, who, of course, had spoken directly with Edkall and Morris, told her it was OK "and to go ahead." She had planned to keep girls and thought she would need to pay "$100 per month for operating the house."[13]

Mildred Brooks, 1718 Bent Avenue, on March 20, spoke to Lt. Colonel

Tom Hembree of the fort's Judge Advocate General's Office. Mildred Brooks also had discussions with Ekdall, Morris, and "Sergeant Ekky." The police officers had agreed to have her pay twenty dollars per week, and she wanted to have girls and whiskey. The officers even told her she could have gambling, but she did not want to include that. "The Chief and the officers didnt [sic] tell me where I could get any girls but did say I could have as many as I wanted but the more girls I had the more I would have to pay. The Chief himself told me that."[14]

Georgia Hill, 2308 Bent Avenue, provided her statement to Hembree on March 20. Hill also spoke to the chief of police in his office. She went to the police station and talked to Violette, who was at the front desk, and she asked if she could see Ekdall. "The Chief of Police told me to come in his office and I did and then Ekky and Jett Morris came in too." The law enforcement officers told her that for twenty-five dollars, "she could have girls and sell whisky and beer, and if she wanted to get girls, she could. I said we hadnt [sic] been allowed to do that before and they said that this was a different administration."[15]

Marie Dixon provided a Denver address, spoke to Hembree on March 20, and submitted her statement. Dixon had been in Cheyenne for about sixteen months. She had lived in Denver but had returned to the Capital City just a few days before March 20. When she returned, she said Georgia Hill "told me the town was open and that I could start work hustling if I wanted to, but that I would have to pay protection. She said I would have to pay $5.00 to a Doctor for inspection and $15.00 for protection." She "went to both Dr. Savery and Dr. Conway for inspection."[16]

Francis Bard, 1709 Bent Avenue, provided her statement also on March 20 to Captain Ralph Rodgers from the fort's quartermaster center. Bard worked as a cook at Joe Eva's Sandwich Shop. She said that it had been a house of prostitution up until three or four months before March. Bard said there were three girls living at 1806 Bent Avenue, and they were "hustling at Joe Eva's." They had been hustling at 1709 Bent until the city closed down that house. The girls hustling for Joe Eva after the city opened up gave her the money after their seven-dollar tricks. The girls kept five, and Joe Eva took two. Bard continued: "She doesn't let many stay there over about fifteen minutes. The house is usually full all the time."[17]

Virginia Butler, 1709 Bent Avenue, spoke to Parker on March 20. Her husband was a soldier serving in Australia at that time. Butler arrived in Cheyenne on March 14 and went to Joe Eva's to get a room. "I asked Joe Eva if the time was ripe for things to open her, I meant by that sexual business with soldiers, etc. ...." Of course, the city did "open." Willa Mae Cox also lived at 1709 Bent, and her husband was stationed in Italy. She said she had been in Cheyenne for four years but had never hustled until she moved to the Bent address. She made it clear her tricks were "all with colored soldiers and sailors."[18]

One other affidavit provided by those detained on March 20 was by Pfc. Pat Johnson, a soldier stationed at the quartermaster center at the fort. He provided his statement on March 23 and spoke to Lt. Col. Tom B. Hembree, from the fort's Judge Advocate General's office. Johnson was picked up by the military police just after ten a.m. on March 20 at 1710 Snyder Avenue. He had left the fort and gone to Cheyenne the day before. That evening, he slept with "two girls whom I know as Louise and Vivian" (aka Pearl Roubideaux). "Vivian is an Indian girl and at one time she told me that Cpl. Bailey brought her here." Johnson knew girls were hustling at Mrs. Burts, 1710 Snyder, and had "sexual intercourse" with Louise before. He paid her seven dollars. That night, she had dates with four soldiers, each of whom paid seven dollars. She kept five and gave Mrs. Burts two dollars. "At one time, Mrs. Burts told me she had to get herself another girl to hustle because she had paid off and she had to get her money back." Apparently, to make the weekly payments, the business owners had to increase their illegal activity while being protected by the mayor and the Cheyenne police.[19]

The statements made by those who were arrested and booked into the county jail were used to gather evidence against Hanna, Ekdall, Morris, and Violette. No information was collected to determine where the alcohol was coming from, although that was L.D. Parker's justification for his participation in the raid. Since it was clear that the mayor and the officers encouraged hustling, gambling, and alcohol, perhaps members of the police department should have been questioned about the source of the whiskey and beer. After all, Ekdall had told Lola West they would supply the alcohol.

The information gathered from the West Side raid likely strengthened Hirst's upcoming court case against the four individuals. It may have been strategic to carry out the raid simultaneously with the arrest of Hanna and the others, so the four would not realize Hirst was conducting an investigation or collecting information. If the raid had happened before March 20, it could have alerted them to Hirst's efforts. But was such a raid necessary? The attorney already had affidavits from Lola West, Pop Grimes, and Susie Stowers, along with eyewitness accounts from federal agents and the court stenographer involved, plus the recording and transcript of that night at the Porters and Waiters Club. That evidence alone would likely have been enough to arrest Hanna, Ekdall, Morris, and Violette. The others detained during the raid could have been approached afterward, following the mayor's arrest, and asked to cooperate. Maybe Lola and Pop could have helped gather statements from those who were told the city was open, and they could do anything they wanted, so long as they paid for protection.

Those West Side residents who were taken from their establishments and hustled into military vehicles and police cars must have wondered what was going on and later wondered why it happened. Those who witnessed the raid through the windows of their homes must have been concerned and possibly frightened as to what was transpiring, and perhaps thought that such a law enforcement operation would never have happened in one of Cheyenne's White neighborhoods. As noted, there were reports of a "city-wide" raid, but clearly it was only on the West Side. Because it was the African American businesses in that part of the city that were being "hustled," seeking statements from West Side residents made sense. Even though the leadership of Fort Warren said they participated in the raid because it was clearly necessary to clean up the community, it does make one wonder what the fort personnel had been told; those who were "arrested" that day during the raid were *victims* of a criminal conspiracy. The business owners were told to pay up, or the city's highest-ranking official, the mayor, and members of the Cheyenne Police Department would put them out of business. The use of the word "arrest" in the newspaper coverage, along with a photo of a few of them being booked into the county jail, made it appear they were the criminals. Yet, even with such treatment, many of them voluntarily provided statements providing information Hirst could use when he took the quartet to court on bribery charges. One other curious item about the "raid" was that shortly after it concluded, Hirst stated, "auxiliary police had been asked to patrol the raided section."[20] It is unclear why it was necessary to patrol the invaded section of the city.

Clearly, the description of the raid as being city-wide was wrong. However, the description was repeated much later to describe what happened on that day in March 1944. In 1970, Hirst completed a "Personal Data Questionnaire." It included the basic personal information one would expect in such a document, but this legal questionnaire asked for descriptions of some of Hirst's most important cases. The former county prosecutor described the case against Hanna and the others. He stated: "These cases changed the attitude in Cheyenne and all of Wyoming with respect to gambling and prostitution, which had been condoned. The places where they were conducted were publicly known and frequented." Hirst mentioned the large number of troops at Fort Warren during the war, which made the vice in Cheyenne "very profitable." He also wrote: "Chicago and Denver vice syndicates were entering the city. Their representatives had offered me, as County and Prosecuting Attorney, very substantial bribes to permit them to continue saying they had bought everyone else. When I refused, some of their agents made threats." According to Hirst, Hanna and Ekdall had "excellent reputations in the community" saying Ekdall was "Director of a mutual fund, was making almost $20,000 per year, and had resigned to become Chief of Police for about $200.00 a month." To help with the investigation he had assistance from federal agents and mentioned the assistance of "two black operators of houses of entertainment" to record a meeting of the mayor and the rest. Hirst went on to describe the arrest of the four, the raid, and the aftermath. After Hanna was arrested, he wrote: "At the same time, by prior arrangement with the Commander of Warren Air Force Base (it was Fort Francis E. Warren), he arrived with jeeps and trucks and armed MPs at the police department and the Sheriff's Office, and they all immediately became interested in joining in making mass arrests at every gambling house and house of prostitution in the City. We obtained pleas of guilty from all concerned." Regarding Schwartz, Hirst wrote: "The representative of the crime syndicates who had threatened me, operated a bar and by coincidence his liquor license was up for renewal on this same day before the City Council." This last line clearly indicates he was speaking about Schwartz. However, regarding the raid, it is odd that he described it as city-wide and that all those arrested were convicted, since they were only held for a short time and never charged with any crime. Certainly, there were other gambling ventures and places of prostitution in the city besides the West Side, and such a raid never occurred in those parts of the city.[21]

The events in Cheyenne on March 20, 1944, the arrests of Hanna, Ekdall, Morris, Violette, and Schwartz, and the raid on the West Side were covered in other Wyoming newspapers. The *Laramie Republican-Boomerang* and the *Casper Tribune Herald* ran stories for a few days, mainly drawing on information from the Cheyenne papers. However, the *Torrington Telegram* on March 23, 1944, provided some strong viewpoints in an editorial. It began that those arrested should not be condemned until they had a fair trial, "but we do think it is unfortunate that the city has become involved in a 'Scandal' that will attract nationwide, unfavorable attention." The editorial continued:

> It has long been the opinion of many citizens of this state that there was "something rotten in Denmark" with regard to conditions in Cheyenne but it was one of those things about which many people talked about but which nothing was ever done. It takes courage on the part of the officials who have brought these conditions to the attention of the people and we hope they have sufficient courage to uncover many other lawless conditions which seem to be rife within the city.
>
> A thorough house cleaning is in order throughout the city and no stone should be left unturned to assure a complete renovation so that Cheyenne may once again be classed as respectable and worthy of being known as our Capital City.[22]

CHAPTER 10 ENDNOTES

1   "41 Negroes Arrested in Raids Here: Cheyenne Police and MPs Carry Out Raid," *Wyoming State Tribune*, March 20, 1944, 1 and 9.

2   Cheyenne Police Department Jail Register, March 20, 1944, Wyoming State Archives.

3   "41 Negroes Arrested in Raids Here: Cheyenne Police and MPs Carry Out Raid," *Wyoming State Tribune*, March 20, 1944, 1 and 9.

4   "Dictograph Employed in Bribery Charge: Statement Released by Hirst," *Wyoming State Tribune*, March 21, 1944, 1 and back page; "Liquor Probe Pushed Here," *Wyoming State Tribune*, March 21, 1944, 1.

5   "Liquor Probe Pushed Here," *Wyoming State Tribune*, March 21, 1944, 1.

6   "Dictograph Employed in Bribery Charge: Statement Released by Hirst," *Wyoming State Tribune*, March 21, 1944, 1 and back page; "41 Negroes Arrested in Raids Here: Cheyenne Police and MPs Carry Out Raid," *Wyoming State Tribune*, March 20, 1944, 1 and 9.

7   "Forty-Seven Arrested In Cheyenne Vice Raids," *Denver Post*, March 21, 1944, 1 and 3.

8   "Forty-Seven Arrested In Cheyenne Vice Raids," *Denver Post*, March 21, 1944, 1 and 3.

9   *Wyoming Eagle*, March 21, 1944, 1.

10   These statements are all in the Byron Hirst Papers, Old West Museum, Cheyenne, Wyoming.

11   Statement by Pearl Roubideaux on March 20, 1944, Byron Hirst Papers, Old West Museum, Cheyenne.

12   Statement by Golden Hall on March 22, 1944, Byron Hirst Papers, Old West Museum, Cheyenne.

13   Statement by Alberta Echoles on March 2, 1944, Byron Hirst Papers, Old West Museum, Cheyenne.

14   Statement by Mildred Brooks on March 20, 1944, Byron Hirst Papers, Old West Museum, Cheyenne.

15   Statement by George Hill on March 20, 1944, Byron Hirst Papers, Old West Museum, Cheyenne.

16   Statement by Marie Dixon on March 20, 1944, Byron Hirst Papers, Old West Museum, Cheyenne.

17   Statement by Francis Bard on March 20, 1944, Byron Hirst Papers, Old West Museum, Cheyenne.

18   Statement by Virginia Butler on March 20, 1944; Statement by Willa Mae Cox on March 23, 1944, Byron Hirst Papers, Old West Museum, Cheyenne.

19   Statement by Pat Johnson on March 23, 1944, Byron Hirst Papers, Old West Museum, Cheyenne.

20   "Dictograph Employed In Preparing Bribery Charge: Statement Released By Hirst," *Wyoming State Tribune*, March 21, 1944, 1 and back page.

21   Hirst Personal Data Questionnaire, 1970, Byron Hirst Papers, Old West Museum, Cheyenne.

22   *Torrington Telegram*, March 23, 1944, 2. *The Salt Lake Tribune* also covered the arrests of the four. It's article, "Cheyenne Mayor, Aids Deny Taking 'Protection' Bribes," was in the March 21, 1944, issue, on page 1.

CHAPTER 11

The Trial

It didn't take long for the trial accusing Hanna, Ekdall, Morris, and Violette of bribery to begin. Just about a month and a half after their arrests, County Attorney Hirst brought them to court. However, during the time between arrests and the trial, much unfolded leading up to the quartet's appearance in court.

Just two days after the arrests, the *Wyoming Eagle* provided some surprising information about what led to that tumultuous day, March 20. According to the article titled "Arrest Was Total Surprise to Officials," "literally scores of Cheyenneites knew for days in advance what was developing and that the 'fireworks' would explode on Monday, apparently not even a whisp of information on the subject reached the ears of any of the four defendants or their confidants." The article claimed the upcoming arrests were a "general topic of discussion" on Cheyenne streets. Some newspaper reporters heard about the "impending explosions" close to a week before the arrests. They approached the investigators and Hirst about what they had heard. According to the article, "The forces of investigation told them pretty much the whole thing, but, and this is the point, in strict confidence." Apparently, the best way to deal with reporters was to let them know about the investigation but tell them what they just heard is "off the record." The reporters did not break the confidence.[1] The article also described the continuation of the investigation just two days before the arrests.

The investigators wanted to plan another trap for those involved in the bribery scheme. However, Hirst and others were advised not to risk any further clandestine attempts to obtain more information. Enough information had been gathered from the recording of the meeting at the Porters and Waiters Club, along with eyewitness accounts from federal authorities who had observed the discussion. Even with these warnings, the investigators decided to proceed with placing a person in an adjoining room while the payments were to be made at the "West End colored house." According to the report, the person stationed in the house, "of course, prepared affidavits covering everything he saw and heard, and they are now a part of the official record."[2]

The affidavit was made by 1st Lt. Kenneth E. Smith, who was described as a "Post Prison Officer." He provided his sworn statement to Tom B. Hembree, a Lt. Colonel in the Judge Advocate General's office at Fort Warren. According to his statement, Smith went to the Porters and Waiters Club late in the afternoon on March 18, two days before the arrests. His charge was to observe "anything of interest" at the club that night. That was a Saturday, which was the weekly pickup day for one of the quartet to collect the money from the African American business owners. He first went upstairs and, from there, saw envelopes with money in Grimes' office. One had "Pop" written on the outside and contained twenty-five dollars, and another, containing one hundred dollars, had "Lola" written on the outside. Just after 6:30, Smith saw Captain Morris drive up in a 1940 Ford Coupe, maroon in color, "driven by a woman with blondish hair." The officer came in and talked to Grimes. When the discussion occurred, Smith walked downstairs and stood outside the door leading into Pop's office. He heard Morris say: "You're a swell guy. You haven't told anybody?" Grimes said, "No." Grimes did not give any of the envelopes to Morris, since he was the wrong pickup person; Violette was supposed to take the money. Smith returned to the club the following morning, and finally, just after four p.m., Violette and Morris arrived. They drove up in a police vehicle, a black 1941 or 1942 Ford sedan. Once they were inside the Porters and Waiters Club, Smith saw Violette, who was standing in front of Grimes' desk, holding the envelopes with the money. The desk sergeant then counted the money, folded the bills, and then "put it in his pocket." As the two police officers left the office, Violette turned to Pop and said, "Everything is all right." In his affidavit, Smith even described their clothing. Morris had on a "greenish suit coat, gray hat, and grayish trousers," while Violette was wearing a "light hat, brown leather jacket, blue denim pants, and tan cowboy boots." Smith provided his statement on March 21, the day after the arrests. What he saw was interesting, although it was unclear if the information would even be needed in the upcoming trial.[3]

The following day, the *Wyoming State Tribune* in an article titled "Money Fails to 'Talk' As 'Whole Town's Talking' of Capital Municipal Scandal." The article began with a serious accusation: that a bribe had been offered to a public official immediately after the arrests of Hanna and the others. The writer described the offer of "filthy lucre" as incredible. If there was such a bribery attempt, it failed. "The official 'propositioned' listened in goggle-eyed amazement, wondering whether his ears were receiving the message registering in his mind. Unhappily, no Dictaphone or 'affidavit man' was among those present and therefore no corroborating evidence is available." The unnamed observer also noted that discussions about the arrest of the four government officials have only intensified since the day of the arrests and the raid on the West Side. The writer also claimed nothing in Cheyenne's history had been as avidly discussed as what occurred on March 20.[4]

One unproven premise, which certainly must have been discussed at that time, was the role of what could be coined as the influence of the "underworld." The column stated: "How far has it been planned that the formula of racketeering should be brought to prevail in Cheyenne?" It mentioned the "tactics of gangsterism" in communities like Cheyenne.[5]

Also mentioned in the article was Lola West's role, although it did not name her. According to the column, "the vital problem of providing money to be paid as 'graft' by the Negro woman whom, as is alleged, was being 'milked' for 'protection.'" Such an event in Cheyenne called for an immediate response, which took place and involved gathering information through a dictaphone recording and a stenographic transcript of the meeting between the quartet and those being victimized.

Finally, the last item mentioned in the list of observations commented on "peanut politicians" trying to inject politics into discussions about the recently publicized illegal activities. Apparently, some blame Republicans, claiming this is what happens when "Republicans get in office." However, this observer quickly dismissed such an accusation by listing many Republicans involved in the investigation and arrests, including County Attorney Hirst, Sheriff Tuck, Juvenile Judge McVicar, Chief of Detectives Harvey Jackson, among others. "Fact is, the petty effort to inject a 'political angle' is unadulterated rot. There is no more a 'political angle' than there is advertisement of a 20th-century automobile in the Scriptures. Democrats and Republicans alike join in praising the activities aimed at ensuring a clean municipal government. Effort to read a 'political angle' into the story is asinine"[6]

After these efforts to provide context and interpretation of the events of

March 20, preparations began for the trials to be held in the upcoming district court session. Sixty Laramie County men were called on the morning of April 10, potentially to serve on juries. One called was Captain Gerald (Jet) Morris, one of the four whose upcoming bribery trial would take place in a few weeks. District Judge Sam Thompson ruled the police captain could serve on any jury except the one hearing his case. Sheriff Tuck's name was also among the sixty, but he was automatically disqualified.[7] Also on April 10, Judge Thompson announced that Judge Harry Ilsley of the sixth judicial district at Newcastle had been selected to try the bribery case against the Cheyenne four.[8] Thompson was not able to hear the case because the defendants had earlier filed an affidavit of prejudice against the judge. Two days later, Thompson announced the trial of Hanna and the others charged with soliciting and accepting bribes would begin on May 1 in Laramie County District Court.[9] The April 30 issue of the *Wyoming State Tribune* stated the case would start at 9:30 on May 1, and it included the two separate "Informations" (charges) Hirst filed on March 20 against the four.[10]

The case filed against Hanna and the others was:

THE STATE OF WYOMING,
Plaintiff,
vs.
IRA I. HANNA, JESS B. EKDALL
GERALD J. (JET) MORRIS, and
E.K. (EKKY) VIOLETTE,
Defendants.

One of the informations filed by Hirst stated: "on or about the 11th day of March, A.D. 1944," the four charged were "officers entrusted with the administration of justice" and "then and there did unlawfully, feloniously, and corruptly solicit, receive and receive from Lola West the sum of one hundred Dollars in lawful money of the United States of America, with the unlawful, felonious intent that said undue reward should then and there influence each and all of them with respect to their official … [and] influence their action with respect to the enforcement by them of the laws of the State of Wyoming and the ordinances of said City of Cheyenne…. " A second information was included citing the money received paid by W.C. (Pop) Grimes in the amount of $25.00. This document also mentioned "that in return for pay of said

$25.00 they would give him protection in said unlawful activities from the Fort Francis E. Warren Military Authorities, and other law enforcement agencies." It also stated: "Said Hanna, Ekdall, Morris and Violette also presented to said W.C. (Pop) Grimes that if he refused to pay said $25.00, refused to conduct a house of prostitution, refused to conduct a gambling game, and refused to sell liquor at retail, then in such case his place of business, known as the Porters and Waiters Club, would be closed up and padlocked forthwith by said Hanna, Ekdall, Morris, and Violette."[11]

The week before the start of the trial on Monday, May 1, Hirst filed four more informations against the four defendants. Hirst was assisted by attorney James A. Greenwood, former state attorney general. Defense attorneys A.D. Walton of Cheyenne, a former U.S. district attorney, and William H. Brown, Jr. of Casper, filed motions to quash the four informations and a motion for demurrer regarding the informations. A demurrer raises a question of law while a motion to quash raises a question of fact. Judge Ilsley overruled the motions. In his dismissal of the motion of demurrer, he required the prosecutors to include in the informations the city ordinances allegedly violated by the defendants. The four already had pled innocent to the first informations and did the same for the new charges. Paragraph six of each of the new informations stated the four "conjointly and while confederating and acting together, unlawfully and corruptly conspire, plan, scheme, counsel, and agree together to make Cheyenne a lawless and open town by permitting gambling, prostitution, and unlawful sale of intoxicating liquor in said city of Cheyenne, and to solicit, offer to receive, receive, and accept bribes." The informations also included the names of other West Side residents who "all charge acceptance of bribes."[12] The defense attorneys made a motion to consolidate all six of the informations. Ilsley ruled against that motion. Hirst then decided to go to trial on the first information he filed, the one charging the defendants with receiving bribes from Lola West.[13]

Following the final rulings on the motions, the process of selecting jurors for the rial began. Three hours in the afternoon were dedicated to interviewing potential jurors. The questioning resumed on Tuesday and concluded around 5:30 p.m. with twelve jurors selected after ten hours of examination by the attorneys. Both the defense attorneys and prosecutors had thirty-two peremptory jury challenges each during the selection. Several spectators were present in the courtroom that day, expecting the trial to start at some point.

However, many left after it became clear it would not begin until Wednesday morning at 9 a.m.[14]

The trial did start on May 3. However, there is no trial transcript, so the sources used to describe the proceedings are the Cheyenne newspapers: the *Wyoming State Tribune,* the *Wyoming Eagle,* the *Laramie Republican and Boomerang,* and the *Casper Tribune Herald.* The reports in the *Boomerang* and *Herald* are identical, so they probably are Associated Press reports. Since the Laramie newspaper only published five days a week at that time, the *Casper Tribune Herald* was used when the *Republican and Boomerang* did not publish.

Materials in Hirst's papers reveal his preparatory work for the trial. Topics included the witnesses he planned to call and the order in which he intended to call them. He also included information about the four defendants, listing who they talked to and when, as well as when they visited the Porters and Waiters Club. Under the heading of "Argument," there are three headings: 1. Jury Performing Function As Officers of State. The points below this heading are for the jury to fulfill their oath to listen to and follow the court's instructions, and to decide guilty or not guilty. If found guilty, the court will decide on the penalty. 2. Defense crimes against public justice (not individual). Here, Hirst included that the four defendants failed in their duty to the public, as well as the mayor, who, as head of the city, represented the city in all affairs. He was expected to serve all the people of Cheyenne, whether Black or White, soldier or civilian. It was also emphasized that the chief and police department were responsible for protecting the city, not leading it into vice, and that good government was the foundation of this "Great Nation." Finally, Hirst stated that the four defendants "prostituted themselves and thereby brought contempt, ridicule and disrespect for our city." 3. Evidence. Here is a partial list of witnesses, including West, Grimes, L.D. Parker, and Fred M. Taylor. The newspapers that day did not report Hirst's opening statement, but one can assume that some or all of the points listed above were heard by the jury that day.[15]

The defense attorneys asked to postpone their opening statement until after the prosecution rested its case. Starting the prosecution, Hirst called city officials, who confirmed that Hanna was elected mayor, that Ekdall, Morris, and Violette were all members of the Cheyenne Police Department, and how everyone was selected for these official positions. After discussing these facts, Hirst called a series of witnesses who testified about the meetings on the afternoon and evening of March 11 at the Porters and Waiters Club. Lola West was first, and she was called to the stand about 11:15. Hirst asked her to identify the defendants, which she did, and then asked about her two one-hundred-dollar payments and what they were for. West responded that they were "not fines, but like a tax, it was a payoff." She then explained that Morris and Violette came to the Black and Tan Café and told her they were planning on opening up the town and asked if she wanted to get in on it. She explained she had some soldiers' wives renting rooms from her, but Morris told her "to get some women, open the doors, start some gambling, and get some liquor." When West asked where she could get the liquor, Morris said, "That's not hard to get." The two police officers left and returned about 7 p.m., and Morris, again leading the discussion, asked West how much she could pay. He was collecting information to present to the mayor and chief. Several days later, according to West's testimony, Hanna and the other three came to her place of business, and the mayor commented that she "had a nice place" and implied she could make some money. At that point, Hirst asked West what types of amusement she had at her place of business. She said she served sandwiches, had some coin-operated machines, and some gambling games. West also said: "The chief said anything I wanted to do was all right, gambling, women, liquor." Nearing the end of her testimony, West explained how she was supposed to take her money to the Porters and Waiters Club and that she complained that one hundred dollars was too much for her to pay, and she wanted to talk to the mayor and chief before she would do that. She was told that if the women staying at the Black and Tan did not hustle, she should kick them out and get some who would.[16]

Defense attorney Brown then cross-examined West. In response to one of his questions, she said her house had fifteen rooms, which she rented to the wives of soldiers at the fort, and added, "I don't rent to no one woman. If their husband's not with them, I don't rent the room." West also testified she had complained to Chief of Detectives Harvey Jackson about the "payoff." Brown then asked if Jackson had ever arrested her. She said yes, and when asked why, she responded, "For whisky," explaining that she had been accused of selling whiskey but denied it. She still paid the fine for the offense because "they said I did." When asked if she had ever done time in jail, West stated she had several years ago for the same charge, selling whiskey. Regarding the payoff, Brown asked her if she had ever handed money to any of the four defendants, and she said no, that it was on the table, and the mayor said, "Pick it up, Ekky." The attorney also asked her if she had received a receipt for the money, and West said she had asked, but they said "no." In response to another question, she said all four defendants were present when she made her first payment, and she believed that the payment was not a fine, but a payoff. "I told them I didn't want no girls, but if they give me whiskey I would bootleg."[17]

After West, Hirst called W.C. (Pop) Grimes to the stand. He testified Captain Morris approached him and asked, "What do you want to do. Things are lined up for prostitution, liquor, and gambling." Grimes said he told Morris he did not want women and could not get liquor, but he might be interested in gambling. The captain told him it would cost $100 per week. Later, Grimes said, Morris and Violette came around and said he had to pay and that it "wouldn't be no chicken feed." The desk sergeant then told Pop to get $100 and put it on the mayor's desk. When he asked what that was for, Violette said, "A goodwill offer." At a later meeting with all four defendants, Grimes asked, "What's this?" and Hanna said, "This is the payoff, and you're gonna pay." Pop protested, and the mayor did relent, saying he only had to pay twenty-five dollars, but that they expected one hundred from West. The four left and returned at 5 p.m. to pick up the money, according to Grimes. There were twenty-five dollars from Pop, twenty dollars from Golden Hall, and twenty-five dollars from West. Violette protested about the less-than-expected amount from Lola and told Grimes, "You tell her take that back and have $100." The captain and the sergeant returned at 8 p.m. to collect the money from West. She complained to Grimes, who told her, "Well, I don't have anything to do with it. I'm just taking orders."[18]

As he did with West, attorney Brown cross-examined Grimes. He asked the witness why he agreed to pay for protection. Grimes responded: "Man I wasn't gonna stan' there and argue with all them men." Brown asked if there had been any violence. "No, sir," said Pop, "but I wasn't gonna run that risk." The attorney then asked Grimes: "How did you escape arrest for gambling before this time?" "By not getting caught," answered Grimes.[19]

That afternoon, Hirst was able to introduce into evidence the three five-dollar bills that had been referenced in a number of headlines following Hanna's arrest. L.D. Parker, one of the federal investigators from the alcohol tax unit and one of the law enforcement officials who witnessed the meetings at the Porters and Waiters Club on March 11, took the stand that afternoon and testified he saw the mayor remove those bills from his pocket in the sheriff's office just after his arrest.[20]

On the second day of the trial, Thursday, May 4, Hirst continued the prosecution and informed the judge that he might complete it that day. Parker took the stand again and continued his testimony. He explained that he, Fred M. Taylor, also an investigator for the alcohol tax unit of the Federal Internal Revenue Bureau, and transcriptionist Clarence Ferguson were concealed in a room of the Porters and Waiters Club on March 11 and were able to observe all of the meetings that day between the defendants and Grimes and West. He described the conversation between Ekdall and West, who complained that $100 was too much for her to pay. She did not have any girls, any gambling, or liquor. The chief of police corrected her, saying he knew she was making money and that she, Grimes, and one other were the "majors" on the West Side. Ekdall described the payment as a "license" for protection and then threatened her by saying he could contact one person at Fort Warren and have her establishment placed out of bounds. According to Parker, Hanna then said: "We're in the driver's seat—from now on, we'll do the telling; we know who was doing the shaking down, but that's different now. If we stick together, we'll be in for eight years, not two."[21] Parker also testified that Hanna told West, "We're in the driver's seat and from now on we'll do the telling." West responded: "If I have to, I have to."[22]

Defense attorney Walton cross-examined Parker. He asked the witness why he had told Mrs. West to pay only the money to the mayor and the chief of police. Parker responded, "They were the head men and the ones we wanted to catch." He then asked Parker to describe the Porters and Waiters Club, its dimensions, and how he observed the meetings. After that answer, Walton asked: "You were the one that devised the plan by which peeking and listening could be accomplished Mr. Parker?" He explained that he became interested in the investigation when Hirst showed him signed statements about liquor being sold on the West Side. He continued that he, Hirst, Bruce Jones, Gus Fleischli, Harvey Jackson, and Glenn Petersen, the head of the bureau of identification in the police department, had discussed the final plans for staging the meeting with the defendants and Grimes and West on March 11.[23]

Hirst's next witness was Joseph L. Filer, a former deputy sheriff with the Laramie County Sheriff's Office. At this point, the prosecutor wanted to confirm that Hanna had the three five-dollar bills on him when he was arrested on March 20. Filer stated that he and Parker compared the serial numbers on the bills found on the mayor with the list of bills Parker had kept in a safety deposit box, along with the three bills. Grimes had testified the previous day that he copied the serial numbers on $70 in $100 bills allegedly paid by West on March 11. His list matched the one Parker described. Pop also testified that, when West complained about the amount of money she was expected to pay, West insisted she had to see the mayor and the chief of police.[24]

Hirst's final prosecution witness that morning was Fred Taylor. Like Parker, he testified that he witnessed the meetings on March 11 at the Porters and Waiters Club. He stated that from his hidden vantage point in an adjoining room, he saw the four defendants talking to West about a "payoff for protection" and saw Violette pick up the hundred dollars from the table where she had counted the money. According to Taylor, West protested because she said she was not engaged in an activity requiring protection. Ekdall responded that she was "paying a license fee" for protection not only from the Cheyenne police but also from the authorities at Fort Warren. Taylor also testified that he and Parker saw the four defendants leave with the money, and even though Hanna did not touch the money, he said he would count it later. Continuing, Taylor testified he had checked the serial numbers of the three bills with the list created by Grimes and held by Parker. Hirst ended the morning session by reading the city ordinances to the jury regarding liquor, gambling, and prostitution in the city.[25]

That afternoon, the prosecution brought in what was described as "an elaborate recording apparatus." John Schooley, a private in the army who had been assigned as a special investigator for the Alcohol and Tax Unit, testified during the afternoon of March 11 that he entered the Porters and Waiters Club and set up the recording device. He also stated that later that night, he heard some of the conversations between the law enforcement officers and Grimes and West. At this point, defense counsel objected to Schooley's testimony "on the grounds he had not actually seen the defendants in the room, and it could not be definitely established the voices carried on the recordings were those of the defendants." The judge sustained the objection; thus, the recordings were not played during the trial at that time. According to the *Wyoming Eagle*, spectators at the trial were disappointed that they would not be able to hear the recordings.[26]

After Schooley left the stand, Hirst called Bernice Favors to the stand. She was the daughter of Lola West and worked at the Black and Tan Club. She testified Morris and Ekdall had talked to her about gambling at the club, and that the captain told her that anytime he called the club and said "wash your neck," that was a sign of an upcoming raid of the club. "He said if Hirst or Harvey Jackson went to come down he would call and say that." Defense attorney Brown cross-examined her and brought race into the courtroom. He asked: "Isn't it a fact that Jet Morris walked in on you when you were in bed with a white soldier in 1933?" She responded: "I've never been in bed with a white man in my life." He also asked if Harvey Jackson had been in the Black and Tan Club, and Favors stated he had never been in the club when gambling was going on.[27]

Next on the stand was prosecution witness Willie Moore. His testimony concerned his discussion with Ekdall about opening his café, the Texas Whirlwind. The chief said he would talk to authorities at Fort Warren to get it opened. Under cross-examination, he was asked why his business had been closed since around early February. Moore explained authorities at the fort had closed it after a "shootin' scrape" took place there. His testimony also described a discussion with Ekdall, where he told him he was considering opening up a house of prostitution, and the chief told him he could have girls and gambling, but he would need to "pay off" in the amount of twenty dollars per week.[28]

Next witness for the prosecution was Mildred Brooks, a "Negro operator of the Cottage Café." She testified that she had to pay twenty dollars a week for girls and gambling at her place of business. Hirst asked if she had made any payments, and she said yes, two to Ekky. Brown cross-examined her, and she testified she "paid Ekky $20 in my bedroom" and also made a payment at her café. The final West Side business owner to testify was Golden Hall. He told the court he had an agreement to pay twenty dollars to operate "a house," and he made two payments to Grimes on March 11 and 18. He also stated that he had made a payment three months earlier to a policeman he did not know.[29]

William Bradley, a captain of the Wyoming Highway Patrol, was the next prosecution witness. He reported attending a peace officer convention in Casper shortly after the election. There, he had a conversation with Ekdall, where the new chief told him he was only planning to serve in the police department for two years and said he was "going to make the best of it while he was there." After Bradley, Hirst called Deputy U.S. Marshall George Smith to the stand. He testified he once was present with Hirst and Hanna when the county attorney asked the mayor whether there was card playing downtown, which could possibly lead to gambling. According to Smith, Hanna denied that would be the case. Brown cross-examined Smith and asked if he had worked for Hirst as a special investigator. He said he had been doing so for three months, and he closed all the gambling in town. When asked by the defense attorney if he had investigated the Plains Hotel for gambling, he said he had, but when he looked into it, he learned there had been some gambling there, but it was not going on during his investigation. Brown asked if Violette had assisted him in closing some of the gambling houses, and Smith said he had. When asked if Ekky had "discharged his duty" at the time, he said yes, he had "as far as I could see."[30]

The last prosecution witness that day was Lieutenant Kenneth E. Smith from Fort Warren. He testified about his observations on March 18 at the Porters and Waiters Club, which were documented in his affidavits provided to the prosecution. Smith noted he saw three envelopes on Grimes' desk, one had Pop written on it, another had Hall on it, and the third said Lola. He later saw Morris walk out with the envelopes. Under cross-examination, Smith was asked to identify Morris in the courtroom, which he did. He also described the car Morris arrived in and what the captain was wearing that day. Smith's testimony ended the trial for that day. Ilsley recessed the case at 5:00 p.m. and said the court would reconvene at 9:00 a.m. Friday, May 5, when defense attorneys Walton and Brown would begin their defense of Hanna, Ekdall, Morris, and Violette.[31]

The trial began that day with Hirst resting the prosecution's case, followed by counsel Walton asking the judge for a directed verdict of acquittal for the defendants. Ilsley denied the motion. Counsel Brown then gave the defense's opening statement, saying that Hanna received $680 that had been collected from the West Side businesses and that he had been arrested before he was given a chance to explain why he had the money and what was to happen to it.[32]

The first defense witness was Ira Hanna, the mayor who had served about three months of his two-year term. During his testimony, Hanna reiterated what was said in the opening statement. He explained he and Ekdall had decided to make the West Side business owners pay fines for their illegal activities since Fort Warren's military police patrolling the area were supposedly aware of prostitution, gambling, and the sale of liquor in the area. According to Hanna, the $680 collected was to be turned into the police court as "fines or forfeitures." He continued that when he and the other defendants were arrested on March 20, it was yet to be determined how the money should be entered into the police docket, although Hanna testified that he had intended the money to be used for city improvements to parks and children's playgrounds.[33]

Some of Hanna's testimony related to his visits to the Porters and Waiters Club. Apparently, one visit was on February 20. Hanna and the other three went to see Grimes at his club. At that time, he testified that Grimes was informed that the business owners on the West Side would need to pay fines for violations. Then, on March 11, after attending a junior chamber of commerce dinner with Ekdall, Morris approached the chief and the mayor, who were also in attendance, and told them that Grimes wanted to see them both. He testified that all four of the defendants went to the Porters and Waiters Club. When they arrived, they saw Lola West, and the mayor asked, "What is the ruckus?" According to Hanna, the ruckus was West complaining about her $100 fine.[34]

To explain how he personally received the money, Hanna testified that Ekdall gave him $340 on March 14 and told him that the money had been collected as fines from West Side businesses. He placed that amount of money in an envelope with the money collected earlier. The mayor continued, stating he kept the money in an envelope in his desk until it was decided to place it on the police docket. After a brief recess, Hanna continued his testimony and, at this point, explained how he came to have the three five-dollar bills in his possession. He said on March 18, he put a twenty-dollar bill in the envelope with the money from fines, took out four five-dollar bills, and gave one of the bills to his secretary to contribute to the Red Cross fund. He put the other bills in his wallet. According to the mayor, his secretary gave him a receipt for the donation, which was presented in court and examined by the jury. Also presented to the court was a list compiled by Ekdall of people who had been fined and the amounts of their fines. This document was also presented in court. Hanna said a total of $680 in fines had been collected, and that was the amount in the envelope. According to his testimony, the mayor took the envelope home with him on March 20 after his arrest.[35]

Hanna's attorney, Brown, followed up about the fines. He asked the witness: "Did you discuss the matter of fines with the other members of the city council, Mr. Hanna?" "I did not," he replied, "because the mayor and chief of police are in charge of the police department." The attorney followed up, asking if the mayor had cooperation with the city council on other financial matters. Hanna answered that he did not.[36]

Prosecutor Greenwood cross-examined the mayor. He asked the mayor whether he had ever consulted with the city attorney about charging and collecting fines. Hanna responded, "No I did not because I intended to turn in the money to police court funds." Greenwood's follow-up question was whether Hanna discussed the fines and how the money would be deposited with anyone? Hanna replied, only Ekdall. After several more questions along these lines, the attorney began questioning the mayor about the method used to determine the fines. He asked Hanna which policemen were involved in the West End operation. Hanna named Ekdall, Morris, and Violette. When asked why only those three, the mayor said: "I had no cooperation from the police department; there were factions down there, one against the other." Greenwood also asked why he had selected Ekdall as chief of police, since Ekdall had no law enforcement experience. Hanna said he had considered Jess Miller, at that time employed by the Wyoming Highway Patrol, but he said he wanted a man in the department "who had never been connected with law enforcement to straighten out the friction in the police department." The prosecutor also questioned Hanna about the meeting at the Porters and Waiters Club on March 11. He asked: "Whatever was done there was done with your approval, Mr. Hanna?" He answered that it was. He also asked the witness whether he commonly visited such places of business on the West Side, such as the Porters and Waiters Club, instead of having people come to his office. Hanna replied that it was the police's duty to collect the fines and return the money to the city. Greenwood then asked him if there had been any arrests between January 3 and March 20 in the West End for prostitution, gambling, and the sale of liquor. The mayor said he did not know and that he was not an arresting officer. At that point, the court recessed.[37]

After the recess, Greenwood went in a different direction and asked Hanna if he knew Syd Schwartz. Hanna answered yes, and the attorney then asked if Schwartz "was appointed as a special police officer?" The mayor said he did not know, but when asked whether such an appointment would go through his office, he answered yes. Greenwood then showed Hanna a special police card with Schwartz's name and the mayor's signature. He responded that he did not sign it, and the only reason Schwartz had such a card was "just so he could keep the law enforced in his bar."[38] The rest of Hanna's cross-examination involved questions about the times he withdrew money from the funds collected for fines. The mayor said he did that three times, although he could not remember the first time. The second time, he put in a twenty for two tens in order to have change to buy groceries. And the last time was when he took out four $5 bills and replaced them with a $20 bill. This was when his secretary took one of the fives and donated that to the Red Cross, and Hanna kept the other three bills, which turned out to be the marked ones found on him when he was arrested on March 20.[39]

The defense continued when the attorneys called C.W. Gibbs of Casper to the stand. Gibbs ran the Casper Bureau of Private Investigation, and he testified that at one time he had conducted a vice investigation for the ministerial association.[40] According to Gibbs, he spoke with Hanna and Ekdall in early March about setting up a merchant patrol in Cheyenne, and the mayor and chief of police asked how fines are collected in Casper. A letter written by Gibbs to Hanna about the collection of fines was introduced as an exhibit for the defense.[41]

The next defense witness was Chief of Police Jess Ekdall. At the start of his testimony, he explained he had dismissed T. Joe Cahill and promoted Morris from sergeant to captain, and Violette from a plainclothes officer to sergeant, at the beginning of his tenure as chief. He also testified that when he took over the police department, he found "quite a clique," and there was considerable friction between the police and detective departments. Harvey Jackson, the chief of detective, told Ekdall that when he took office, a police officer had broken into the Tyrrell Chevrolet company garage, and another officer had stolen items from Jack's Appliance store, and "the department had never done anything about it." Ekdall then discussed when the topic of raiding the West Side came about. Hanna called him into his office and asked the chief what he knew about the situation on the "West End." They both agreed that the best course of action was to raid it. They called Morris and Violette into the office to get their opinions. Ekdall testified that Morris said, "Okay any time you say we'll do down and knock 'em off." Violette, however, said they should wait "until they had a chance to talk to some of them and see what they could find out." According to Ekdall, Hanna and the chief made a trip to the West Side to gather more information. Later, Ekdall suggested "closing them up." However, the mayor, according to Ekdall's testimony, said that the houses in that part of the city should not be closed down because there had been so much rape and "slugging" going on that closing the houses might make things worse. Hanna proposed organizing the businesses and attempting to collect fines. According to the chief, the fines would serve to discourage illegal activities and generate revenue for the city.[42]

Later in his testimony, Ekdall discussed visiting the Porters and Waiter Club. He explained they had talked to Grimes and others, telling them they would "knock 'em off" every two weeks, apparently referring to the schedule for collecting fines or, as Hirst described them, bribes. According to Ekdall, it was Grimes who, not wanted to get arrested, suggested he be the one to collect the money for them. When Pop asked Ekdall who would handle the weekly collection, Grimes said, "Let Ekky do it because he's been awfully nice to us down here." Regarding collecting money from the West Side businesses, Ekdall explained the mayor asked, "What are we doing with this money?" This was after the chief had given Hanna $340, and Ekdall then mentioned they should run it through the books.[43]

Hirst cross-examined Ekdall, and the only part of that testimony involved four guns the chief had taken from his office at the police department. Apparently, he refused to surrender them until city council passed a resolution requiring him to do so. Ekdall denied this. Hirst also asked the witness whether the city clerk stated that if the guns were not returned, the purchase price would be deducted from his paycheck. Ekdall replied, "Yes."[44]

Next on the stand for the defense was Violette. He testified he had been assigned to control the West End in the summer of 1943. After he received that assignment, Lola West approached him and asked if she could run a slot machine that summer. Violette told her he would need to ask Harvey Jackson, the chief of police at that time. Jackson said it would be all right during the week of Cheyenne Frontier Days. Later in his testimony, Violette mentioned a meeting he and Morris held on February 21 with Ekdall, who asked them if there had ever been any payoffs on the West Side. Ekky testified about this, "I said there must have been some kind of a payoff as I'd tried to raid some places several times and was never able to get away with it." Under cross-examination, Violette stated that he had collected $320 from West Side businesses on March 11 and turned that money over to Ekdall the following day.[45]

The last witness that day was Morris, who testified that Ekdall first asked him how things were on the West Side, and he responded that it was no worse than before. "The chief asked me how they had paid before, and I said some came to the chief's office and he'd come out and hand me a receipt." Ekdall then asked about gambling on the West Side, about whether it had stopped after law enforcement said all gambling in the city had been stopped. Morris said, "I don't know if it ever quit." Regarding the collection of fines, the captain said he only collected once, and that was when he walked into George (Kid Rabbi) Howard's business, the Red, White and Blue Café, and, "not even thinking about it," an envelope was placed in his hand. When asked what he did with the payment, Morris said he took it to the chief. When asked if he was ever paid any money "as the result of business transactions on the West Side, Morris replied emphatically: "Not a dime." That concluded his testimony and the judge recessed for the day with court to begin again on May 6.[46]

The final day of the trial to determine if Cheyenne Mayor Ira Hanna, Chief of Police Jess B. Ekdall, Captain G.J. (Jet) Morris, and Desk Sergeant E.K. (Ekky) Violette were guilty or innocent of soliciting and accepting bribes took place on Saturday, May 6. That day, as had been the case every day of the trial, the courtroom was filled to overflowing.[47] The specific charge was soliciting and accepting $100 on two occasions for "protection" from Lola West, the proprietor of the Black and Tan Café on the city's West Side. The first person on the stand was Morris, who returned to complete his testimony, which had begun the day before. He testified that during the last ten years, the collection of fines from prostitutes had been booked through the police court and receipts had been issued to the violators or the "landladys." Following the captain, the defense team had four Cheyenne businessmen and the county surveyor testify "to the good reputation, honesty and good citizenship of the four defendants," according to the *Wyoming State Tribune*. Those who testified for the defense were T.H. Baldwin, county surveyor; Mark A. Chapman, local insurance agent; William Hays, Cheyenne druggist; Edward F. Murray, local insurance man; and Jack Speight, Cheyenne grocer. After the jury heard these witnesses, the defense rested its case at 10 a.m.[48]

In response to the defense case, the prosecution called several rebuttal witnesses. Apparently, because Morris had spoken about a visit to George (Kid Rabbi) Howard's café, Hirst called Howard to the stand. Howard testified he made four payments of $75, $50, $25, and $75 to a "tall fellow and a short fellow and the other three times (to) a short fellow." (Violette was the shorter of the two police officers). He could not state the exact dates of the payments, and when asked to identify the two men, he said, "I know their pictures." He was also asked if his café had been raided, and he responded: "They done something to it." The affidavit Howard made and signed shortly after the four defendants were arrested was presented in court.[49] The prosecution also recalled Lola West to the stand. She testified that she made a list of the serial numbers of the bills paid to the defendants for protection. The list was introduced by the state as an exhibit, and the numbers of the three five-dollar bills found on Hanna after his arrest were included on the list. Hirst also recalled Pop Grimes, L.D. Parker and Fred Taylor to review their earlier testimonies. Finally, the state called Mrs. Alma Wilkinson to the stand. She was Hanna's secretary, and she testified she received five dollars from the mayor "about 10 or 11 days before his arrest" to pay for a membership in the Red Cross. She typed out his membership card. With that, the calling of witnesses ended. Judge Ilsley called a recess and instructed the jury to return by 1:30 p.m. when closing statements would be heard.[50]

The trial reconvened at 1:30 that afternoon, and both sides presented closing arguments. Unfortunately, the newspapers did not include anything about the closings in their stories about the trial. The *Laramie Republican and Boomerang* only reported on the length of the arguments, with the defense taking an hour and fifteen minutes and the prosecution an hour and ten minutes. Later that afternoon, the judge ordered the jury to deliberate on whether the four defendants were guilty. About 9:40 p.m., the jury announced the four were guilty of soliciting and accepting a bribe. Ilsley immediately announced the sentences. Hanna and Ekdall were sentenced to not less than seven years and not more than ten years in the Wyoming State Penitentiary. Morris was sentenced to not less than one year and not more than two years. Violette's sentence was not less than two years and not more than three years.[51] The official "Judgment and Sentence of Court" stated, "having been tried before a jury according to law and said jury duly having found" all four guilty of bribery.[52] All of the convicted men were immediately taken to the county jail. Whether the convictions would be appealed had still not been decided. The judge set bonds of $5,000 for Hanna and Ekdall, $3,000 for Violette, and $2,000 for Morris. By Thursday, May 11, all four had posted bond and were free until May 13.[53] Also on May 11, Violette and Morris filed a motion for a new trial. The grounds for this action were: "1. That the verdict in said cause is contrary to the evidence; 2. That the verdict in said cause is contrary to law; 3. That the judgment in said cause is contrary to law." The defendants wanted the verdict set aside and to be given a new trial.[54] Ilsley denied the request.

On Monday, May 8, the two city council members, Jones and Fleischli, met and approved a resolution declaring the mayor's office vacant after Hanna's conviction two days earlier. The resolution stated Hanna was "unqualified, unable, and incompetent to serve and act as mayor" of Cheyenne. That action also names Jones as acting mayor. Also that day, Hirst and the new Chief of Police McVicar issued a joint statement saying they were determined to "effect a general cleanup of persistent law violators." Both Jones and Fleischli pledged their full cooperation in that effort.[55]

Shortly after the convictions, on May 9, the *Laramie Republican and Boomerang* published an editorial about the arrests and convictions of Hanna and the three law enforcement officers titled "The Cheyenne Scandal." It began with a mention of the convictions, then stated that the trial and sentences "may have a cleansing effect on the governments of other cities throughout Wyoming and the Rocky Mountain west." The editorial described how the prosecuting attorney and judge handled the case admirably. It went on to state the "scandal is going to reflect on the city commission for government," and said many government observers believe a city council of more than three persons is desirable for many reasons. "In the first place, it is not such a tight little fraternity, and the more official eyes there are looking out for things, the more likely it is that an unsavory condition will be uncovered. The checks and balance system of our council and manager government, it seems to us, would make any kind of fraud difficult."[56]

The editorial's last two paragraphs spoke directly about the Cheyenne case: "They are laughing in Cheyenne about how a 'dumb' woman of questionable reputation, arrested about 15 times by her own admission, outsmarted Cheyenne's 'smart' erstwhile city officials. One Lola West ordered to pay regular 'hush money,' arranged to have all of the culprits come to her place of business where they could be seen or heard by investigators, working with her to trap them. It was an ordorous case. We hope there won't be another one like it in our state for many years to come."[57]

Of course, the actual meeting between the four defendants, Lola, and Grimes took place at the Porters and Waiters Club. But it was West who insisted she wanted to speak to Hanna and Ekdall, which brought them there that evening of March 11, so that the meeting could be observed by law enforcement, recorded, and transcribed.

A few weeks after the *Laramie Republican and Boomerang* editorial, the case and the resulting convictions received national attention when an article appeared in *Time: The Weekly Newsmagazine*. It was a brief article titled "Western Dewey" in the section about what was happening across the country during the war.

> A young Harvard-educated prosecutor who likes to think of himself as the Wild West's Tom Dewey last week could carve four more notches in his briefcase. His victims: Cheyenne, Wyo.'s mayor, chief of police and two cops.
>
> Cheyenne's dilapidated, frame-built West End district was a wide-open haven for girls, gambling and guzzling until last summer, when Army authorities from nearby Fort Francis E. Warren cracked down. Sin spots went under cover, which meant they had to begin buying protection. Soldiers (mostly Negroes) from Fort Warren still had a million-a-month payroll to blow. In sleazy backroom dives, blackjack stakes ran as high as $200 a game. Nightspots bootlegged whiskey because they could not get liquor franchises, limited in Cheyenne to 20 a year and unofficially valued at $50,000 each. Negro service wives were forced to prostitute themselves or be thrown out of their rooms in the congested Negro district.
>
> All this became known to blue-eyed baby-faced Byron Hirst, 31, the new county attorney. He also heard that the mayor was in on the take, and warned him: "I'm not interested in being a conquering hero around here, but everybody is beginning to think you're a crook." Finally Hirst set a trap. He got the buxom Negro madam of the "Black and Tan Club" to insist on paying off to the mayor and police chief in person. Hirst's men watched through a peephole, recorded the transaction on a dictograph. Last week Attorney Hirst got his conviction.[58]

The Dewey referred to in the *Time* article was Thomas E. Dewey, who served three terms as New York's governor from 1943 to 1955. During the 1930s, he served as a U.S. Attorney in New York, and from 1935 to 1937, Dewey served as a special prosecutor on the state's organized crime unit, which successfully convicted Lucky Luciano, a gangster and major figure in American organized crime. The *Time* writer made a number of errors. There were more White soldiers at Fort Warren than African American soldiers, and, of course, the four defendants met West and others at the Porters and Waiters Club, not in the implied Black and Tan Club.[59] Prostitution, alcohol, and gambling were not only found on the West Side, as implied by the article, but in other parts of the city as well.

CHAPTER I I ENDNOTES

1   "Arrest Was Total Surprise to Officials," *Wyoming Eagle*, March 22, 1944, 1 and back page.

2   "Arrest Was Total Surprise to Officials," *Wyoming Eagle*, March 22, 1944, 1 and back page.

3   Affidavit provided by 1st Lt. Kenneth E. Smith, to Tom B. Hembree, March 21, 1944, Byron Hirst Papers, Old West Museum, Cheyenne.

4   "Money Fails to 'Talk' As 'Whole Town's Talking' of Capital Municipal Scandal," *Wyoming State Tribune*, March 23, 1944, 4.

5   "Money Fails to 'Talk' As 'Whole Town's Talking' of Capital Municipal Scandal," *Wyoming State Tribune*, March 23, 1944, 4.

6   "Money Fails to 'Talk' As 'Whole Town's Talking' of Capital Municipal Scandal," *Wyoming State Tribune*, March 23, 1944, 4.

7   "District Court Jury Called: 60 Names Drawn, Including 'Jet' Morris, Who Faces Bribery Charge During Term," *Wyoming State Tribune*, April 10, 1944, 1 and 9.

8   "Judge Thompson Calls District Jury: Ilsley to Preside at Bribery Hearing," *Wyoming Eagle*, April 11, 1944, 8.

9   "Trial of Four City Officials Set May 1: Docket Revealed," *Wyoming Eagle*, April 13, 1944, 1 and back page; "Trial of Four On Bribery Counts Fixed: Will Open May 1 in Court Here," *Wyoming State Tribune*, April 13, 1944, 1. See also "Thompson Disqualified In Trial of Four City Officials: Defendants Ask Change In Petition," *Wyoming State Tribune*, March 22, 1944, 1 and 11. In the petition against Thompson the defendants charged him with "bias and prejudice" and that they "cannot receive a fair and impartial trail before" Thompson.

10   "Judge Ilsley Will Hear Bribe Charges," *Wyoming State Tribune*, April 30, 1944, 1.

11   Copies of legal filings are located in Byron Hirst Papers, Old West Museum, Cheyenne.

12   "Defense Plea to Squash New Charges Against City Officials Here Denied: Argument Holds Up Opening of Trial for Four," *Wyoming State Tribune*, May 1, 1944, 1; "Naming of Jurors in Trial of Four City Officials Under Way: Formal Beginning of Case May Be Delayed Until Tomorrow; Challenges Take Time," *Wyoming State Tribune*, May 2, 1944, 1 and 11.

13   "Motion to Consolidate Six Counts In City Case Denied," *Wyoming Eagle*, May 2, 1944, 1 and 8; "Naming of Jurors in Trial of Four City Officials Under Way: Formal Beginning of Case May Be Delayed Until Tomorrow; Challenges Take Time," *Wyoming State Tribune*, May 2, 1944, 1 and 11.

14   "Jury in City Bribery Trial Is Picked: Testimony Starts at 9," *Wyoming Eagle*, May 3, 1944, 1 and 8.

15   Byron Hirst Papers, Old West Museum, Cheyenne. The notes also included a list of ordinances which applied to the case. These included the role of the Cheyenne Police Department and the appointive officers of the city as well as the ones related to gambling, alcohol, vagrancy, immorality, and elections.

16   "Testifies to Paying Hush Money to Run Illicit House: Café Proprietor Initial Witness to Take Stand in Cheyenne Trial," *Laramie Republican and Boomerang*, May 3, 1944, 1 and 4; "Lola West Swears She Was Asked for Money: Testimony of City Officials Takes most of Opening Hours of Hearing," *Wyoming State Tribune*, May 3, 1944, 1 and 9.

17   "Federal Man Tells Court of Hearing 'Payoff Discussions,'" *Wyoming Eagle*, May 4, 1944, 1 and back page.

18   "Federal Man Tells Court of Hearing 'Payoff Discussions,'" *Wyoming Eagle*, May 4, 1944, 1 and back page.

19   "Federal Man Tells Court of Hearing 'Payoff Discussions,'" *Wyoming Eagle*, May 4, 1944, 1 and back page.

20   "Federal Man Tells Court of Hearing 'Payoff Discussions,'" *Wyoming Eagle*, May 4, 1944, 1 and back page.

21 "Investigators Say They Saw 'Payoff,' Expect to Hear Many More Hours of State Testimony," *Wyoming State Tribune*, May 4, 1944, 1 and 11.

22 "State To Rest Case Today In City Trial: Recordings Not Entered As Evidence," *Wyoming Eagle*, May 5, 1944, 1 and back page.

23 "Investigators Say They Saw 'Payoff,' Expect to Hear Many More Hours of State Testimony," *Wyoming State Tribune*, May 4, 1944, 1 and 11.

24 "Investigators Say They Saw 'Payoff,' Expect to Hear Many More Hours of State Testimony," *Wyoming State Tribune*, May 4, 1944, 1 and 11; "U.S. Agents Testify They Saw 'Payoff,' Swear on Stand Cheyenne Officials Collected $100 Bribe," *Laramie Republican and Boomerang*, May 4, 1944, 1 and back page.

25 "U.S. Agents Testify They Saw 'Payoff," Swear on Stand Cheyenne Officials Collected $100 Bribe," *Laramie Republican and Boomerang*, May 4, 1944, 1 and back page; "Investigators Say They Saw 'Payoff,' Expcet to Hear Many More Hours of State Testimony," *Wyoming State Tribune*, May 4, 1944, 1 and 11.

26 "State To Rest Case Today In City Trial: Recordings Not Entered As Evidence," *Wyoming Eagle*, May 5, 1944, 1 and back page; "Hanna Testifies He Received 'Fines' for Illicit Activities, Says Money Was To Be Used for City Playground," *Laramie Republican and Boomerang*, May 5, 1944, 1 and back page.

27 "State To Rest Case Today In City Trial: Recordings Not Entered As Evidence," *Wyoming Eagle*, May 5, 1944, 1 and back page; "Hanna Testifies He Received 'Fines' for Illicit Activities, Says Money Was To Be Used for City Playground," *Laramie Republican and Boomerang*, May 5, 1944, 1 and back page.

28 "State To Rest Case Today In City Trial: Recordings Not Entered As Evidence," *Wyoming Eagle*, May 5, 1944, 1 and back page.

29 "State To Rest Case Today In City Trial: Recordings Not Entered As Evidence," *Wyoming Eagle*, May 5, 1944, 1 and back page; "Hanna Testifies He Received 'Fines' for Illicit Activities, Says Money Was To Be Used for City Playground," *Laramie Republican and Boomerang*, May 5, 1944, 1 and back page.

30 "State To Rest Case Today In City Trial: Recordings Not Entered As Evidence," *Wyoming Eagle*, May 5, 1944, 1 and back page.

31 "State To Rest Case Today In City Trial: Recordings Not Entered As Evidence," *Wyoming Eagle*, May 5, 1944, 1 and back page.

32 "Hanna Testifies He Received 'Fines' for Illicit Activities, Says Money Was To Be Used for City Playground," *Laramie Republican and Boomerang*, May 5, 1944, 1 and back page.

33 "Hanna Testifies He Received 'Fines' for Illicit Activities, Says Money Was To Be Used for City Playground," *Laramie Republican and Boomerang*, May 5, 1944, 1 and back page; "Hanna Testifies Money Collected Was 'Fines,' Mayor Called As Witness in Bribery Trial," *Wyoming State Tribune*, May 5, 1944, 1 and 11.

34 "Hanna Testifies He Received 'Fines' for Illicit Activities, Says Money Was To Be Used for City Playground," *Laramie Republican and Boomerang*, May 5, 1944, 1 and back page; "Hanna Testifies Money Collected Was 'Fines,' Mayor Called As Witness in Bribery Trial," *Wyoming State Tribune*, May 5, 1944, 1 and 11.

35 "Hanna Testifies Money Collected Was 'Fines,' Mayor Called As Witness in Bribery Trial," *Wyoming State Tribune*, May 5, 1944, 1 and 11; "Hanna Testifies He Received 'Fines' for Illicit Activities, Says Money Was To Be Used for City Playground," *Laramie Republican and Boomerang*, May 5, 1944, 1 and back page; "City Case May Go To Jury Sometime Today," *Wyoming Eagle*, May 6, 1944, 1 and 8.

36 "Hanna Testifies Money Collected Was 'Fines,' Mayor Called As Witness in Bribery Trial," *Wyoming State Tribune*, May 5, 1 and 11.

37 "Hanna Testifies Money Collected Was 'Fines,' Mayor Called As Witness in Bribery Trial," *Wyoming State Tribune*, May 5, 1944, 1 and 11.

38   "City Case May Go To Jury Sometime Today," *Wyoming Eagle*, May 6, 1944, 1 and 8. The questions asked Hanna about Schwartz being a "special police officer" probably related to why Schwartz had a siren and red light on his private car.

39   "City Case May Go To Jury Sometime Today," *Wyoming Eagle*, May 6, 1944, 1 and 8.

40   "Casper Detective Made Investigation," *Casper Tribune Herald*, June 25, 1943, 4.

41   "Casper Detective Made Investigation," *Casper Tribune Herald*, June 25, 1943, 4.

42   "City Case May Go To Jury Sometime Today," *Wyoming Eagle*, May 6, 1944, 1 and 8.

43   "City Case May Go To Jury Sometime Today," *Wyoming Eagle*, May 6, 1944, 1 and 8.

44   "City Case May Go To Jury Sometime Today," *Wyoming Eagle*, May 6, 1944, 1 and 8.

45   "City Case May Go To Jury Sometime Today," *Wyoming Eagle*, May 6, 1944, 1 and 8.

46   "City Case May Go To Jury Sometime Today," *Wyoming Eagle*, May 6, 1944, 1 and 8.

47   "Servicemen's Newsletter," *Wyoming Eagle*, May 6, 1944, 26.

48   "Preparing Instructions For Jury—City Case Nears End, Character Witnesses on Stand," *Wyoming State Tribune*, May 7, 1944, 1 and back page; "Four Convicted by Jury at Cheyenne, Mayor Hanna and Former Police Chief Sentenced to Terms of Not Less Than Seven Years by Judge Ilsley," *Casper Tribune Herald*, May 7, 1944, 1 and 2.

49   A copy of the affidavit by George (Kid Rabbi) Howard referenced during the last day of the trial is not included with the other affidavits in Hirst's Papers at the Old West Museum.

50   "Preparing Instructions For Jury—City Case Nears End, Character Witnesses on Stand," *Wyoming State Tribune*, May 7, 1944, 1 and back page; "Four Convicted by Jury at Cheyenne, Mayor Hanna and Former Police Chief Sentenced to Terms of Not Less Than Seven Years by Judge Ilsley," *Casper Tribune Herald*, May 7, 1944, 1 and 2.

51   "Bruce Jones Named Acting Mayor, Four Officials Convicted on Bribe Charges, Group Being Held In County Jail; Bonds Not Posted," *Wyoming State Tribune*, May 8, 1944, 1 and 9; "Four Convicted by Jury at Cheyenne, Mayor Hanna and Former Police Chief Sentenced to Terms of Not Less Than Seven Years by Judge Ilsley," *Casper Tribune Herald*, May 7, 1944, 1 and 2.

52   "Judgment and Sentence of Court," In District Court, First Judicial District, The State of Wyoming vs. Ira L. Hanna, Jess B. Ekdall, Gerald J. (Jet) Morris, and E.K. (Ekky) Violette, Doc. 8, No. 222, May 6, 1944, Wyoming State Archives.

53   "Four Convicted by Jury at Cheyenne, Mayor Hanna and Former Police Chief Sentenced to Terms of Not Less Than Seven Years by Judge Ilsley," *Casper Tribune Herald*, May 7, 1944, 1 and 2; "Bruce Jones Named Acting Mayor, Four Officials Convicted on Bribe Charges, Group Being Held In County Jail, Bonds Not Posted," *Wyoming State Tribune*, May 8, 1944, 1 and 9; "Former Cheyenne Officials Freed on Appeal Bonds," *Laramie Republican and Boomerang*, May 11, 1944, 4; "City Officials Free on Bonds Until May 13," *Wyoming Eagle*, May 11, 1944, 1 and back page.

54   "Motion for a New Trial," Filed in the District Court, The State of Wyoming vs. Ira L. Hanna, et al, May 11, 1944, Wyoming State Archives. "Ex-Cheyenne Police Officers File for New Trial," *Laramie Republican and Boomerang*, May 12, 1944, 4.

55   "Move Is On To Declare Mayor's Office Vacant," *Laramie Republican and Boomerang*, May 8, 1944, 1 and back page; "Four Officials of Cheyenne Convicted On Bribery Charges; All Are Given Prison Terms, Jones Acting Mayor," *Lusk Free Lance*, May 11, 1944, 1 and 10.

56   "The Cheyenne Scandal," *Laramie Republican and Boomerang*, May 9, 1944, 4.

57   "The Cheyenne Scandal," *Laramie Republican and Boomerang*, May 9, 1944, 4.

58   "Western Dewey," from TIME © 1944 TIME USA LLC. All rights reserved. Used under license. *Newsweek* also mentioned Hirst and the "Cheyenne Scandal" as did John Kennedy on the Blue network. "Hirst Is Praised by Commentator in Bribery Case Here," *Wyoming State Tribune*, May 22, 1944, 10.

59   The information about Thomas E. Dewey is from the National Governors Association website, www.nga.org/governor/thomas-edmund-dewey/.

To Prison?

Ira Hanna, Jess Ekdall, Gerald Morris, and E.K. Violette only had a few days after their trial before they were on their way to Rawlins and the Wyoming State Penitentiary. Sheriff Tuck ordered the four to gather at the county jail on Sunday, May 14, by 9:30. They all arrived fifteen minutes early and waited for the prison's warden, A.S. Roach, to come and drive them to Rawlins to begin their sentences. While waiting, some of their friends and some employees at the city-county building talked with them and shook their hands. According to the *Wyoming State Tribune*, "Ekdall seemed in particularly good spirits, joking with everyone. Morris had little to say. The mayor, who looks much thinner than on the day when he was arrested, thanked the county jail officers for their kindness during the five nights he was imprisoned. Violette appeared to be unconcerned throughout the whole proceeding." At 11:15, Tuck took the four "Bribe-Takers," as described by the *Laramie Republican and Boomerang*, to lunch at a local restaurant, and half an hour later, they all climbed into the back seat of Roach's large sedan and left for Rawlins.[1]

All four entered the prison on May 14, 1944. A "Description of Convict" was completed for each one. For Hanna, No. 6046, his occupation was listed as bookkeeper, and he had a wife and three children. He had finished one year of high school. Ekdall, No. 6047, occupation listed as "Investments and Bond Salesman," and he was married with one child. He was a graduate of the University of Wyoming. Morris, No. 6049, was listed, of course, as a police officer, with a wife and one child. He had completed 8th grade. Like Morris, Violette, No. 6048, was a police officer, and he also had a wife and one child. He had completed 9th grade.[2]

Within five days of their incarceration, Warden Roach granted the Cheyenne quartet "trustyship" and assigned them to outside work at the prison. The warden explained that when he considered a prisoner trustworthy, he made him a trustee.[3] The warden also said the four would receive the same treatment as the other prisoners. The topic of sending the four to the prison farm at Riverton came up quickly after their convictions. Good behavior was one of the criteria for prisoners to be sent to the prison farm. Roach transferred the four to the farm, but their stay lasted less than a month. According to the warden, Hanna and the others wanted to be in Rawlins at the penitentiary so their families could visit them more easily. It was customary for prisoners with good records who wanted to be returned to Rawlins to request the transfer.

Back in Cheyenne, a few days after the four defendants were convicted, the Cheyenne Police Department took steps to "clean up" the West Side. This was the part of town where businesses had just been encouraged by the mayor and chief of police to engage in gambling, selling whiskey, and bringing in girls to "hustle" because they planned to "open up" the city. To start the clean-up, the police arrested George "Kid Rabbi" Howard and Terry Masiel. Sergeant Harold R. Blocker charged Howard with operating a "disorderly house." In the Cheyenne City Ordinances, a disorderly house was defined as "… as any room, house, building, vehicle or any other place within the City of Cheyenne, for the purpose of fornication, adultery, prostitution, or any other lewd or immoral practices." After his arrest, Howard was released on a $100 bond, although he failed to appear the following day, so he forfeited his bond. Masiel was arrested and charged with immorality. While at Kid Rabbi's, Blocker had given her seven dollars for committing an illegal act. She was unable to pay the fine and was sent to the county jail. Her sentence was a $100 fine or ninety days in jail. Acting Police Chief F.B. McVicar repeated a promise he made several days earlier that "law violations in the city must stop or violators will be prosecuted to the full extent of the law." He also warned that future violations would result in places being padlocked by the police department. Shortly after that, the Cheyenne City Council named McVicar as the permanent chief of police.[4]

As for the Cheyenne convicts at the state penitentiary, all four would be out of prison by the end of 1945. Morris, who had the shortest sentence, not less than one year and not more than two, was placed on parole May 5, 1945, one day before the anniversary of his conviction. He was officially discharged on August 30, 1945. Prisoners at that time could earn good time for good behavior. Morris earned 155 days of good time. Also, his citizenship was restored.[5]

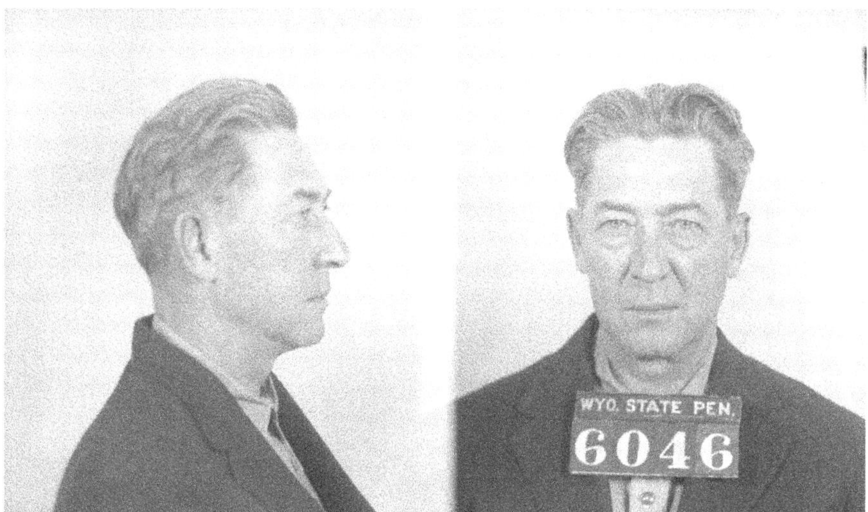

Wyoming State Penitentiary photo of Ira Hanna. He was convicted of bribery on May 6, 1944. Hanna was sentenced to not less than seven years and not more than ten years in prison. He entered prison on May 14, 1941, was paroled on December 15, 1945, and the sentence was officially discharged from parole on December 15, 1945. Photo courtesy of the Wyoming State Archives.

Wyoming State Penitentiary photo of Jess Ekdall. He was convicted of bribery on May 6, 1944 and sentenced to not less than seven years and not more than ten years in prison. He entered prison on May 14, 1944. Ekdall was paroled on June 15, 1945, and officially discharged from parole a year later. Photo courtesy of the Wyoming State Archives.

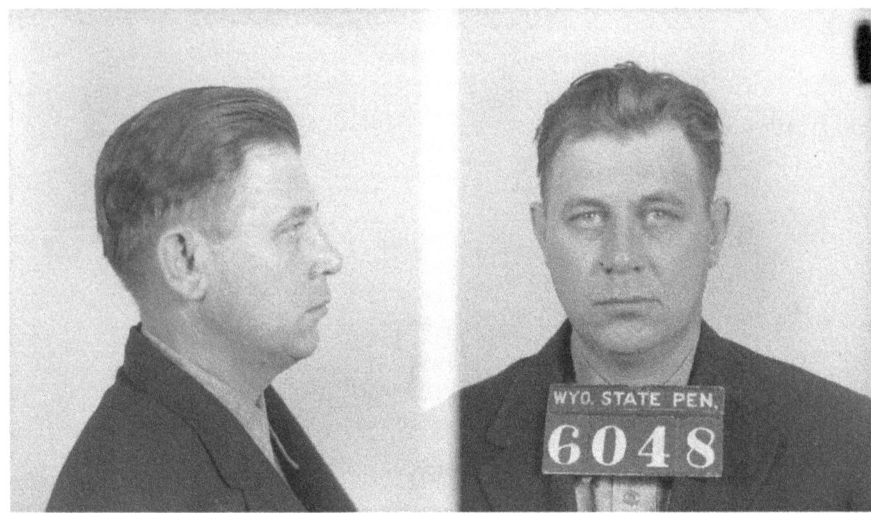

Wyoming State Penitentiary photo of E.K. Violette. He was convicted of bribery on May 6, 1944, and sentenced to not less than two years and not more than three years. He entered prison on May 14, 1944. Violette was paroled on July 11, 1945, and officially discharged from parole September 5, 1945. Photo courtesy of the Wyoming State Archives.

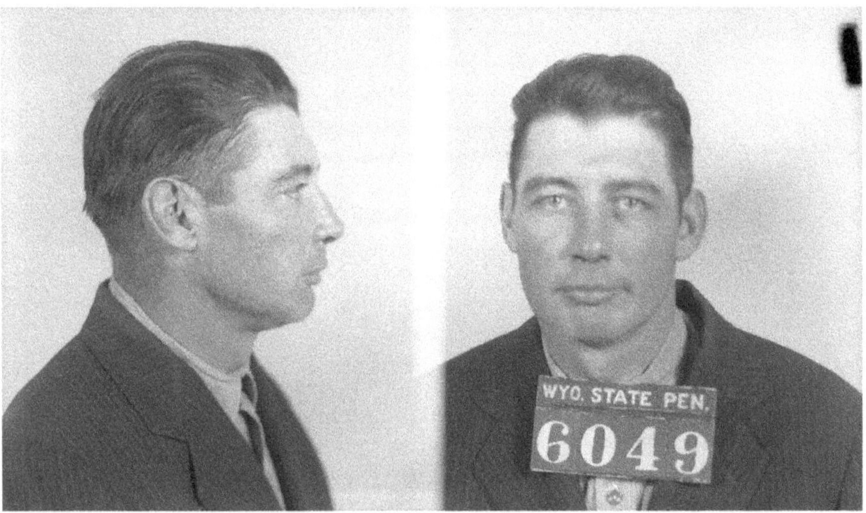

Wyoming State Penitentiary photo of Gerald Morris. He was convicted of bribery on May 6, 1944, and sentenced to not less than one year and not more than two years. He entered prison on May 14, 1944. Morris was paroled on May 19, 1945 and officially discharged from parole August 30, 1945. Photo courtesy of the Wyoming State Archives.

When Morris was paroled, the other three made news due to their work status during their confinement. The *Wyoming Eagle* ran a story on May 19, 1945, titled "Jess Ekdall Now Working Here at Governor's House." The day before, the *Wyoming State Tribune* featured a story titled "Jess Ekdall Is Working At Mansion." The former chief of police was in Cheyenne working as a handyman at Wyoming's governor's mansion. At that time, the governor was Lester Hunt, who said the prisoner was a yard, garage, maintenance, and repair man. The governor contacted the prison and, because it was hard to find adequate help during the war, asked then-warden Alex McPherson if it would be possible to assign a trusted inmate to work around the mansion. The warden recommended Ekdall. This was permitted because the practice of assigning prison trusties to jobs at various state institutions was already in place. Ten prisoners were assigned to various positions at the time. Besides Ekdall, one was assigned as a janitor at the home of the Catholic prison chaplain; four worked at the state park at Saratoga; another worked at a Rawlins dairy; and three worked on maintaining the grounds of the prison warden's home. It is unclear where Ekdall would have been incarcerated in Cheyenne at this time. Still in Rawlins, Hanna and Violette also had interesting job opportunities, although not so far afield as Ekdall. Hanna, as a trustee, worked as a bookkeeper in the chief clerk's department at the prison, and trustee Violette was the warden's chauffeur.[6] Their tenures in these positions were short because they soon followed Morris and were paroled.

Violette was the next of the four to be out of the state penitentiary. In July 1945, he sought a reduction in his two-to-three-year prison term. The State Board of Pardons met on Wednesday, July 11, and, along with ten others, considered the former desk sergeant's early release from the Wyoming State Penitentiary. According to the minutes of the meeting, "Governor Hunt moved that the sentence be commuted to a term of 1 to 2 years (and) to go on parole immediately." The motion received a second and was carried, and Violette was no longer incarcerated. As governor, Hunt served as president of the board. Violette was the only one considered by the board that day who was granted a parole. His official discharge date was September 5, 1945, and, like Morris, his citizenship was restored.[7]

Even before Violette was paroled, there was an indication that Hanna and Ekdall might soon be considered for parole. In mid-June 1945, the *Wyoming Eagle* ran a short story on page one of the June 15 edition titled "Pardon

Board Not To Pass On Hanna, Ekdall." Both inmates requested that their parole cases not be addressed at that time, but Hunt and the secretary of the pardon board had already received letters from around the state recommending that the two be considered for parole.[8] It is not known why they might have been averse to meeting with the board in June, but those concerns must have diminished as they met with the board on October 3, 1945. That day, the cases of Hanna and Ekdall were the first two addressed by the State Board of Pardons. Several people met with the board to speak in Hanna's favor. They were attorney E.C. Raymond of Newcastle, Edwin Hanna, and the former mayor's wife. The board "moved and seconded that Hanna be placed on parole December 15, 1945." Motion was carried and his sentence of "7 to 10 years to a term of 1 year 7 months 10 days (reduced) to 5 years to allow parole" in mid-December.[9]

Following Hanna, Ekdall's case had the same result. Speaking for him were attorney Harold Huber, the president of Hamilton Depositors Corporation of Denver, Colorado,[10] and Mrs. Ekdall. Sentence commuted similarly to Hanna's, and therefore, he was eligible for parole on December 15.[11] The day following the result of the pardon board meeting, both Cheyenne newspapers published stories about the two winning parole and would be released on December 15, but the stories also reported that weeks before the hearing many letters were received by the governor's office and the pardon board in support of clemency for the two convicted of soliciting and accepting bribes only a year and a half earlier. Even Judge Ilsley, who presided over the trial of the four, wrote identical letters in support of both Hanna and Ekdall. He wrote: "It is certainly the intent of the law that there be proper efforts made toward the rehabilitation of inmates of our penal institutions. Therefore, I would recommend that if the above-named inmate has made proper efforts toward his own rehabilitation and has obeyed the rules of the institution where he is confined, the board consider favorably the matter of his parole, and I am glad to add my recommendation in his favor." There were many more letters in support of clemency for Ekdall than for Hanna. According to the *State Tribune*, the pardon board files contained 158 letters supporting the former chief of police, including letters from Representative Frank Barrett, Edward F. Murray, Reverend Ralph Veit, James Greenwood, and one from a number of Cody citizens, among many others. Letters requesting clemency for Hanna were far fewer and included Edward F. Murray,

James Greenwood, Reverend Ralph Veit, Walter J. Bradley, J.K. Stoddard, William O. Wilson, and W.A. James.[12]

Cheyenne's former mayor was paroled on December 15, 1945. According to a document dated November 16, 1946, from the Wyoming State Penitentiary, Hanna earned 410 days for good behavior, including 165 days while on parole. As stated, his final discharge was December 15, 1946, as noted on the form. However, for some reason, Ekdall's final discharge was earlier. According to the Wyoming State Penitentiary form dated June 12, 1946, he also had earned 410 days for good time, including the same amount as Hanna for his time on parole. Noted on the form, however, was that Ekdall's sentence had been commuted on June 13, 1946, to a term of "1 Yr 7 Mos 10 days to 3 Yrs 8 Mos 10 Days." This occurred because, on April 3, 1946, Ekdall appeared before the pardon board and again asked that his sentence be commuted so he could be discharged from parole as soon as possible, since the company employing him wanted him to work in Montana. He needed to be off parole so he could move out of state. At the meeting, Hunt moved to allow discharge from parole on June 15, 1946. The vote was three in favor and one opposed, so Ekdall was discharged from parole that day in June.[13] Both inmates had their citizenship restored.

At the beginning of their imprisonment, Roach, then warden of the state penitentiary, stated the four found guilty in a Cheyenne courtroom of soliciting bribes would be treated like any other prisoner. Of course, once they were granted trustee status, that certainly changed and allowed for much more freedom for the prisoners. Morris was the only one who served nearly his full sentence. Violette spent his time serving as the warden's chauffeur and received a reduced sentence. Ekdall, apparently the most popular of the four convicts, benefited the most, spending months working around the governor's mansion in Cheyenne and having his sentence reduced twice. Hanna had a job as a bookkeeper, apparently working with the accounts of prisoners at the penitentiary. The sentences given by Judge Ilsley to both Ekdall and Hanna, ranging from seven to ten years, were severe, but even he supported their early release.

CHAPTER 12 ENDNOTES

1   "Four Former Cheyenne City Officials Taken to Prison, Turned Over To Warden A.S. Roach," *Wyoming State Tribune*, May 14, 1944, 1 and 9; "Four Cheyenne Bribe-Takers In Pen At Rawlins," *Laramie Republican and Boomerang*, May 15, 1944, 4; "Former City Officials Enter Rawlins Prison," *Wyoming State Tribune*, May 15, 1944, 1.

2   "Description of Convict," State Penitentiary, Rawlins, Wyoming, Wyoming State Archives.

3   "Former Cheyenne Officials Made Trusties At State Pen, Four May Be Moved To Farm," *Wyoming State Tribune*, May 19, 1944, 1 and 11; "Four Former City Officers Are Trusties," *Wyoming Eagle*, May 20, 1944, 18.

4   "Police Act to 'Clean Up' West Side," *Wyoming Eagle*, May 13, 1944, 1; "McVicar Is Appointed Chief Here," *Wyoming Eagle*, May 17, 1944, 11.

5   "Convict's Discharge, Wyoming State Penitentiary Inmate File Gerald J. Morris, Reg. No. 6049," Board Records, RG 0080, Board of Charities and Reform Records, Wyoming State Archives.

6   "Jess Ekdall Now Working Here at Governor's House," *Wyoming Eagle*, May 19, 1945, 9; "Jess Ekdall Is Working At Mansion," *Wyoming State Tribune*, May 18, 1945, 1.

7   "Treat and Violette Seeking Reduction In Prison Terms, State Poard [sic.] in Session At Rawlins," *Wyoming State Tribune* July 11, 1945, 1 and 9; "State Pardon Board Grants Parole To Former City Policeman E.K. Violette," *Wyoming Eagle*, July 12, 1945, 1 and 21; "Violette to Be Freed; Treat Aided," *Wyoming State Tribune*, July 12, 1945, 1; "Minutes of State Board of Pardons," July 11, 1945, 509-510, Wyoming State Archives; "Convict Discharge, Wyoming State Penitentiary, Inmate File Elwood K. Violette, Reg. No. 6048," Board Records, RG 0080, Board of Charities and Reform Records, Wyoming State Archives.

8   "Pardon Board Not To Pass On Hanna, Ekdall," *Wyoming Eagle*, June 15, 1945, 1.

9   "Minutes of State Board of Pardons," October 3, 1945, 511, Wyoming State Archives. The meeting was held in the governor's office.

10   Hamilton Depositors Corporation was the employer of Ekdall before he became chief of police and after prison he worked there again.

11   "Minutes of State Board of Pardons," October 3, 1945, 511, Wyoming State Archives. The meeting was held in the governor's office. Ekdall may have known Hunt before he became chief of police, but he certainly knew the governor then since he had been working at the governor's mansion.

12   "Hanna and Ekdall Win Parole Pleas, Become Eligible for Release December 15," *Wyoming Eagle*, October 4, 1945, 1 and 8; "Hanna and Ekdall May Be Freed From Prison Dec. 15, Clemency Is Granted by State Board," *Wyoming State Tribune*, October 4, 1945, 1 and 11; "Many Prominent Persons Speak For Hanna, Ekdall," *Wyoming Eagle*, October 5, 1945, 4.

13   "Convict's Discharge, Wyoming State Penitentiary Inmate file Ira L. Hanna, Reg. No. 6046," Board Records, RG 0080, Board of Charities and Reform Records, Wyoming State Archives; "Convict's Discharge, Wyoming State Penitentiary, Inmate File Jess B. Ekdall Reg. No. 6047," Board Records, RG 0080, Board of Charities and Reform Records, Wyoming State Archives; "Hanna and Ekdall Freed on Parole," *Wyoming State Tribune*, December 16, 1945, 1. Minutes of State Board of Pardons, April 3, 1946, 515, Wyoming State Archives.

Epilogue

IRA L. HANNA

Ira L. Hanna was born in Indiana in 1889. By the early 1900s, he was attending high school in Cheyenne. He worked for several years as a clerk for the Union Pacific Railroad and then managed the Western Coal Company. Hanna served as the Laramie County Deputy Treasurer for several years before becoming the county treasurer after winning the election in 1926; he was re-elected to the same position in 1934. In 1938, he was elected Laramie County Assessor and re-elected in 1942, serving in that role until he became Cheyenne's mayor in January 1944. Hanna was quite popular, winning some elections by more than three thousand votes. In 1914, Hanna married Edo Jessen Heaney, and they had three children. She died in 1935.[1]

After only two months in the mayor's office, he participated in the effort to "sell protection" to Cheyenne's West Side African American businesses. Why he chose to engage in and possibly lead this criminal activity as the city's top official remains unknown, raising several questions. Did he start planning this criminal activity before or during his campaign for mayor? Was he being encouraged or assisted by others in the community? Even as he campaigned for office, claiming he had an "unquestioned reputation for honesty" and promising "Good, Clean Government," he may have been plotting actions that contradicted his campaign promises. Within his first two months in office, members of the African American business community were urged to place $75 or $100 in an envelope and send it to the mayor's office.[2]

Various acquaintances of Hanna believed there were reasons behind his involvement in extorting Black business owners. Byron Hirst, in a conversation with Vaile Ward of the sheriff's department, did not name him directly but indicated it was Sydney Schwartz who told the mayor he could do it and get away with it. Ward also thought it was Schwartz. He told Hirst, "Ira got pushed into it that way." Hirst even told Lola West, speaking of Schwartz: "He was down there, as I understand it, between the primary and the general election, and said that he wanted Ira Hanna elected, and if Ira was elected

Ira Hanna was a longtime resident of Cheyenne. He attended high school in the city and then worked for the Union Pacific Railroad and the Western Coal Company. In 1926 he was elected to the position of Laramie Country Treasurer and then reelected and Hanna then served six years as Laramie County Assessor, resigning that position after his successful run for Cheyenne mayor. As mayor he served from January 1944 to May 1944. After his conviction in May on the charge of bribery he served his sentence in the Wyoming State Penitentiary. Photo courtesy of the Wyoming State Archives.

they'd open the town up, 'cause they were trying to get you to vote for Ira, I suppose." John McInerney, Hanna's opponent in the general election, warned in one of his primary ads that "Cheyenne's Mayor Must Lead—or Be Led." The ad mentioned that a strong commissioner could lead a mayor, but he was also concerned that an outsider could lead a mayor and "be the Mayor in fact, if not in name." Did McInerney know something about Hanna and Schwartz? Additionally, City Council member Bruce Jones made an astonishing statement on March 20, the day Hanna was arrested, telling those present: "The laws have been corrupted. One man made boasts and brags about what he was going to do, how he was going to have things his way. I think he selected a man who he was going to use as a tool." This clearly refers to Schwartz and how he was going to use Hanna. Hirst believed Schwartz was involved with the Denver and Chicago mafias, but he apparently lacked proof; the only charge against Schwartz was hiring a female barmaid. Still, it seems others besides Hirst suspected Schwartz was behind the protection-selling plot. At one point, Hirst told Vaile Ward that he almost had "very nearly enough to charge him (Schwartz) and believed he was as guilty as Hanna, Ekdall, Morris, and Violette, but nothing came of his investigation. Another possibility was that Hanna needed money. During Hirst's conversation with Lola West and Bernice Favors, he asked: "Well, didn't the chief (Ekdall) say something like that, too, about how the mayor was a poor man and he (Ekdall) didn't need any money because he made a lot, and it was for the mayor principally? I thought that was in there." Lola responded, "Yes."[3] After twenty years of service in Laramie County government, Hanna would have had a steady income, but perhaps circumstances arose that led him to believe he needed more money, or at some point, he felt he deserved more. That certainly does not discount the idea of someone on the outside leading the criminal activity, but it may partially explain Ekdall's participation.

Why did the quartet only target Black businesses? There is no documentation explaining their motivation, but they likely believed that West Side business owners would not complain or seek legal recourse against the extortion because the highest elected Cheyenne official and members of the police department were involved. After all, they were the minority in a segregated Cheyenne, and some, like Lola West, had previously been arrested by the Cheyenne police. The raid on the West Side on March 20 shows how law enforcement viewed the city's African Americans, and they did not expect any complaints or legal action in protest of their treatment during the raid.

Another important issue is prostitution in Cheyenne. During Ed Warren's time as mayor, Fort Francis E. Warren exerted significant pressure on the city to completely eradicate prostitution. This effort took place in 1942 and 1943, and Hanna would have known about the challenges Warren faced on this issue since he was working in local government, and the newspapers covered the story extensively. Yet, shortly after Hanna became mayor in early January 1944, he and his associates almost immediately told the West Side African American business owners that the town was now open to all kinds of vice, especially prostitution. They warned that if these business owners did not pay for protection, the mayor and police would shut them down. If they chose to participate, it was up to them to hire more women to "hustle," even implying that if they had female residents in their boarding houses, those women should engage in prostitution, or else they should be kicked out and replaced with women willing to hustle. The reason given for encouraging more prostitutes on the West Side was to protect the women of Cheyenne. Susie Stowers, who ran a boarding house there, was approached by Ekdall and encouraged to have prostitutes. He told Stowers they "were opening up the houses because of the rape cases," and that they "had to do something to protect the city." This reflects the widespread fear many in Cheyenne felt about the perceived danger posed by the African American soldiers stationed at the quartermaster center. Before Hanna became mayor, the Cheyenne police were sufficiently concerned about the supposed threat of Black soldiers to list and document their arrests, though they did not do the same for White soldiers. The police list of Black soldiers' arrests did not include many rape cases, raising the question of whether Ekdall and others were acting to open the town to "protect the city" or for personal financial gain through extortion. During the March 11 recorded meeting with Grimes, West, Hanna, Ekdall, Morris, and Violette, Lola at one point admitted she was willing to agree to pay for protection. She told the mayor, "You will be in charge for two years." Hanna promptly corrected her, stating he would do this for eight years, meaning he expected four terms as mayor. His reaction to West clearly showed Hanna's involvement in the criminal activity, though maintaining it for that duration might have been unlikely, as once the war concluded, the army would have shut down the quartermaster center, decreasing the number of African American soldiers near Cheyenne and thus lowering income for West Side businesses.

After Hanna was released from the state prison on parole, he returned to Cheyenne. At some point, he moved to Temple City, California. Hanna remarried and worked in a liquor store. In June 1957, he and his wife traveled to Wyoming to visit relatives and friends in Cheyenne and to see his sister in LaGrange. A few months later, Hanna died on September 18, 1957, in California.[4]

LOLA WEST

Lola West led the effort by Cheyenne's African Americans to gather information about the criminal activities of the mayor, chief of police, and two police officers, which resulted in the conviction of all four in a Cheyenne courtroom. Lola was the owner of the Black and Tan Club on 18th Street on the city's West Side and had a long, mixed history in Cheyenne. She arrived in the city in the mid-1920s, apparently with her husband, William. According to the 1940 federal census, Lola was born around 1890 in Oklahoma.

William first appeared in the *Wyoming State Tribune* in July 1925. The Cheyenne police arrested him and Sam Lenly on charges of possessing whiskey. Apparently, West sold Lenly the alcohol; later, police searched West's house and found "a quantity of whiskey." At West's trial, Judge William Riner sentenced him to ninety days, but when West said he would leave town, the judge reduced the sentence to thirty days. That was during Prohibition, and Cheyenne Frontier Days was underway. Part of the headline in the newspaper read "Frontier Disturbances Keep Officers Busy." According to the article, others were charged with drunkenness, "wreckless" driving, intoxication, possession, and speeding.[5]

At the start of 1926, William West was again in the newspaper, this time for assaulting his wife and striking her in the face with his fist. Police took him into custody based on Lola's complaint. In court, he first pled not guilty, but when made aware of the evidence against him, changed his plea to guilty. Justice Argesheimer sentenced him to six months in the county jail. The judge realized West said he would leave town at his earlier trial, so he asked him why he was still in Cheyenne. He responded that his wife would not go with him, so he remained in the city. They had five children.[6]

In June 1928, tragedy struck the West family. Their thirteen-year-old son, William Windal West, died at Memorial Hospital and was laid to rest in

Lakeview Cemetery. A newspaper article about his death said he was survived by his mother, three brothers, and one sister. The father was not mentioned. Perhaps he did leave town after his second sentence.[7]

Beginning in 1929 and extending to the World War II years, Lola West was arrested numerous times, often for illegal possession and sale of alcohol, but sometimes also for running a disorderly house. In June 1929, she was arrested and fined for possessing five pints of "moonshine whiskey." The sentence included a $100 fine and thirty days in jail. A few months later, she and T.B. Walls faced charges of operating a disorderly house. They and twenty-nine others were rounded up by Cheyenne police on October 1, 1929, mostly for visiting disorderly houses.

Even with the legal challenges she faced, Lola stayed active in the African American community. One example is from November 1935, when the West Side's Pre-Collegiate Club, which was organized to support members through college, hosted a "play trip" for African American children in the city.

Portrait of Lola West. Date of photograph is unknown. Courtesy Alonzo Reed Family.

Cheyenne Mayor Archie Allison and City Commissioner Ed Warren arranged for a Union Pacific bus that stopped at six homes. Each home was decorated to represent a different country, and food typical of that country was served to the participants. This also served as a fundraising event, with the money raised used to send Miss Epsylu Green to St. Louis to start her nursing training at a hospital. Members could join the club when they entered seventh grade, and through their efforts, they helped support older members attending college. "When they come of college age, they in turn will be helped." Lola hosted one of the houses that the members visited during that event.

The Cheyenne Police Department was also busy early in 1930. During the first week of February, officers arrested twenty-six people. Those who were soldiers at the fort were turned over to Fort Warren authorities. The rest were jailed by police—four for being drunk, four on charges of creating a disturbance, and three for possessing "intoxicating liquor." Others faced charges of gambling, vagrancy, and prostitution. Lola was one of those arrested for having liquor. Police apparently found seven pints of alcohol in her house. She was fined $75 and sentenced to thirty days in jail. In early 1934, she was arrested, pled guilty, and received a suspended three-month sentence. Four years later was charged with selling liquor on a Sunday. Probably the most interesting charge occurred during the late summer of 1940.

During August 1940, West was arrested by federal officers after an FBI agent filed a complaint for violating the White Slave Traffic Act, also known as the Mann Act. *The Wyoming Eagle* published a story titled "Lola West Faces White Slave Charge" and reported: "Lola West, a 48-year-old Negro proprietress of a colored nightclub and rooming house, was arrested and jailed on Wednesday on a federal complaint charging violation of the White Slave Traffic Act. Mrs. West was accused of transporting Eris Johnson, a 21-year-old Negro woman, from Denver to Cheyenne last week for immoral purposes." The charge also involved another Denver woman, Ruthy Gean Smith, allegedly brought across the state line by West. Both women were held as witnesses. Another witness against West was Mildred McDonald of Cheyenne. One newspaper mentioned she was one of West's employees, but it is unclear why she was considered a witness. Officers arrested McDonald as a material witness, although she posted a $500 bond and was released. West pled not guilty when she appeared before U.S. Commissioner Francis J. Bon, who set her bond at $1,500. Unable to pay the bond, she remained in the county jail. Federal officers stated this was the first Mann Act charge in Cheyenne in more than a year.

The federal charge of violating the Mann Act against West may have been the first in Cheyenne for a while, but it was not the only one filed in the state that fall. In September, federal officers arrested Judd Theodore Wilkins from Pine Bluffs, Arkansas, also for violating the Mann Act. The charge against him stated he had transported his wife, Eva Wilkins, and a second woman, Lucille Frances White, from Pine Bluffs to Laramie "on May 20, Aug. 15, and Sept. 15 for immoral purposes." Like West, he pled not guilty.

At the time, federal charges in Wyoming were heard by a grand jury in Casper, Wyoming. During September, West and the witnesses were transferred to the Casper jail to testify before the federal grand jury later in the fall. U.S. District Attorney Carl Sackett had prepared twenty-six cases to present that session. These ranged from "embezzlement and automobile theft to burglary and white slavery…." An article in the *Wyoming Eagle,* published a few days before the beginning of the grand jury, repeated the white slavery charges against West and Wilkins.[8]

The twenty-man federal grand jury convened on Tuesday, November 12, to consider the numerous cases presented by the prosecutor. Judge T. Blake Kennedy presided over the courtroom and session. That day, more than eighty witnesses were called to testify about the cases, including the white slavery cases, one of "selling liquor to Indians," and many others. In the *Wyoming Eagle* edition, the following day, an article stated that "the jurors were believed to have decided to return indictments" against West and Wilkins. However, that was not true. The grand jury announced its verdicts on Thursday. There were two "not true" rulings, meaning the charges would be dismissed, and thirty true bills resulting in indictments. One of the not true bills was the white slavery charge against Lola West.

However, the other white slavery case against Wilkins was confirmed as true, leading to his indictment and charges of violating the Mann Act. The three witnesses in the West case — McDonald, Smith, and Johnson — were released and sought payment for fees owed to them for their detention. As mentioned, the charges against West were dismissed, and the bond was released. She returned to Cheyenne. A few years later, as we know, Lola was instrumental in gathering evidence and helping to convict Hanna, Ekdall, Morris, and Violette in May 1944. She and others approached Chief of

Detectives Harvey Jackson and then Byron Hirst regarding the selling of protection. The transcript of the recorded meeting on March 11 at the Porters and Waiters Club showed Lola assisting in getting all four — the mayor and police officers — to admit their involvement in the criminal scheme. She then testified twice during the May trial that resulted in their convictions.

After the trials, life probably returned to normal for Lola and the Black and Tan Cafe. However, by 1948, she had legal issues again. In December of that year, police raided her club and charged her, fining her for running a disorderly house. In June 1950, she was charged again for the same offense and released on a $50 bond, which she forfeited. That year appears to be the last time the Black and Tan Cafe is listed in the Cheyenne City Directory, so her business likely closed around then.

Lola West has not yet received credit for her assistance to law enforcement in gathering evidence and participating in the sting that would convict Hanna and the others, and for her willingness to testify against them in court. She died on August 24, 1975, and is buried in Lakeview Cemetery.[9]

BYRON HIRST

Byron Hirst, who investigated and led the effort to convict Hanna, Ekdall, Morris, and Violette, had a long and distinguished legal career in Cheyenne. He served only one term as the County and Prosecuting Attorney for Laramie County, 1943-1947, and certainly his most notable case was the conviction of Hanna, Ekdall, Morris, and Violette. He returned to private practice when his term in that office expired. Besides his successful law practice he served as a Wyoming State Senator from 1953 to 1956, and on many boards and committees, including president of Cheyenne Chamber of Commerce in 1956, Rotary Club, Newcomen Society, Young Men's Literary Club, president of Cheyenne Downtown Association, and member of the executive committee of the Warren Air Force Base Civilian Advisory, among many others. During his time as a member of the Wyoming State Bar Association, he chaired many of its committees. He founded the firm Hirst and Applegate with James L. Applegate. Hirst passed away on August 20, 2002.[10]

JESS EKDALL, GERALD (JET) MORRIS, E.K. (EKKY) VIOLETTE, SYDNEY A. SCHWARTZ

Shortly after Jess (Jesse Boyce) Ekdall was released from the Wyoming State Prison, he moved to Billings, Montana, to continue working for the Hamilton Management Corporation, an investment firm. In 1955, Ekdall was listed as the regional manager for the corporation. He later moved to California. He died December 24, 1979, and is buried in Cheyenne's Lakeview Cemetery.[11] Gerald (Jet) Morris remained in Cheyenne. At the time of his death in January 1965, he worked as a maintenance man for the Cheyenne Police Department.[12] He was buried in Beth El Cemetery in Cheyenne. E.K. (Ekky) Violette moved to Eugene, Oregon, and during the 1950s and 1960s worked as the head custodian at a high school in the city.[13] Sydney A. Schwartz left Cheyenne and moved to California.

JOHN MCINERNEY

John McInerney ran unsuccessfully for the office of Cheyenne mayor in 1939 and 1941; in 1943, he lost in a close race to Hanna. However, with the former mayor in the state prison, he ran again in 1945 and defeated W.L. (Bill) Cook in a close election. Bruce Jones, who had served as mayor after Hanna's conviction, ran that year but lost in the primary. He received fewer than one thousand votes. In McInerney's 1945 campaign, he did not need to warn about someone possibly controlling the mayor or express concern about gambling in the city. He campaigned on the idea that his only interest was a "Better Cheyenne." To improve the city, his ads stated he would maintain and repair the streets, improve street lighting, and plan for a far-sighted airport program. The *Wyoming State Tribune,* in its campaign coverage on November 7, 1945, the day after the election, stated Cheyenne's voters "settled for a complete change in city government." Gus Fleischli did not run for reelection to the city council, so Cheyenne's city offices changed hands, with McInerney as mayor and A.W. (Art) Trout and O.E. (Oc) Erickson as city council members. The *Tribune* also ran a short editorial on the front page that day, and the first line read:

"Testimony of so many elections to the contrary notwithstanding, politics can be clean when practiced by clean men."[14]

EPILOGUE ENDNOTES

1   "Pretty Home Wedding," *Cheyenne State Leader*, May 21, 1914, p.3; "Hanna Funeral Service Is Set For Saturday," *Wyoming State Tribune*, September 12, 1935, 1 and 8.

2   Byron Hirst interview with Lola West and Bernice Favors. Interview is on a sound scriber disk in Byron Hirst's Papers at the Old West Museum, Cheyenne, Wyoming. The interview transcript is in the author's collection.

3   Byron Hirst interview with Lola West and Bernice Favors. Interview is on a sound scriber disk in Byron Hirst's Papers at the Old West Museum, Cheyenne, Wyoming. The interview transcript is in the author's collection.

4   "Ira Hanna, Once County Assessor, Dies on Coast," *Wyoming Eagle*, September 18, 1957, 17; *Wyoming Eagle*, June 12, 1957, 18; California Death Certificate.

5   "Frontier Disturbances Keep Officers Busy," *Wyoming State Tribune*, July 21, 1925, 2; "William West Gets 6 Months in Jail," *Wyoming State Tribune*, January 19, 1926, 2.

6   "William West Gets 6 Months in Jail," *Wyoming State Tribune*, January 19, 1926, 2.

7   "William West Dies Tuesday," *Wyoming State Tribune, Cheyenne State Leader*, June 27, 1928, 2. According to the Laramie County Sheriff Prison Calendar/Register, William was in the county jail from April to July 1926 for a parole violation. A notation in the register stated "To leave the State." RG1003, Laramie County Sheriff Prison Calendar/Register, January 1921-August 1927, vol. 3, 104-105. Five years later the family endured another scare after Lola's daughter was hit by a car. She apparently suffered a "severe injury to her eyelid and needed surgery, but was not seriously injured in any other way. The driver of the car was detained by police and questioned and then released. The driver said the accident was "unavoidable." "Injured Child Improves," *Wyoming State Tribune*, August 10, 1933, 5.

8   "26 Cases To Come Before Grand Jury," *Wyoming Eagle*, November 8, 1940, 1 and 7.

9   "Lola West Funeral Is Here Friday," *Wyoming State Tribune*, August 27, 1975, 26.

10 Hirst biographical information taken from "Biographical Outline," Byron Hirst, Byron Hirst Papers, box 1, Americana Heritage Center, University of Wyoming; "Former State Senator Hirst Dies," *Wyoming Tribune-Eagle*, August 21, 2002, 3.

11 "Mrs. Jess Ekdall Dies At Casper," *Lusk Herald*, May 12, 1960, 6; Advertisement for Hamilton Management Corporation in the *Billings Gazette*, June 1, 1955, 21; California, U.S. Death Index, 1940-1997.

12 "Gerald Morris Rosary Tonight, Funeral Friday," *Wyoming State Tribune*, January 21, 1965, 2; Wyoming Certificate of Death.

13 *Eugene Guard*, October 29, 1961, 20. The short article is about Violette's son, John E. Violette, who served in the U.S. Navy.

14 "Elect McInerney for Mayor," *Wyoming Eagle*, November 6, 1945, 3; "McInerney Elected Mayor; Trout and Erickson Victors," *Wyoming State Tribune*, November 7, 1945, 1; "An Editorial," *Wyoming State Tribune*, November 7, 1945, 1. "Men Successful In Business Urged To Seek City Offices: Gus Fleischli Says He Will Not Run for Reelection; Gives Advice to Successor," *Wyoming State Tribune*, October 11, 1945, 1.

Bibliography

MANUSCRIPTS AND ARCHIVES

American Heritage Center, University of Wyoming
  Adams, Gerald M., Papers
  Byrd, Harriett Elizabeth Family Papers
  Ehrenberger, James, Papers
  Hirst, Byron, Papers

Cheyenne Frontier Days Old West Museum
  Hirst, Byron, Papers.

Wyoming State Archives
  City of Cheyenne, Cheyenne Mayor Records
  City of Cheyenne, City Council Records
  Laramie County Jail Dockets

NEWSPAPERS

Casper Tribune Herald
Laramie Republican and Boomerang
Lusk Herald
Salt Lake Tribune
Torrington Telegram
Tribune Stockman Farmer
Wyoming Eagle
Wyoming State Tribune
Wyoming Tribune-Eagle

PUBLISHED WORKS

Adams, Gerald M. *The Post Near Cheyenne: A History of Fort D.A. Russell, 1867-1930.* Boulder, Colorado: Pruett Publishing Company, 1989

______. *"Fort Francis E. Warren and the Quartermaster Corps of World War II, 1940-1946.* Fort Collins, Colorado: Citizen Printing, Inc. 1994.

Baffoni, Allison, "It is the promiscuous woman who is giving us the most trouble": The Internal War on Prostitution in New Orleans during World War II" (2015) University of New Orleans Theses and Dissertations. 2055.

Blasi, Brigida R. "By All Who Knew Them: The Collins Family and the Making of a Black Community in Wyoming Coal Camps," *Annals of Wyoming*, Winter 2022, 10-41.

Buchanan, John G., "War Legislation against Alcoholic Liquor and Prostitution," *Journal of the American Institute of Criminal Law and Criminology*, February 1919, vol. 9, no. 4, 520-529.

James D.Calder PhD (2011) *Eliot Ness (April 19, 1903–May 16, 1957)*:

Gangbuster to Security Executive—A Meandering Career of Great Highs and Tragic Lows, Journal of Applied Security Research, 6:2, 196-208, DOI: 10.1080/19361610.2011.552005

Collins, Jan MacKell. *Good Time Girls of the Rocky Mountains: A Red-Light History of Montana, Idaho, and Wyoming*. Helena, Montana, Two Dot, 2020.

Davis, Sammy, Jr. and Jane and Burt Boyar. *Why Me? The Sammy Davis, Jr. Story*. New York: Farrar, Straus and Giroux, 1989.

Delmont, Matthew F. *Half American: The Epic Story of African Americans Fighting World War II at Home and Abroad*. Viking Press, 2022.

Drury, Tawnya K. "Disorderly Dollars: Penalty, Prosperity and Prostitution, Cheyenne, Wyoming, 1915-1922" (M.A.T. Thesis), History Department, University of Wyoming, 2002.

Dubois, William R. and Shirley E. Flynn. *We've Worked Hard to Get Here: The First One Hundred Years of the Greater Cheyenne Chamber of Commerce*. Cheyenne: Greater Cheyenne Chamber of Commerce, 2007.

Ewig, Rick, *Cheyenne: A Sesquicentennial History*. San Antonio, Texas, HPN Books, 2017.

Field, Sharon Lass, ed. *History of Cheyenne, Wyoming, Laramie County, Volume 2*. Dallas, Texas: Curtis Media Corporation, 1989.

Gish, Robert F. *Cheyenne, Wyoming 1940-1955: World War II National Defense Work, Shortage of Living quarters, Justifying the Construction of Federal Housing Projects*. Privately printed.

Glasrud, Bruce A., and Cary D. Wintz, *Black Americans and the Civil Rights Movement in the West*, Norman: University of Oklahoma Press, 2019.

Hallberg, Carl V. "Ethnicity in Wyoming." In *Readings in Wyoming History: Issues in the History of the Equality State,*" edited by Phil Roberts, 132-136. Laramie, Wyoming: Skyline West Press, 2004.

Hegerty, Marilyn. *Victory Girls, Khaki-Wackies, and Patriotutes: The Regulation of Female Sexuality during World War II*. New York: New York University Press, 2008.

Humphrey, David C. (1995) "Prostitution in Texas From the 1830s to the 1960s," *East Texas Historical Journal*: Vol. 33: Issue 1, Article 8.

Ibach, Kim and William Howard Moore, "The Emerging Civil Rights Movement: The 1957 Wyoming Public Accommodations Statute as a Case Study, *Annals of Wyoming*, 2001, 2-13.

Jacob, Matthew Frye, *Sammy Davis, Jr. and the Long Civil Rights Era: A Cultural History*. Oakland, California: University of California Press, 2023.

Johnson, Sydney. "How the USO Served a Racially Segregated Military Throughout World War II.

Jones, Walter R. *The Sand Bar: A History of Casper, Wyoming's Controversial Lowlands*. Casper, Wyoming: Natrona County Public Library, 2nd ed., 2012.

Kassel, Michael B. "Thunder on High Cheyenne, Denver and Aviation Supremacy on the Rocky Mountain Front Range" (M.A. Thesis), History Department, University of Wyoming, 2007.

Kaufman, Reagan Joy, "Discrimination in the 'Equality State': Black-White Relations in Wyoming History," *Annals of Wyoming*, Winter 2005, 13-27.

Knapp, Gretchen, "Experimental Social Policymaking During World War II: The United Service Organizations (USO) and American War-Community Services (AWCS), *Journal of Policy History*, 2009-04, Vol. 12 (3), 321-338.

Larson, T.A. *History of Wyoming*. Lincoln: University of Nebraska Press, 1965.

______. *Wyoming's War Years, 1941-1945*. Cheyenne: Wyoming Historical Foundation, 1993.

Lee, Ulysses. *The Employment of Negro Troops*. Washington, D.C.: Center of Military History, U.S. Army, 2001.

Mackey, Mike. "Cheyenne's 100-Octane Plant." In *Readings in Wyoming History: Issues in the History of the Equality State,"* edited by Phil Roberts, 125-131. Laramie, Wyoming: Skyline West Press, 2004.

"A Matter of Color: African Americans Face Discrimination: While We Do Not Discriminate, We Do Segregate," Oregon Secretary of State Web Site.

McGuire, Christy, ed. "Northern Racism," Chapter 8, *Taps for a Jim Crow Army: Letters from Black Soldiers in World War II*, University Press of Kentucky, 2021, 165-182.

McGuire, Phillip, "Judge Hastie, World War II, and Army Racism" *The Journal of Negro History*, October 1977, vol. 62, No. 4, 351-362.

Modell, John, Marc Goulden and Sigurdur Magnusson. "World War II in the Lives of Black Americans: Some Findings and Interpretations," *The Journal of American History*, December 1989, vol. 76, no. 3, 838-848.

Nash, Gerald D. *The American West Transformed: The Impact of the Second World War*. Lincoln and London: University of Nebraska Press, 1985.

Ness, Elliot, "Federal Government's Program in Attacking the Problem of Prostitution," *Federal Probation*, vol. 67, no. 3, December 2003, 10-12.

O'Neal, Bill. *Cheyenne: A Biography of the "Magic City" of the Plains*. Austin, Texas: Eakin Press, 2006.

Parascandola, John. "Quarantining Women: Venereal Disease Rapid Treatment Centers in World War II America," *Bulletin of the History of Medicine,* Fall 2009, vol. 83, no. 3 431-459.

Perry, Douglas. *Eliot Ness: The Rise and Fall of an American Hero.* New York, Viking Press, 2014.

Stanton, Fred, ed., *Fighting Racism In World War II; A Week-By-Week Account Of The Struggle Against Racism And Discrimination In The United States During 1939-45; From the Pages of* The Militant, Pathfinder Press, 1980.

Thompson, Troy. "A Black Spot': Florida's Crusade against Venereal Disease, Prostitution, and Female Sexuality During World War II," *Florida Public Health Review*, 2005, vol. 2, Article 20, 115-120.

Wood, Anthony W. "The Blackest City in the West: A Decade of Hope and Hardship in Cheyenne, Wyoming," *Annals of Wyoming*, Fall 2022, 2-19.

Woodford, Tyson R. and Billie L.M. Addleman, "Byron Hirst's Case Against Cheyenne Corruption," *Wyoming Lawyer*, October 2022, Vol. 45, No. 5, 34-37.

Woodward, John P., "The Taming of Front Street: Prostitution in Southeastern Wyoming, 1930-1960" (M.A. Thesis), History Department, University of Wyoming, 2010.

Index